The New Theatre
of the Baltics

ALSO BY JEFF JOHNSON

William Inge and the Subversion of Gender:
Rewriting Stereotypes in the Plays, Novels, and Screenplays
(McFarland, 2005)

Pervert in the Pulpit:
Morality in the Works of David Lynch
(McFarland, 2004)

The New Theatre of the Baltics

From Soviet to Western Influence in Estonia, Latvia and Lithuania

JEFF JOHNSON

foreword by Daniel Gerould

McFarland & Company, Inc., Publishers
Jefferson, North Carolina, and London

Some of this material has appeared in slightly different form in *Slavic and East European Performance* and *Teatras*.

LIBRARY OF CONGRESS CATALOGUING-IN-PUBLICATION DATA

Johnson, Jeff, 1954–
 The new theatre of the Baltics : from Soviet to Western influence in Estonia, Latvia and Lithuania / Jeff Johnson ; foreword by Daniel Gerould.
  p. cm.
 Includes bibliographical references and index.

 ISBN-13: 978-0-7864-2992-9
 softcover : 50# alkaline paper ∞

 1. Theater — Estonia — History — 20th century. 2. Theater — Latvia — History — 20th century. 3. Theater — Lithuania — History — 20th century. 4. Theater — Baltic States — History — 20th century. I. Title.
 PN2859.E7J64 2007
 792.09485 — dc22   2006038453

British Library cataloguing data are available

©2007 Jeff Johnson. All rights reserved

No part of this book may be reproduced or transmitted in any form or by any means, electronic or mechanical, including photocopying or recording, or by any information storage and retrieval system, without permission in writing from the publisher.

On the cover: Airida Gintautaitė and Egidijus Bakas in Marius Ivaškevičius's *Close City* at the Art Fort, Vilnius (photograph by Dmitrij Matvejev)

Manufactured in the United States of America

McFarland & Company, Inc., Publishers
 Box 611, Jefferson, North Carolina 28640
 www.mcfarlandpub.com

for Loreta Rudaitienė
(1958–2006)

Acknowledgments

A Antonia, la mia musa favorita di Piccolino...
Thanks first to those who helped finance this project, especially the Northeast Modern Language Association for awarding me their Summer Fellowship Research Award, and Dr. Rosemary Layne from Brevard Community College for generous Staff and Program Development funding.

Thanks again to Dr. Mike Kaliszeski, Provost at the Melbourne campus of Brevard Community College, for his patronage and sympathetic indulgence in yet another improbable project.

None of this research would have been possible without the incredibly kind, professional help of so many people in Lithuania, Estonia and Latvia who, with genuine enthusiasm and commitment, helped arrange interviews, translations, entry to performances and generally provided assistance in all aspects of this project.

Especially, I want to thank Giedrė Liūgaitė, Manager of the Theatre and Cinema Information and Education Centre in Vilnius, and theatre critic Elvyra Markevičiūtė in Kaunas; Katrin Talts, Managing Director of the Information Center for the Estonian Theatre Union, Ene Paaver, Literary Manager of the Estonian Drama Theatre, and Triin Sinissaar, Dramaturge, Tallinn City Theatre; Zane Kreicberga, Director, and Agnese Bite, Information Project Manager, at the New Theatre Institute of Latvia.

Thanks also to Rita Palienė, Helen Parry, Kathleen Jaeger, Gene Floersch, and Ron and Suzanne McClung for their advice and refreshments, and to my parents for putting up with me.

As usual, thanks to Carla for everything.

Finally, I could not have written this book without the encouragement, guidance, and scholarly advice from Daniel Gerould.

Contents

Acknowledgments — vii
Foreword by Daniel Gerould — 1
Preface — 5

1. The Crisis of Relevance — 11
2. Lithuania: Catholic Spectacle — Directors' Theatre — 30
3. Estonia: The Lutheran Narrative — Writers' Theatre — 93
4. Latvia: Focus on Process — Actors' Theatre — 156

Notes — 211
Works Cited — 213
Index — 217

Foreword
by Daniel Gerould

Even for someone unusually curious, with a lively interest in modern drama and the stage, the question arises: why take the trouble to learn about the theatre in Lithuania, Estonia, and Latvia, three very small countries, each with a different and difficult language unrelated to the major linguistic families of Europe? Jeff Johnson, a writer and scholar who has visited Lithuania, Estonia, and Latvia, experienced the theatre there, and talked with the major artists, feels that the effort has been well worthwhile, and in this book he shares his discoveries with the reader.

Among the many reasons that Johnson advances for us to pay serious attention to the theatre in Lithuania, Estonia, and Latvia, the one that strikes me as the most compelling and interesting is this: the micro-stories of these theatres' struggle for existence in the face of annihilating pressures offer us paradigms for understanding broader issues and general problems confronting cultural institutions in the twenty-first century.

The New Theatre of the Baltics is less a handbook or tourist guide than a speculative investigation into the means by which small countries must fight to retain their cultural identity. How, Johnson asks, has each of the Baltic countries attempted to solve the problem of keeping its theatre alive and relevant through a series of dizzying changes and upheavals? First colonies of Tsarist Russia, then tyrannized by Nazis and Bolsheviks during World War II and the Cold War, the Baltic countries were finally liberated in the 1990s only to be inundated by Western popular culture and lost in a homogenized European Union in which they seem destined to be very minor players. Countries that survived occupation and suppression of native culture under cruel totalitarian regimes now face audiences with a declining appetite for theatre, vulgarized taste, and increasingly short attention spans. Once the theatre in the Baltic states suddenly lost its heroic role as opposition and resistance to communism, it became a prey to market economy, mass media, and rampant consumerism.

Vaclav Havel has called theatre "a living instrument of social awareness ... lodged in its own time." But how can this lofty role be maintained in the face of rapid cultural change and loss of national identity? These are the urgent questions at the heart of this book, for what is at stake is nothing less than the preservation of one's own culture.

Johnson shows us what has happened in the Baltic states after the transition from the Soviet-imposed system — with its lavish state support of the arts, containment and censorship, and tolerated safety-valve dissent — to independence and adaptation to the Western economic model and assimilation to capitalism. The sudden absence of state financing and sponsorship characterize the trauma of privatization.

The Baltic states have produced a number of internationally celebrated directors, to whom Johnson introduces us. He lets us hear them debate what cultural policies their countries should take and what artistic choices they themselves should make if the theatre is to remain relevant. Among the issues debated none is more vital than that of language, both literal and, in the sense of scenic language, figurative. In the times of political oppression, theatre was a means of preserving the language when its use was forbidden by occupying powers. Theatre with its shared language and culture had been a means of unifying the population and giving a sense of national identity. Now the language was perceived as an obstacle making the artistic products less exportable.

Writers, artists, and audiences in English-speaking countries simply take for granted that the world will be interested in their art, will be able to understand it, and then will wish to imitate it. For Lithuanians, Estonians, and Latvians, language is the source and strength of their culture and at the same time a seemingly insurmountable barrier. How can a national theatre of a small country retain its own cultural identity and yet at the same time speak to cross-cultural audiences? These are the kinds of important questions about the nature and purpose of art that Jeff Johnson raises in this book. Is theatre a local art written for native audiences? Or should playwrights and theatre artists strive to reach a wider audience and subscribe to a pan–European aesthetic by creating in a generic, transportable style that transcends any particular social contexts? Baltic theatre artists realize that theatre must talk about all mankind, but how is this best done? Can a national identity be located within a larger cultural identity of the European Union?

Some Baltic theatre companies adopt a "nomadic philosophy" of traveling from international festival to international festival, erasing boundaries and intentionally failing to establish permanent ties to any particular audience. Will this produce a theatre without roots that plays in different countries and venues on an international circuit, ignoring audience expectations? Some of the Baltic directors with whom Johnson talks hope to make their theatre by abandoning text-based scripts and creating visually dynamic performances that speak a universal scenic language.

The artists in today's Baltic theatre realize that they must forget old obsessions, adapt to new circumstances, and create afresh. But they must look both backward and forward, reckon with the past, constantly consider where their theatre came from and what its future can be. In the Baltic countries theatre and history are inseparably connected.

In this book we are exposed to a full panoply of possibilities. Johnson has talked with writers, artists and critics and heard their ideas about the kinds of cultural policy and organization that can keep these small and fragile cultures from being swallowed up in the European Union. He has also heard from directors and listened to their views. Some favor the old psychological realism inherited from the Russians; others advocate the new and innovative, the director-dominated visual theatre of metaphor and image. Nothing is yet settled. History is still in process. One of the strengths of Johnson's book is that the author does not give easy answers or neat formulas. He does not speak dogmatically in his own voice, but rather listens well and hard. The story is largely told in the words of those who have both witnessed the course of events and also influenced and shaped them. Those words describe different ideas and advance different opinions. The one thing that the speakers all agree upon is the importance of theatre in shaping and defining their country's history and culture.

Daniel Gerould is Lucille Lortel Distinguished Professor of Theatre and Comparative Literature at the City University of New York.

Preface

I found Kaunas, Lithuania, by chance. I'd just finished a Fulbright teaching assignment in Denmark, and instead of returning to the States after the academic year I took a summer job at Kaunas Technological University. With the vaguest notion of Lithuania, and having never heard of Kaunas, I bought a *Lonely Planet* guide and flew in.

What I found was a thriving theatre scene. Whether staged in spacious houses or cramped lofts, the performances were striking and unusual, an alluring mix of physical theatre, metaphor and stylized acting. And the theatres were full of engaged students, actors, directors, artists and regulars — a community of aficionados that actually cared enough about theatre to make it an integral part of their lives. I felt compelled to share my enthusiasm with a wider audience in the West that, I assumed, due to the geo-political situation during the Soviet years, had little exposure to the dynamic theatre I was encountering. But because I spoke, after all, no Lithuanian, it was extremely difficult to find people to translate the plays, much less conduct interviews. Most of the young theatre professionals spoke Russian and German but only broken English. Nevertheless, I managed by group effort to form what might best be described as "meaning by consensus," enough to write profiles of individual theatres in the city that were eventually published in *Slavic and East European Performance*, the journal of the Center for Advanced Theatre Studies, City University of New York.

Daniel Gerould, editor of *SEEP*, encouraged me to situate the Lithuanian material within the broader context of the Baltics generally, exploring the effects on the theatre first regarding the transition from the Soviet times into the era independence, and then the impact of the integration of the Baltic countries into the European Union.

Given the encouragement and support from Gerould, my approach to Vilnius was more methodical. I was awarded a research grant from the northeast chapter of the Modern Language Association (NEMLA); then, through a series of scattershot emails, I procured invitations from all the major players in Vilnius, especially with the help of two main resources: Asta Jonusaitė at the Lithuanian National Drama Theatre and Giedrė Liugaitė, Manager of the Theatre and Cinema Information Center. I timed my visit to Vilnius to coincide with the New Drama Action Festival, sponsored in part by the Information Center and showcasing some of the best productions of the year by Lithuanian directors.

Well aware after my Lithuanian experience that what was once the significant topic of contention — coping with the transition from the Soviet system to independence and the adaptation of a Western economic model — was being displaced by theoretical and aesthetic concerns, by the time I approached the theatre community in Tallinn, Estonia, I was prepared for a different line of inquiry. I knew that for those old enough to have lived during Soviet domination, displays of residual bitterness are common and inform their aesthetics as much as their politics. But for the younger generation, the issues of the transition period are settled. Many have grown up without firsthand knowledge of enforced deprivations, and even for those with a trace of that experience, so many new and more immediately relevant issues crowd the agenda that to dwell on past injustices seems obsessive, backward-looking and obstructionist when most people want to focus on the future.

As with my experience in Lithuania, I had no firsthand reconnaissance on Estonia. I was familiar with Jaak Rähesoo's *Estonian Theatre*, and from that and other research I had enough historical insight to understand Estonia's cultural identification with Scandinavia, contrasted sharply with Lithuania's affiliation with Poland and East Prussia. I had also been clued in to the rivalry — if not hostility — exhibited by the Lithuanians toward Estonians. My contacts in both Kaunas and Vilnius characterized the Estonians as haughty and superior, as if the relative prosperity of the Estonians and their connections to the west via Finland during the Soviet era somehow compromised them. This perception, at least from the point of view of some Lithuanians, that Estonia's Scandinavian connections allowed them to be better positioned than other Baltic states to take advantage of the new economy, generated an enmity based in envy that perversely created in the Lithuanians a sense of supremacy in theatre arts — especially in producing talented directors.

Though my main line of enquiry in Estonia was still twofold — the impact on theatre of the transition from the Soviet era to independence, and the imperiling of their national identity as Estonia is assimilated into the European Union — I now identified a definitive contrast between the Catholic, visual-based theatre of Lithuania and the Lutheran, text-based approach of Estonia, as well as the corollary issue of distinguishing the Lithuanian style that privileges the director from the Estonian tradition of privileging the playwright (or the actors) in determining the production values of a performance.

My schedule put me in Tallinn at the end of the regular season, but the quality of the summer programs ensured an opportunity for me to witness excellent performances. In any case, I had no problem procuring DVDs of the most seminal works, most of which have become standards in repertoires at the major theatres. My best shot at gathering firsthand material was to use the same methods as in Lithuania: interviewing as many of the principals as I could, viewing productions and framing a cultural perspective from academics and critics. As in Lithuania, the younger artists spoke better English than the older generation, but mostly the discussions were all productive and rarely necessitated the use of a translator.

Two main resources in Tallinn were Katrin Talts, Managing Director of the Information Center for the Estonia Theatre Union, and Ene Paaver, Literary Manager of the Estonian Drama Theatre, both of whom were invaluable in arranging interviews and access to performances and generally assisting in all aspects of the project in Tallinn. Leasing a room from the Theatre Union in their complex off Uus Street in the center of Old Town, I began my work comfortably ensconced in the center of the major theatre resource organization in Tallinn, within walking distance of every important theatre, editor and critic in the city.

My approach to Latvia was even more calculated. When I first tried to visit Latvia I was dissuaded by Aivars Līnis, the Artistic Director of the Art Theatre, because the season, basically throughout the country, was over by mid–May and I couldn't be there until late June. So I cancelled any plans of trying to include Riga in my initial research. Luckily, I met Zane Kreicberga, Director of the New Theatre Institute of Latvia, during the New Drama Action festival in Vilnius and we made arrangements for me to visit Riga that November for Spēlmaņu Nakts ("actors' nights"), an annual showcase of Latvian plays organized by the Latvian Theatre Union in Riga. That year, eight of the plays nominated by a jury of prominent theatre critics for best performance, best director, best actor, and so forth were performed by various major theatre ensembles. Following the performances was a conference featuring independent experts, critics and guests from around Europe. The experts included critics from Denmark, Belarus, Poland, and the Czech Republic. Other invited professionals in attendance represented Finland, Poland, Slovakia, Russia and Lithuania. The festivities culminated in an awards ceremony held on November 23 to commemorate the birthday of the famous Latvian theatre director Eduards Smiļģis.

Hosting all of the major theatres in Latvia, the showcase represented an impressive array of styles — traditional, modern and postmodern — underscoring the diversity (and critical controversies) driving Latvian theatre today. Of the performances, the less traditional plays were shunned by the critics, with a production of Turgenyev's *A Month in the Country*, an unapologetic exercise in strict nineteenth century Stanislavskian psychological realism, sweeping the awards, winning in every major applicable category, including best play, best acting, and best costumes. This privileging by the jury of realism over more meta-theatrical approaches exposes a rift within the Latvian critical community, with the established critics supporting the tendency of the traditional repertory theatres like the National to stage pro forma classics and young directors insisting on plays that challenge the very idea of "theatre," who prefer to explore the possibilities and limitations of what sustains a "performance."

The difficulty, many critics explained, began after independence, when the dominance of Stansilavskian realism was challenged or modified by the novelty and "pop" appeal of Western influences, and even though now contemporary Latvian directors are well versed in postmodern tendencies, the older generation of audiences, echoed by the critics in the popular press, continues to demand and promote the typical psychological realism that dominates repertories at most of the major theatres. The younger audiences, meanwhile, prefer more adventurous directors, or at least a rethinking of how to stage classical plays, maintaining the uniqueness of the original but translating the action into more contemporary theatre language. Luckily, festivals such as Spēlmaņu Nakts continue to frame the issue, allowing traditional artists and the avant-garde to argue their cases in performance before an appreciative audience actively engaged in the ongoing cultural debate.

This book is not meant to be comprehensive or definitive. It is a snapshot, not a portrait. To write authoritatively about a subject that is so quickly evolving, and so foreign both in language and culture from my experience, takes a lot of audacity *and* a lot of humility. Even so, this book serves as an introduction, a summary and a forum of ideas about the current scene in Baltic theatre, a detailed account of my experience in the region that both defines the situation up to the flash of the photograph and exposes a loose schema for the future. This study is not a prediction. It is a depiction of what is happening in Baltic theatre now.

1

The Crisis of Relevance

Although Estonia, Latvia and Lithuania share a common modern history, they are culturally distinct. Jaak Rähesoo points out in his *Estonian Theatre*, "For foreigners Lithuanians, Latvians and Estonians are all lumped together in the geopolitical notion of the 'Baltic States/nations'" (13). They were independent states annexed by the Soviet Union in 1940, occupied by the Germans from 1941–44, re-occupied by the Soviets after World War II, only to emerge in the early 1990s as independent states again, intoxicated with liberation but suspect of the libertine, unregulated, promiscuous availability of a new, Westernized, profligate media.

Culturally, Estonia is aligned more with Lutheran Scandinavia, especially with Finland, while Lithuania shares affinities with Catholic Poland, and Latvia splits along a porous religious fault line with the German Lutheran influences in the northwest and Russian Orthodox in the east (nearly half the population is Russian-speaking). The Baltic states have experienced a common history of external oppression, their separate identities shaped most acutely by the years that demarcate Soviet dominance after World War II. The collective ebb and flow of their artistic freedom is directly tied to the years of strict Stalinist control before 1953, the easing of cultural restrictions during Khrushchev's tenure ('53–'64), the end of Czech-style liberalization after 1968 (which inspired resistance and experimentation, depending on the leniency of the various civic authorities), finally to Gorbachev's "restructuring" (*perestroika*) and "openness" (*glasnost*) in 1988 and independence after 1991.

Marvin Carlson, editor of *Western European Stages*, writing about the changes in Estonia after the occupation, insists that the situation of the theatre was precarious. It had lost its viability and appeal to mere entertainment, challenged not only by a demand for "popular" shows in its own venues but by the infusion of new media suddenly available that offered mainly ephemeral, instant gratification — the sort of cultural experience that, perhaps, fit the prevailing *zeitgeist* but caused consternation among the country's intelligentsia who worried that the new market driven entertainments were lowering both cultural and educational standards. Carlson notes:

> When I last visited Estonia, in the summer of 1993, Soviet occupation (and Soviet support and domination of the theatre) had recently ended, and the theatre was struggling to find its place in the new society. With political commentary allowed in all public venues, this function of theatre diminished sharply, and, in the period of financial strain, the theatres of Estonia struggled to find a new role and a new public. [...] Many regular theatre-goers, uninterested in [...] lighter fare, stopped attending... [62].

Carlson's comments are particular to Estonia but applicable to Latvia and Lithuania as well. Theatre directors and educators in all three Baltic countries make the same point, and most attribute the cause to the sudden turn from a limited, repressed media to a society with no regulation and no control. Culturally, the situation resembles that of a man dying of thirst who suddenly has unlimited access to gallons of water: he must sip or he'll make himself sick, and if he drinks too much too fast, he might die. Rähesoo writes, "Theatre as a public art [...] had to re-think its role: for years a channel for expressing [...] opposition to Soviet rule, it now had to obtain a new function" (71).

Financially, the case immediately after liberation was even more precarious. In all three Baltic states before independence, the Soviets had in place an intricate system of state-supported theaters. The forced move toward private funding put a strain on many of these companies, and to compete with television, movies, and the general trend that began to privilege entertainment over more politically engaged theatre, many of the formerly avant-garde houses revised their repertoire to accommodate a less discerning but more affluent audience capable of sustaining subscription-based seasonal programs.

The roots of modern drama in Estonia, Latvia and Lithuania, once it shed its German classicism, can be characterized as a theatre of resistance, first to reinforce the fledgling independence movements in each country during the years between 1918–1940, then as a response to Nazi occupation, and again as an ideological weapon countering the post–World

War II annexation under strict Soviet ideology. (Lenin's influence permeates Baltic postwar history, from the formation of the early independent states to the popularity of socialist realism in art.) Theatre, however, maintained its integrity by proving a cogent tool for reformers. Just as it worked (at times) for the Soviet apparatchiks trying to indoctrinate patriotism on a reluctant citizenry under occupation, in the hands of partisan artists in the Baltics theatre became a necessary vehicle of nationalist propaganda for the young states. The idea of theatre as a "weapon" reflects the nationalist agenda of Baltic theatres at the end of the nineteenth and beginning of the twentieth centuries, and that same intense nationalism allowed Baltic theatres to be regarded by Russian playwrights during this time as among the most daring and Western.

A new phenomenon emerged after liberation, in which the politicized "theatre of resistance" during the Soviet era was transformed into a "theatre of entertainment" many critics feel is detrimental to the states' cultural vitality, both collectively and individually. This anxiety about the relevance of theatre in the Baltic countries embodies what many social theorists — Jean Baudrillard, for one — describe as a displacement of reality, in which ideology is diluted by consumerism and simulation replaces actuality, where politics, production, and economy form a capitalist paradigm that disrupts the cultural importance of art, reducing it, some believe, to a meaningless exchange of signs and images with no ameliorative purpose.

What Baudrillard identifies as an "ecstatic" (23) phenomenon is clearly discernable within the context of contemporary Baltic theatre and its sudden cultural displacement from a socially relevant theatre to one driven by consumerism. Each state, exiled, as it were, from European affairs, subsumed within the anti-western cultural thrust of the Soviets, had been resituated within the cultural tradition of Europe. Even so, many students, faculty and theatre personnel still felt marginalized. Critics blame this lack of cultural relevance in theatre on the pernicious aspects of Western (especially American) influences in the arts.

In 1941, under German occupation, theatre in the Baltics virtually disappeared — along with many of its most talented writers who were executed or sent to concentration camps. After Stalin's death, the situation became more favorable for artistic productions, even though the theatre was relentlessly scrutinized and censored by Soviet commissars. Yet, even with the restrictions (or because of them), the theatre thrived as both entertainment in a country starved for popular cultural venues and as a vehicle for political and spiritual nourishment. It was only after the Baltic countries achieved independence that the theatre began to suffer a tangible loss of relevancy. Frustrating many new writers was the difficulty of being read or performed for specialized language-specific audiences. Their works were seldom translated. But it was the influence of Western media, specifically music, cinema and television fueling the pernicious skepticism about Western cultural hegemony and undercutting the once thriving theatre community in the Baltics. Many critics describe the new age as one of extreme individualism, competitiveness, and market cultures, and they fear that morality has been privatized. (Kaunas theatre critic Elvyra Markevičiūtė describes the situation as a state of "collapse.") These critics also worry that the abrupt change to moral relativism related to unprincipled capitalism may lead to social disintegration. Ironically (and irrespective of the backlash against George W. Bush's foreign policy) an anti–Western bias may now displace the anti–Soviet activism that historically played such a significant role in the life of an intensely politicized citizenry.

From about 1957 to 1988, drama in the Baltics developed rapidly, especially effective in preparing the countries for their eventual independence. But many of these influential playwrights, their reformist mission accomplished, became members of parliament, editors of influential newspapers or ministers, and ceased writing plays. This created a crisis in theatre, when between 1988 and 1993 the most important and most interesting dramas were not staged in the theatre; instead, the favorite works of critics were adapted dramatically to reflect periods of crisis. To counter this aesthetic turn to pragmatism, many Baltic theatres "discovered" (as it were) Western dramas. These "discoveries" and the playwrights' turn to politics explain why immediately after independence very few plays from the Baltics appeared on the contemporary stage.

During periods of repression, censorship legitimized theatre at a time when those coded Aesopian parables containing clever, politically critical commentary concealed within ironic allusions were shared by the audience and players but lost on the Party bosses. Though many artistic directors recall the absurdity of the Soviet censorship, they also lament the loss of social influence from which the theatre suffers today. During the Soviet period, theatres were crowded with people hungry for ideas; the significance of the "coded" productions was either lost on the commissars or became part of an elaborate game that for the censors simultaneously pacified and encouraged the political opposition.

One of the central ironies during this period is that, with censorship, the officials had to attend the performances, but without it, they quit coming. The situation changed during the transition: "between 1991 and 1993, theatres emptied. [...] the 'theatre of life' had become more interesting and exciting than the performing arts" (Čakare 87). The political situation demanded direct action, and people began taking ideas from the theatre into the street. The theatre suddenly seemed tame, worse than irrelevant, and though many directors were keen to recover its significance, most were unsure about how to renew its relevance. During the transition, the focus had been so centered on message and resistance that talent suffered: theatre had become a political vehicle at the expense of aesthetics. But when the audience no longer felt any political necessity, theatres struggled. Many influential directors complain that after liberation, theatres, especially as they competed with the influx (or onslaught) of popular Western entertainment, were undermining the educational level of the people. These directors (and other critics) insist the moral aim of theatre is to restore to both the audience and the productions a sense of intellectual integrity.

The same tune is sung, albeit in a different key, in nearly all of the former Soviet states. In Croatia, for instance, Dubravka Vrgoč reports how in the early 1990s, "young dramatists departed from a long tradition lasting from the mid nineteen fifties to eighties, in which politics was a central theme of the Croatian theatre [...] [so that] the plays written and performed in Croatian theatres in the first half of the nineties were free from ideology" (52). In Poland, Wieslaw Górski writes about the change from a more personal level, recalling how after living in New York City for six years he returned home in 1994 to discover that "Poland was free. [...] Censors went to other jobs. Solidarity was in demand no longer. Money was" (45). Amazed at the influx of Western culture, of "McDonald's [...] Western clothes [...] Western cars" Górski notes: "in 1989 our spiritual life looked [...] devastated" (45). In a 2000 interview with Michal Bragant, then curator with the Czech National Film Archives, James Buglewicz, explains that "[i]n the sixties, the new films were totally financed by the state" (36). But after 1989, many filmmakers "were absolutely upset by the privatization of the film industry" (36). Bragant even jokes that "many artists, writers, and filmmakers after 1989 complained, lamenting the lack of ideological oppression. [...] it made people more inventive [...] it was good for the imagination" (36).

Most theatres in the Baltics (as well as in other formerly occupied states) had no organizational system in place to replace the loss of state sponsorship, to mitigate the trauma of privatization and the impact of coming out of the cultural and economic isolation imposed by the Soviets only to encounter the dramatic irruption of possibility afforded the citizens after 1989. The Baltic Theatre Policy Review of 2000 summarizes the situation:

> Since the collapse of Soviet regime crucial changes in economics, politics, society and culture have occurred. Along with the development of the democratic society and market economy changes had to be obvious in the cultural policy as well. However, transition period has generated loss of criteria and confusion instead of a serious input into the change of cultural policy and distribution of public funds to culture. During the last 10 years numerous non-governmental organisations have been established performing innovative activities in performing arts field. Contemporary dance, international events, inter-sectoral projects, alternative training projects are few of those activities. However, performing arts policies on the state level are still ignoring all these developments mainly focusing on sustainability of existing state institutions.

Viktor Avotins, who reported on the 2000 conference in Riga, cites disparities between the state arts funding agencies and the reality in the theatres as an acute problem the Baltics must resolve in order for the theatre to recover its vitality. Funded by the Soros Foundation and organized by the New Theatre Institute of Latvia and Intercult of Sweden, the Baltic Theatre Policy Review conference allowed a forum in which participants tried to harmonize the various strategies of the three Baltic countries regarding cultural policy within the context of the state support for the arts. Participants from the Baltics, Sweden, the Netherlands, Russia, Bulgaria and the Czech Republic attempted to develop common recommendations for the Baltics. Avotins notes how "the theatre people and people from other art fields make an appeal to authority, based in the nature of art, but directives of the cultural policy are made based on the nature of authority." He cynically sums up the situation: "Even if the situation in Latvia, Lithuania and especially in Estonia, is better than in Russia and the authorities have done also good things (created foundations etc.) the discussions at the conference remind us of the inability to pragmatize adequately the future of the art, that the Ministries of Culture cannot conceive the contemporary theatre as anything other than a coat-hanger."

Others at the conference concurred. According to Baiba Tjarve from Latvia, "Lithuania has policy of reaction slowly responding to deep crises or burning issues. [...] Estonia has a policy of stability: adjusted legislation, set criteria, high subsidies. [...] Latvia has do-nothing-policy, which is carried out in quite a conservative political and artistic framework"

(Tjarve, "Performing Arts Policy"). Irena Viesaitė from Lithuania adds, "In Lithuania the ideological pressure has not completely disappeared, including also the conservative pressure from the society. Theatres request educated society but who will finance and further these things? The best directors still leave the state theatres and create their own theatre companies." Audronis Liūgą from Lithuania echoes Viesaitė's point: "When the talented directors (not only Eimuntas Nekrošius and Oskaras Koršunovas) left the state theatres nobody asked them — why are they doing that? Only thanks to the Soros Foundation it was possible to talk about new organizational forms in Lithuania." Jaak Allik from Estonia recalls how "[i]n 1989 in Estonia theatres were attended by 1.5 million people. Nowadays there are many more economic possibilities and the theatre is not any longer the only place to talk about life. [...] However, if we support only projects, then the theatre structures will be destroyed and the repertory theatres will become project theatres." The consensus of the attendees, according to Avotins, is that the funding processes are still politicized, and the only remedy is transparency in the distribution apparatus. The recommendation is for each state to organize "priorities and criteria for the distribution of the money" and to avoid competition between "the state and independent organizations" because "the state acknowledges the independent sector only when it is convenient for the state" (Avotins).

Along with the complaints about funding priorities, many participants at the conference noted the loss of relevancy and the drift toward pure entertainment in the theatres, a situation rooted in the economic crisis as the drama companies compete with popular media for a shrinking audience. As Allik puts it, "I am a little bit afraid for the reforms in culture. Because the cultural reforms are run by people who haven't succeeded in their own field." Many also linked the debasement of theatre repertoires to the "lack of mass education and modern cultural education [...] the social values are subject of the popular culture, but the art is free to think only about esthetical values." Edward Boyakov, at that time the Russian Director of the Golden Mask Festival, cautions that "actors and directors of younger generation leave the repertory theatres and start to work in TV, advertising or show-business structures."

Estonia, Latvia, Lithuania: the refrain is the same: "the theatrical atmosphere more and more will be taken over by TV and media" (Rudzīte).

On the other hand, and with perhaps a wistful does of optimism, Avotins notes that "some [at the conference] pointed out that arts education will be important, because there will be need to think how to keep the actor in the theatre, who will be attracted by TV, soap operas, movie." Many attendees were convinced that, in the Baltics, "repertory theatres will be the backbone of our theatre system [...] and will not become the Netherlands, Italy or England, where there are no repertory theatres." But this symbiotic paradox, of trying to compete with popular media while maintaining funding from the state, coupled with the need to uphold aesthetic integrity in a society saturated and infatuated with MTV and naked weather forecasters, presents a dilemma for both fledging and established theatres. The fact remains that "de-monopolisation (sic) and diversification of the structure is necessary. In a real field of competition the repertory theatres have to exist as well."

In her report on the third Baltic Theatre Policy Review, Ilze Rudzīte writes, "As in Estonia and Lithuania, also here in Latvia a performing arts policy does not exist at the highest, state level." Privatization came as a shock to a system that, though repressed, had long functioned at the pleasure of the state. So while theatre was "ideologically shaped and carried out by the Ministry of Culture" (Tjarve, "Performing Arts Policy"), it was also fully funded and immune to the volatile market forces the Baltic states experienced after the collapse of the Soviet Union, including the less ideological but maybe even more stressful issues such as "considerable inflation, crucial political, economical and social changes which have affected cultural institutions."

In Tjarve's view, the result, more by necessity than design, was "a strange mingle of the Soviet and market management running cultural institutions (commercial shows and business sponsors on one side; improvident, inefficient management on the other)" (Tjarve, "Performing Arts Policy"). In her report Tjarve cites Dragan Klaić, a director of the Theatre Institute in the Netherlands, who identifies the problem as endemic and common in all former satellite states: "Similar problems," he says, "were found in the theatre in Eastern European countries" (qtd. in Tjarve, "Performing Arts Policy"). Yet, even though all three Baltic states share the same structural and financial difficulties, according to Tjarve the individual responses from each, in theory and practice, differ significantly, with Estonia — long associated with the Scandinavian countries, especially Finland — recovering more quickly than Latvia or Lithuania and enjoying "a new cultural policy," Latvia "in the process of developing planning documents [...] to change the existing legislation," while Lithuania "demonstrates sharp discrepancies between reality and level of cultural policy" (Tjarve, "Performing Arts Policy").

Funding issues will be resolved. And from the look of things, the status of theatres will play out as predictably as it does in Western Europe, Britain and the United States: politicized but domesticated, alternately stressing a national civic identity and an existential social critique while maintaining a comfortable dialectic guaranteed to satisfy the whims of the preservationists, the traditionalists, the folklorists, and those promoting history and cultural artifacts. The more difficult issue to resolve involves immediacy and relevance: What will keep the general public interested in Baltic theatre?

I was introduced to Baltic theatre at its smallest venue, Kaunas Little Theatre, a three story brick and mortar building off a cobble-stoned shop-lined street in the old-town section of Lithuania's second city. (Physically the theatre is tiny, but "little" in this sense derives from the Russian signifying "elite" or "exclusive.") The first floor features a cafe, a cozy artistic hub for local actors and students. The second floor houses administrative offices, and the third floor serves as the stage, an intimate loft-style space with seating for 70. The crowd mainly consists of university students and young professionals.

Alma Bukšnaitytė, the former theatre manager, typifies the attitude of the theatre-going public active both during and after the Soviet occupation, especially in her ambivalence toward Western-style capitalism. Young enough to remember both the Soviet grade school propaganda and the intellectual liberalization, especially at the universities after *perestroika*, Bukšnaitytė remembers the country torn in a "cultural schizophrenia," convinced the ability to adapt to "the new way" must come from "inside."

"In 1989," she says, "after liberation the people were confused because, instead of making individual choices they all wanted to think one way. They were the products of collective thinking."

During her university years, when she visited her parents they accused her of being "cosmopolitan," of "bad thinking." But her ambivalence is also typical: "The Russians have beautiful anecdotes," she explains, her smile betraying a sense of guilt in the fondness of the memory. "A Russian teacher says now in Russia is day and in the West is night, so boy stands up and says, 'Yes, and it is right because of their black capitalism.'"

Neat, explicit...

"Absurd," she says, her nostalgia suddenly ironic. When she hears Russian, she says "it smells like old times coming back — like in Proust — a mixed impulse. Because I miss the influence of Russian culture, especially in movies and art." But after 1989, the major Russian influences came from the "nauji Rusai"— the new Russians, the bourgeoisie, the nouveau riche, in her mind no different from the Red Capitalists of 1917, partycrats allowed to earn individual income from private enterprise.

If the money comes from Russia in U.S. currency, the culture now comes from the West — German MTV, American movies, Mexican soaps.

The philosophy of the Kaunas Little Theatre has evolved in response to the sense of disruption following Lithuania's independence from the Soviets. Before independence, Bukšnaitytė says, there was a cause, a purpose, a unifying sense of relevancy in "a theatre of resistance." During the occupation the Soviets not only tolerated and approved of a subversive theatre but they encouraged it, as if by sanctioning political dissent they could contain it, could allow the intellectual community, to ease discontent, to thrive while at the same time maintaining a convenient, identifiable scapegoat.

"But what are the subjects now?" asks Bukšnaitytė. "And how does the theatre respond? The society is evolving and theatre needs to evolve with it. We don't have a new language for the new time. With so much Western influence, ideas are open, but Lithuanian theatre lacks the language which can investigate the problems of *now*."

She complains that many theaters, responding to Western trends and a market economy, were ineluctably moving away from a theatre of ideas towards popular entertainment, and in an attempt to retain an audience risked becoming irrelevant.

"Nowadays," she says, "it's Shakespeare as can-can."

Bukšnaitytė is philosophical about the Westernizing of the economy. She prefers a middle way, something between Marxism and Capitalism, expecting the free-for-all market mentality to evolve into some kind of vague hybrid akin to the French model, a sort of "third way" ideal bandied about so vocally during the Clinton/Blair years. "The 'Black Capitalism' of the 1990s is over," she says. "Things are settling down."

Some disagree. A woman named Ina, another Little Theatre cafe regular, considers herself a professional. During the Soviet era, she took her degree in design and graphics from an art school in Kaunas, but ended up working in an import-export firm wholesaling clothes from China. After independence, she lost her job and moved into a house she believed was cursed. Her husband, in prison in Germany for doing business with the Mafia, had inherited the property from his grandfather who, according to Ina, was given the house by the Nazis for turning in the original owner, a Jew. Her only support came from her husband sending Deutsch marks hidden between split Polaroids, and what little his brother, on leave from the Lithuanian navy, also living there, could bring in. The brother, before becoming a sailor, served in the Russian army and told horror stories of young Lithuanian soldiers ordered to clean up at Chernobyl. Several he knew were already dead, most from leukemia. Ina reminds him that when the Soviets sent troops to Lithuania, she and her friends met the tanks on the bridge over the Nemunas River. "We stopped them with our hands," she says, "not with Kalashnikovs."

After liberation she began to earn a "Western salary" coordinating truck deliveries between Warsaw and Moscow. Later she became the manager of a store selling designer furniture, financed (of course) by a German entrepreneur whose support was based in part on her agreeing to be his lover. "I have a child to think of," she said, shrugging in a fatalistic gesture so common in the expression of many liberated Lithuanians when they talk about what they understand as the necessities of Western-style economics. "All money in Lithuania is black," she says.

With that introduction, my two central issues were set: the change in theatre during the transition from Soviet occupation to after independence in 1991, and the impact on Lithuanian national identity after its later integration into the European Union — that is, how a small country with a small language can maintain its cultural uniqueness as it is assimilated into ever larger spheres of influence, as a former satellite nation, as a Baltic state, then as a full-fledged member of this so-called "New Europe."

One trend in Lithuanian theatre distinguishing it from both the approaches to theatre in the other Baltic states and from what the Lithuanians called "Western" approaches allows the director auteur status, freeing him to consider the text little more than a suggestion. This approach, of course, in practice is not as rigidly enforced as its apologists imply, but the disdain for the sanctity of the text and the cavalier attitude exhibited by the most distinguished Lithuanian directors toward rewriting, reworking or, often, merely abandoning the text, distinguish them from mainstream directors in the U.S. and U.K. who tend to respect, if not revere, the text, and where, in practice if not in theory, directors and actors — unless they are "stars"— are subordinate to the writer's work. These directors, privileging visual content over text, reject any shared operating principle with the writer. Critic Elona Bajorinienė agrees. "The best Lithuanian directors oppose literary theatre dominated by text." She cites Eimuntas Nekrošius, Rimas Tuminas and Jonas Vaitkus as the three main figures, "the 'Olympus' of contemporary Lithuanian theatre."

Still, prominent professional directors like Vaitkus insist no theatre can be successful without the mediating influence of a strong director. Others, especially those associated with two of the most influential directors in the country — if not in Europe — Rimas Tuminas and Oskaras Koršunovas — were equally adamant about the importance of an auteur director. Even so, new writers like Marius Ivaškevičius and impresarios like Liūgą challenge this approach, condemning it as a product of the old-fashioned centralized state system that institutionalizes mediocrity and the status quo. This new generation of writer/directors hopes to create a "post-dramatic" theatre that actually diminishes the authority of the director and reinstates a more egalitarian, improvisational and intuitive ensemble approach to staging a play.

Jurgita Staniškytė, Coordinator for International Studies at Vytautas Magnus University and former Fulbright Scholar, explains this new approach as actually a return to the authentic historical roots of Lithuanian theatre which had been distorted by the introduction of psychological realism in the nineteenth century, and thus the antagonism toward text-based realism is itself a political act, as relevant today as the coded "Aesopian" language during the Soviet occupation. "The tradition of visuality has its deep roots in the poetic metaphorical tradition of Lithuanian theater." For her, "this new approach to textual and performative elements in contemporary Lithuanian theatre is closely linked with the attempt to restore the heterogeneous, harmonic relationships between the two." Rūta Skendelienė, a theatre critic from Kaunas, agrees:

> [...] a paradoxical construction principle of sight-action-text connections developed in Lithuanian theatre. In the theatre of metaphors, performances spoke about certain things on the superficial level, but conveyed utterly different meanings on the deeper level [...] The purpose of the directors was to create a performance structure consisting of many layers, so that on the surface it would be understood in one way and the deeper layers would have an absolutely different meaning.

Throughout the Baltics, each country develops its own socio-political system of cryptography, but the process — the use of theatrical performances to unify the population and to provide a coded critique of the cultural situation (this Aesopian language) — was for all three the prime generator of relevance during the Soviet period. The problem, according to Skendelienė, is that after independence, because there were essentially no more taboo topics or forbidden subjects, to win back audiences who found the theatre irrelevant many directors tried to compete with pop entertainment, diluting the intrinsic theatrical experience, or they sought new avenues of relevance, but these attempts often seemed overly didactic and ineffective at revitalizing theatre. "This was how the ethical ESOP language, which flourished in Soviet times, became transformed to an aesthetic" (Skendelienė).

I approached Tallinn from Finland, where colleagues at the University of Helsinki had identified a delicate balance of politics and culture that united *and* separated the two regions. I heard for the first time how this Lithuanian tendency to stress the visual over the oral in performances might be explained by the prominent role of miracle plays, relics and visual stimulants in the Lithuanian Catholic liturgy (the most common analogy was to compare Italian *commedia dell'arte* with Ibsen). What I would find in Estonia, I was assured, would be a theatre stylistically closer to the tradition of Scandinavia: preachy narrators, a penchant for text-based performances, a reliance on intellectual story-telling. This tactic of logical analysis adapted to theatre, attributable to the Reformation, specifically to the Lutheran tradition of literacy and the sermonizing tendencies of Reformation preachers, had over the years created the operating stereotypes commonly associated in the Baltics with "traditional values" and "spiritual decadence," and the Lutheran/Catholic split, acknowledged since the Thirty Years War, is still present in the national experience of each country; indeed, the differences in the directorial approaches — the Catholic, visual-based theatre of Lithuania and the Lutheran, text-based approach of Latvia and Estonia — distinguish the Lithuanians from their northern neighbors.

I began with Tallinn City Theatre where Jaan Tätte is based. Tätte's work not only represents the ability of an Estonian playwright to have his work translated and performed internationally but also exemplifies the Lutheran-inspired, text-based, story-telling approach to Estonian playwriting. Tätte establishes both a normative "type" of theatre and the model to reject by other directors intent on creating a more physical, metaphorical theatre. Tätte's plays are a foil, setting at one end the nearly nontheatrical narratives of Merle Karusoo's recollections-performances and at the other the chameleonic, "total theatre" shock-cabaret of Peeter Jalakas's Von Krahl, locating Eva Klemets, Tiit Ojasoo, Mart Koldits, Hendrik Toompere and Andrus Kivirähk somewhere between these extremes. (As late as the summer of 1998, only one of the playwrights under consideration in this study — Kivirähk — was cited by Külli Paulus in his "Estonian Dramaturgy — a Moment of Stage" published in *Estonian Literary Magazine*.)

Aesthetics dominated the discussions in Tallin, as the issues that dominated the theatre during the Soviet years are waning with the new generation of writers. Priit Kruus, in a 2005 article for *Estonian Literary Magazine*, writes that the "youngest representatives of Estonian literature, born at the end of the 1970s and early 1980, are the children of the transition period [...] [that] lost their societal innocence and lived through a critical period that was as long as their teenage years." The pressing issue for the new generation, according to Kruus, is "their relations with mass media." Like many of his counterparts in other Baltic states, he disparages the corrosive effects of Western pop culture: "One freedom that we haven't used until now is the freedom to be independent from something — the image of Western hype literature, market economy book-selling strategies, or the need to try all kinds of swearwords and dabble in postmodernism."

No matter how diminished, the hangover from the Soviet years is still evident: not that the new generation of writers wants to forget or dismiss the repression, hardships and atrocities, but in a time of prosperity and freedom — a description most theatre practitioners in the Baltics subscribe to — many appreciate the luxury of not having to confront with such intensity and seriousness sociological and political issues, entertaining instead debates about aesthetics, the nature and purpose of art and its role within the larger question of mass-marketing and consumer-based entertainment.

The debate about the role of theatre in Estonia during the later years of the Soviet era is unsettled. Anyone remotely involved in theatre during the Soviet period remembers the theatre as a place where people could go to hear the "hidden message of hope," to enjoy the sport of defeating the ideology of the censors, to mock the occupiers while resisting the occupation.

Anneli Saro, Lecturer in the Department of Literature and Folklore at the University of Tartu, adds a different twist to the common perception that theatre during the Soviet occupation was a noble exercise in collective resistance. Saro's point is to attempt to explain the popularity of theatre during the Soviet times that qualifies the popular notion (especially in the West) that the theatre offered some noble collective act of resistance, a romantic, mythical idea Saro debunks not to denigrate the value of the theatre during that period but to frame it in a more realistic perspective.

First, as she remembers, censorship was not as extreme as many reactionaries in the West would like to believe. American and British playwrights were frequently performed — Miller, Beckett and Albee, for example — although authors who were provocatively anti-communist — like Pinter — were automatically banned. To appear ideologically correct, the official position from Moscow was that at least one third of the performances in any given repertory were supposed to be Soviet, but research, according to Saro, suggests that this "ideological correctness" was never strictly enforced, much less realized by any local repertory theatre.

Far from being an apologist for Soviet policy, Saro nevertheless is quick to point out that the popularity of theatre during Soviet times may have had less to do with resistance or defiance than with, oddly, the market realties of supply and demand. In the Soviet period, people earned what can be called, relatively, a normal salary. However, consumers then were in the unusual position of having money but nothing to buy. People needed permission to buy a car, and only one car per family was allowed. It was equally difficult to buy a house, and in Estonia Russian nationals were first on the list for available property. On television, irrespective of the anomalies noted above, most people had access to two channels, one Russian and one Estonian, but both tended to feature mainly Soviet propaganda or films from what were considered by the authorities as "friendly" countries, especially, in Saro's recollection, movies form India. Restaurants were also scarce; standing in line to wait for a table was normal even on weekdays. Travel, obviously, was restricted, so vacations were limited to trips within the Soviet Bloc. In short, opportunities for cultural, culinary and recreational activities were so restricted or unavailable that people had nothing better to do than to go to the theatre.

In Saro's scenario, the theatre of resistance, revered by the West as an idealized act of defiance, more realistically resembles a theatre of necessity. Her view represents, perhaps, an historical correction, exposing the tendency of critics in the West to mythologize and romanticize (while patronizing) the role of theatre during the Soviet occupation, often to feed their own sense of righteousness.

Saro's view does not diminish the truly serious threat the Soviets imposed on the cultural identity of Estonia and the other Baltic states. As in Latvia and Lithuania, no directors were allowed to study their craft in Estonia.[1] Directors were required to attend academies in Russia, usually in Leningrad or Moscow, where their ideological points of view could be monitored and, in theory, the Soviets could inculcate the potentially powerful theatre tyros with the proper Soviet ideological training and education to ensure that they would remain loyal comrades. Like nearly everything else the Soviets tried to micromanage, their attempt to control the ideas of theatre directors was undercut too, either by directors who nodded on cue, then returned to their native countries to pursue their own visions (Padegimas in Lithuania, for instance, among others), or, as in Estonia, by local actors who, with no professional training in directing, assumed the task, thwarting the censors and at the same time creating ensemble groups adept at keeping the theatre free from the ideological interference of Soviet apparatchiks. (The first group of directors, four in all, including Merle Karusoo, graduated the Drama Studio of Tallinn State Conservatoire in 1976.)

After suffering the same cultural and financial upheavals as the other Baltic states after independence, Latvian theatre since the 90s has gone through a similar period of rejuvenation, having repositioned itself at the center of the critique of cultural values, practical and aesthetic, inherent in the capitalist Western economic social model. But questions of funding, inextricably tied to controversial issues such as the relationships between audience expectations and artistic autonomy, subsidized repertories and independent theatres, creative license and quality control, continue to plague development and experimentation. For instance, Eduards Liniņš, representing the Latvian Ministry of Culture, acknowledged "a psychological barrier: the state theatres, funded previously, do not think of the newly established independent theaters seriously" (36).

Baiba Tjarve, in her role as former director of the New Theatre Institute of Latvia, summarizes the situation in the 90s:

> Everything has changed. Myself, my colleagues and my contemporaries from ex-communist countries have gained invaluable experience in setting up new organizations and lobbying for reform in cultural policy. We needed to change the entire legislative set-up, to find unusual new ways of fundraising... [Tjarve, "Passing on Knowledge" 146].

How successful this project has been rates a qualified optimism:

> Performing arts in Latvia still adhere to Stanislavskian approach where psychorealism and a strong text are dominant. The use of multimedia, visual arts, contemporary dance, and an intersectoral approach is still peripheral. [...] However, there does exist a young generation of both artists and audiences who are open to experiencing a different concept of theatre... [147].

Indeed. After independence the dominance of Stanislavskian realism was challenged and/or modified by the novelty and "pop" appeal of Western influences — what one of Latvia's most famous experimental directors, Pēteris Pētersons called "'bankrupt foreign trends'" (qtd. in Zeltiņa 39).

Contemporary Latvian directors are now well versed in postmodern tendencies, although, perversely some of the early experimental directors have moved away from avant-garde styles and have returned to the traditional realistic approaches of "straight" drama.[2] Regnārs Vaivars, for instance, notorious for his early meta-theatrical productions challenging the limits of theatre, staged Albee's *Who's Afraid of Virginia Woolf* (*Kam no Vilka kundzes bail?*) with an uncharacteristic fidelity to the text, eschewing any directorial pyrotechnics for an acute sense of psychological precision. Such confidence in the material itself and respect for the playwright's intentions demonstrate a maturity too seldom seen in fledgling directors out to impress audiences and critics clamoring for anything considered "new." This eclectic impulse, according to Guna Zeltiņa, a prominent critic and scholar at the Latvian Academy of Sciences, proves that post-nineties Latvian theatre "is striving to overcome its long-term isolation from the contemporary developments in the world theatre and [...] to crystallize a style and directions of its own" (47–48).

This split in allegiance — between the nationalists and the Europhiles — mirrors the schizophrenic attitude with which many in Riga's theatre community struggle, manifest in an arrogance — a cultural defiance — regarding their status (especially when compared to the other Baltic nations) undercut by an equally intense diffidence — a self-defeating impotence — that qualifies their confidence as innovators and central players in the contemporary theatre community in Europe. Tjarve, almost militantly, rejects what she perceives as the apprentice status assigned to Latvian theatre (and to Baltic theatre generally):

> Sometimes I wonder why there is such a strong belief that it is the so-called Western European experts, trainers and professionals who have experience and knowledge that must be passed on to their Central/Eastern European colleagues. And why not the other way around? [Tjarve, "Passing on Knowledge" 146].

Much of the critical commentary feeds this perception, and some of it can be taken as condescending. Critics from former Soviet bloc countries identify with Latvia's attempts at recovery, both financially — learning to survive without heavy state subsidies — and thematically — reestablishing theatre again as a viable social force once it became redundant after independence. Other critics from more advanced nations within the Euro zone but who share the geo-cultural situation of being a small country at play in a field dominated by cultural behemoths like Germany and Russia sympathize with Latvia's struggle to have its voice heard in the larger cultural sphere beyond its borders. (Annelis Kuhlmann, a Danish critic from the University of Aarhus, suggests that Latvian theatre, like theatre in Denmark, is essentially conditioned by its dilemma of "facing the world outside a small country.") Even when foreign critics move beyond the socio-political events of recent history and address the aesthetics of Latvian theatre they tend to view Latvian theatre as an emerging phenomenon cleft by desire: for the older generation, a craving for the past glory of Stanislavskian realism, evoking a golden era of actors superbly trained in the Russian tradition; for the younger generation, a demand for new forms and experimentation driven by a disdain for tradition, yet qualified by an awareness of their own appropriation of postmodernity without necessarily contributing anything wholly original to the mix.

Latvia shares the same issues uniting the other Baltics, traceable to the pagan resistance against the Christian crusades, the impact of the Reformation, the Hanseatic influence, various foreign occupations and now independence. But these common histories provoke an odd intramural rivalry among the Baltic countries. In Estonia, a critic told me she would not be at Spēlmaņu Nakts (the Showcase of the Best Latvian Performances, held annually in November) because she had attended the year before and, in her words, "the plays were so awful that I don't think I'll go back." Critics in Lithuania had spoken derisively of Latvian theatre as an actors' theatre. And in Latvia, Lauris Gundars, head of the Theatre, Cinema and TV drama course at the Latvian Academy of Culture, actually turned the Lithuanian's reputation for strong directors into an opportunity to criticize them, explaining, "There are almost no new writers.... The biggest problem in Lithuania is the strong directors." Feeding this bickering is skepticism on the part of the Latvians about the value of trying to "globalize," of creating plays that can be exported into a pan–European aesthetic that will place Latvia on the map as a major EU cultural player. This scrimmaging, expressed in Latvia as a defensiveness, a weird blend of belligerence and diffidence, has, in a positive spin, caused some of the best directors to rethink their narrow concern for aesthetics and instead decide to revisit the essence of psychological realism — not in the traditional sense but in a post–Stanislavskian concentration on intense inner states of expression and the ability of theatre to express them in a more contemporary mode.

In all of the Baltic states, the directors whose reputations have been recognized in "greater Europe"— Gintaras Varnas and Marius Ivaškevičius in Lithuania, Tiit Ojasoo and Hendrik Toompere in Estonia, and Alvis Hermanis and Gaļina Poliščuka in Latvia, et al.— established themselves as innovators challenging the idea of theatre while adhering to traditional principles of character and action. These directors have self-consciously moved away from what most now consider decadent psychological realism, experimenting with new forms of expression. Other writers and directors — Jonas Vaitkus and Rimas Tuminas in Lithuania, Jaan Tätte and Eva Klemets in Estonia, Māra Ķimele and Indra Roga in Latvia — seek to revitalize the Stanislavskian model by approaching classics with a new perspective, informed by modern theatre language and techniques that modify without destroying the strategies of realism.

Before independence from the Soviets, Baltic theatre was a dynamic driving social force, drawing a loyal audience attuned to the Aesopian parables the political writers managed to sneak past the regional commissars. They came to protest. They came to be pacified. They came because no other interesting media could provoke such intensity, such connectedness, such defiance — the rhetoric quickly turns purple with romantic notions: still, the influence, the seriousness, the irreverence inherent in Baltic theatre before the Soviets' withdrawal set a high bar for post–Soviet repertory companies, and how they hope to renew that former vitality is the subject of this book.

2

Lithuania: Catholic Spectacle — Directors' Theatre

    Lithuanian theatre can be traced back to the pagan street, when a Vaidila, a combination priest, actor and minstrel bard was wreathed and masked for his performance in religious rituals and folk festival celebrations. The role of the Vaidila evolved over the centuries, and in the Middle Ages he was identified as the chief performer of romantic allegories, miracle plays, and the elaborate street theatres common to the period. Some critics suggest that even contemporary trends in Lithuanian theatre can be traced back to its earliest manifestations in pagan rituals and spiritual culture. Skendelienė suggests that "Lithuanian theatre is very much connected with the mythology of the nation [...] it can only be understood in the context of its history." After 1795, when Lithuania (which by then had merged with Poland) fell under Russian rule, theatre was inextricably tied to a national yearning for independence, the kindling of Lithuanian patriotism and resistance to what the citizens recognized as Czarist oppression. According to Skendelienė, "At the end of the nineteenth century Lithuania theatre was not hedonistic; its principle function was to preserve national identity." These performances were, however, seditious and therefore "the organizers [...] were persecuted and punished, many of them being deported to Siberia."

    Lenin's influence permeates Lithuania's history, even during the formation of the early independent state (circa 1918). Theatre proved a useful tool for the reformers, just as it had worked for the Soviet apparatchiks as a perfect vehicle for patriotic indoctrination. In the hands of partisan artists, theatre became a necessary vehicle of propaganda for the young state. Just as it had during the late nineteenth century, theatre again was directly associated with Lithuanian national identity. "For spectators it was not entertainment so much as a secretive act of civil disobedience, a form of resistance" (Skendelienė). After World War II, Juozas Grušas and Justinas Marcinkevičius began to use traditional techniques in their plays, but with some innovative elements. Kazys Saja, considered the first to use modern dramatic techniques, mixed allegorical subjects with sarcasm and became popularly recognized as one of the new Lithuanian writers able to express what Markevičiūtė describes as "the wounds in the human soul." Juozas Glinskis, influenced by Artaud's "theatre of cruelty" and a flagrant nonconformist, achieved a Pyrrhic victory when he provoked the Soviet censors into prohibiting some of his pieces. In the 1960's and 1970's, Saulius Šaltenis created a special kind of drama, presenting on stage an array of simple village people. His non-heroic leading characters expressed simple values and authenticity in an epoch of total untruth.

"Untruth," or inauthenticity (*mauvais foi*), is a potent theme in contemporary Lithuanian theatre, fueling the skepticism about Western cultural hegemony felt most acutely in the once thriving theatre community. Loreta Rudaitienė, a Ph.D. candidate at Kaunas Technological University, accuses the West of having a "consumerist mentality." Rudaitienė cheers for the Chetchnyans in their struggle against Russia, and is convinced that the conflict was started to sap Yeltsin's power. She stresses that the conflict was for Yeltsin a moral defeat. "Any unfair deal," she says, "has negative consequences on personal matters first, which later influence other activities (in his case, political). The same happened to Gorbachev, since he has the blame for killing Lithuanians the night of January 13, 1991." As for Yeltsin, she says simply, "He lost his will to govern." In Rudaitienė's mind, Marxism and Capitalism are merely two sides of the same extremist coin. Both cause a loss of identity: on one side, the self is subsumed in a collectivist obscurity; on the other, through materialism, it is taken for granted.

"I was a child of Lenin," she says. "A star pupil. I believed Lenin was the great father who would care for his children." At fifteen she began "freethinking." After a fellow student died in self-immolation over the Russian occupation, she said her rejection of Soviet ideals was instinctive. She frames the issue succinctly: "What is happening to the Lithuanian spirituality in an age of individualism, competitiveness, and market cultures?" She complains that "morality has been privatized" and fears that the abrupt change to moral relativism related to unprincipled capitalism may lead to social disintegration. The real problem, she believes, is psychological: the Soviet system created an existential crisis because the ideological propaganda was so baseless in fact. "Every social ill was blamed on the West. For instance, a soldier goes to war and is killed. His wife's grief is caused by Western bourgeoisie economies."

This anti–Western bias echoes the central role theatre played historically in the life of the politicized citizenry. In the thirty years from about 1957 to 1988, Lithuanian drama developed rapidly, mastering both contemporary subjects and techniques. Lithuanian playwrights strongly influenced their audiences, playing a pre-eminent role in preparing the renewal of independence in 1988. Because of this, the most interesting of the artists (Šaltenis, Saja and Glinskis) became members of parliament, editors of big newspapers or ministers, and ceased writing plays. According to Staniškytė, "The image of Lithuanian theatre as [...] a theatre which has lost its privileged status in society and become a marginalized art form governed by the vision of authoritative directors, is still wide spread among Lithuanian theatre critics."

Earlier, having been isolated from the world theatre processes or suppressed in the rigor of socialist realism, Lithuanian theatre has seen a rebirth of the so-called "theatre of relativity" promoted by aggressively independent directors nourished by a new sense of aesthetic freedom. Where in its incipient stages, Lithuanian theatre was grounded in the dogmatism of socialist realism, later styles developed an anti-naturalist movement inspired by the influence of Brecht, Meyerhold, Evgeny Vakhtangov and Michael Chekhov, reflecting a new awareness of technique on the contemporary Lithuanian stage. Staniškytė admits that "Lithuanian theatre for a long time has been a 'director's theatre,' where the director's concept dominated all other representational elements in performance." However, after independence and the sudden crisis of relevance in theatre, more directors became interested in an aesthetic approach to performances, expressing a "tendency toward a deconstruction of the process of theatre production and its inherent technologies of representation."

This new spirit was exhibited in the autumn of 1988 at a defiant festival titled "Atgaiva" ("spiritual re-nourishment") organized in Šiauliai by Gytis Padegimas in which every Lithuanian theatre company presented new work or plays that had been banned, including texts by exiled Lithuanian playwrights. This festival marked a turning point in Lithuanian culture, important as both a cultural and political event. But no amount of optimism can counter what young Lithuanian writers must confront: they are working in a small language, and because most Lithuanian writers can be read or performed only by and for Lithuanian audiences, this linguistic stricture can become fatally frustrating. Few Lithuanian writers are translated. As a result, many writers concentrate on non-verbal performances, or they turn away from their native language, many choosing to compose in English.

It is this cynical spirit that many like Rudaitienė feel is diminishing the nature of the people. She casts her criticism in both spiritual and social terms: for her, free-for-all capitalism has stolen the soul of the Lithuanian people, and the abrupt changes in Lithuania have created a present chaos in values.

The question for many boils down to this: Because unbridled capitalism has allowed influences from so many different cultures to permeate a space as small as Lithuania, the society is struggling to find a way to cope with the present chaos in values. Whether the country's theatre can create a language to express this anxiety, or whether it will succumb to the market pressures of entertainment — appropriated by the very system it intends to critique — remains to be seen.

Kaunas

Regional nationalism pervades Kaunas. The city is a second city to Vilnius the way Arhus is to Copenhagen, or Manchester to London: the real and perceived sense of inferiority breeds rivalry, competitiveness and a deep pride in the spirit of the locals. One night, an English-language radio broadcast people being interviewed in Vilnius, a decidedly more cosmopolitan and international city. They regarded Kaunas as a parochial backwater. "The people in Kaunas have too many moral constraints," said one. "It's an industrial city," said another. "All they think about is business." Vilnius, for them, was the center for art and intellectuals. Not surprisingly, the people interviewed in Kaunas insisted that their city was the "true capital," accused Vilnius of being "Russified," and, expressing the view of many people in the central region, they considered people in Kaunas "real Lithuanians."

"Real" Lithuania is not a concept. By the end of the nineteenth century, the Czarist regime forbade literature in the Lithuanian language, one of the reasons for the late emergence of a Lithuanian national dramaturgy. At that time, thousands of disobedient Lithuanians were executed for rioting against the Russian Empire, while others were refused the right to their land, schools, writing and language. Russia's repression led to a resistance movement that held patriotic performances on farms, in rural barns or on village thrashing grounds, where intellectuals and peasants plotted liberation. To encourage Lithuania's national independence movement, a new form of theatre developed called "thrashing house" or "barn theatre."

Since Kaunas was the capital (from 1920 to 1940), the population has consisted of nearly one hundred percent ethnic Lithuanians. During the crucial 1994 election, the voters in the Kaunas region voted overwhelmingly for the Lithuanian-American candidate, while Vilnius and the rest of Lithuania voted for a former communist. In the next watershed election, 1998, one hundred per cent of the last returns from Kaunas were cast for the Lithuanian-American Valdas Adamkus, votes that decided the presidency. Some in Kaunas described the 1998 vote as "revenge."

The main pedestrian promenade in Kaunas is Freedom Street (Laisvės Alėja). At one end, a huge green and white Kalnapilis beer sign flashes a hundred feet above a communist era block-and-mortar business complex, while underneath it, beside a busy Benetton boutique, black-caped penitents kneel and pray for hours on the sidewalk, eyes rolled back, hands cupped in supplication. At the other end of the "high street," nearly two kilometers away, as if to spiritually offset that huge green and white neon Kalnapilis beer sign dominating the opposite end of the promenade, a Russian Orthodox Church, dilapidated but imposing, its gilded dome wrapped in scaffolding, shadows the employment commission.

On any given afternoon, Freedom Street is transformed from a sleepy morning pedestrian by-way into a tableau of controlled anarchy, indicative of the contradictions and incongruities inherent in the emerging Lithuanian socio-economic system. Women living in abject poverty (by American standards) splash out in fashionable glamour for a trip to the market for milk. Crumbling pre-war apartments and abandoned buildings litter the block before the park where a new hotel in the "historical section" (old town) charges hundreds of US dollars a night for a single room. Communist-era cars — Žigulis, Škodas and Ladas, still popular with university students — rust beside polished new Mercedes, Jaguars and BMWs ("Big Mafia Wheels"). Bobutės selling fruit and flowers in the alleys of stylish restaurants pay pennies for greasy black sausages in musty meat stores behind posh pizza joints charging American prices. Often in summer there is no hot water in parts of the city, but everyone complains about it on a cell phone.

For years, the hip cultural buzz in Kaunas centered on the Little

Theatre of Kaunas (Kauno Mažasis Teatras), established in 1992 by Rolandas Atkočiūnas, one of the post-*perestroika* "New Wave" of Lithuanians. Atkočiūnas, after studying directing in Moscow, wanted an alternative, independent theatre that stressed experimental, non-traditional works by international writers. In 1991, Atkočiūnas returned to Kaunas and convinced the municipality to seed an innovative theatre that, according to its directive, would "approach the spectator and the actor ... and evolve in the direction of cafe-theatre."

In 1994, Arvydas Lebeliūnas assumed the job of artistic director and continued to develop the Little Theatre in the direction set by Atkočiūnas. Lebeliūnas preferred expressionistic plays with minimalist staging, especially ones that mix genres and appeal to students and young people eager to be challenged by experimental work. All jobs were done "in house." The actors, drawn from open casting in Kaunas and Vilnius, created the sets, costumes and props. During his tenure, Lebeliūnas staged four productions a season, developed during two months of workshops and rehearsals, which ran simultaneously during the season. "It's a matter of pragmatism," explains Lebeliūnas. "We have no promotional budget." The remedy was simply to run the shows long enough for word to get around.

"It's an actor's theatre," he says. "Stress is placed on acting, on the physical."[3] A Little Theatre production of *Charlie!* (*Karol*) by the Polish writer Slawomīr Mrożek offers a good illustration of what Lebeliūnas means. In his adaptation, which only loosely follows Mrożek's original, the play centers on a visit by a gangster and a soldier to an ophthalmologist who has just cured a young woman's blindness. In the course of the interrogation of the doctor by the two men, Lebeliūnas created a simple Manichean context framing insight and blindness, knowledge and ignorance, within a dramatic chiaroscuro. His engrossing treatment, relying on the symbolic use of music, metaphorical lighting, and a surreal sense of minimalist staging, visually, seamlessly, welds the past and the present, demonstrating, both within the action of the play and the staging under his direction, the insidious abuse of symbols as weapons. In one particularly haunting moment, underscoring Lebeliūnas's deft minimalist's touch, the young woman with newly restored vision dances as if in memory, behind the black back drop, flooded in light, while the three other characters freeze in a potential murder. Playing to the audience, mixing drama and farce, the stock characters managed to attain a psychological depth beyond their archetypes, effectively revealing the absurdity of terror, the intrinsic comedy of desperation.

Aside from the iconoclastic bent of its material, what sets the Little Theatre off from other theaters in Kaunas is evident in its eclectic seasonal programs. One year, for instance, the ensemble invited Norwegian Ingve Sundvor to direct a play, presented puppet shows by Lithuania artist Valdis Aleksaitis, produced three short plays by the French writer Jean Michelle Ribes, and staged *The Sad Ballad of Johnny Reb and His Pretty Wife Cecilia* by American playwright Scott Turner. Lebeliūnas concedes that when he was in charge, he was not averse to producing traditional pieces — Chekhov's one-act comedies, for example — but he insisted that they be staged with "a new twist, and an emphasis on action."

When Lebeliūnas ran The Little Theatre, he clearly aligned its philosophy with Baudrillard. In *The Ecstasy of Communication*, for example, Baudrillard writes, "There is no longer any transcendence or depth, but only the immanent surface of operations" (12). The loss of vitality in the contemporary Lithuanian theatre reflects his thesis: "The everydayness of the terrestrial habitat hypostatized in space marks the end of metaphysics, and signals the beginning of the era of hyperreality [...] entirely without metaphor [...] the absolute space of simulation" (16).

A production of Tonino Guerra's *The Fourth Chair* at the Little Theatre explicitly illustrates Baudrillard's notion of a theatre in crisis, reflecting a cultural "state of terror which is characteristic of the schizophrenic, an over-proximity of all things" (27). The Little Theatre has a reputation for doing quite a lot with very little, but with its staging of Guerra's *The Fourth Chair* seldom does a theatre have the opportunity to conflate contemporary political ideas with the aesthetics of theatre while also addressing the unique (and local) social, cultural and psychological problems faced by former Soviet satellites emerging into independence.

Guerra is perhaps best known for his work as a screenwriter, working with Italian icons of cinema like Antonioni (*L'Avventura, Blow Up, Zabriskie Point, Red Desert*), Fellini (*Ginger and Fred*) and the Taviani brothers (*Night of the Shooting Stars*). He also scripted *Nostalgia* with the Russian director Andre Tarkovsky. Given Guerra's pedigree, the didacticism one might expect from such a scathing critique of Western cultural hegemony as *The Fourth Chair* is refreshingly absent. And in the hands of Lebeliūnas, the treatment is light and lively, the "message" appropriately oblique, the drama perfectly complemented by a set that deflates the symbols into a tidily packaged minimalist spectacle.

The action involves a chance encounter between Luisa, a young sales representative for a detergent company, and Emilio, a successful businessman

Ieva Zelionkaitė and Ramūnas Šimukauskas in *The Fourth Chair* at the Little Theatre, Kaunas, directed by Arvydas Lebeliūnas. The play reflects Lithuania's cultural schizophrenia. Stampeded by cowboy capitalism, with many of its citizens ill-equipped to handle the sudden influx of Western materialism, the prophylactic "closet" expresses the murkiness of a disposable identity (photograph by Gintautas Kažemėkas).

Luisa interrupts on the verge of hanging himself. Dressed in an outlandish silver and pink outfit, tall in her platform heels, pushing her grocery cart full of washing powder, she is the epitome of a "material girl," a self-centered "Barbie," as artificial as her hair, her heavily made-up face barely masking the child beneath. She is so obsessed with hawking her wares that she utterly fails to notice that Emilio is literally one step from suicide. An expert at selling, she knows everything about her product, her job, but understands nothing of life, of human relationships. Blinded by her materialism, she communicates only with things.

Emilio, clean-shaven, wearing his modest but rich double-breasted suit, dapper and correct even with his neck in the noose, tries to explain to Luisa that his wife has left him, and he doesn't know how to live without her. His life, he thought, had been perfect: his apartment, after all, is fully automated; his life as precise as a clock; and neither he nor his wife had ever wanted for anything. Having never faced a crisis before, he doesn't know how to deal with his wife's sudden desertion. He is completely baffled as to why she left, and more curiously, why she didn't take any of her possessions with her. At a loss to explain his predicament, his life in pieces like a broken watch, he decides his only recourse is to kill himself.

As he relates his story to Luisa, he begins to notice that, for the first time, he is actually talking about honest feelings, expressing an emotional life. But conditioned by sales logic, able to think only in slogans and the generic impersonal sincerity of advertisements, Luisa fails to recognize the intimacy, the potential for human understanding that Emilio tries to convey. She thinks his problems can simply be washed away as easily as dirt from his shirt (which she mechanically washes to demonstrate the cleansing power of her product.) Meanwhile, during his confession, Emilio realizes how he, too, has become a slave to things. He finally understands that his wife left him because his perfect, automatic, clockwork world was totally artificial.

Luisa, condemned to listen, never to hear, becomes obsessed with Emilio's chairs. In a manic epiphany, he sells her one. But it is not enough to slake her craving — her appetite for things is insatiable — so finally he sells her everything he owns. Disillusioned, left with nothing, not even his rope and noose, he decides that resistance is futile — if you can't beat 'em, join 'em — so he relents, embracing Luisa's vision of the advertising life, emerging in the final scene as a clown, dancing in a green spangled jump suit to a disco version of the theme from The Pink Panther.

The chairs represent obsessive materialism, but they are also necessary as a means to suicide. The prophylactic "closet"—a tube of cellophane—ironically offers a temporary shelter, a retreat from the awful reality of the situation, but it also provides a startling image of distortion expressing the murkiness of identity. The "washing machine" suggests easy, wash'n'wear solutions to life's problems, but also a window, a framing device to contain chaotic spasms of abandonment. Even the costumes, which establish a vivid contrast in the personalities of the characters, highlight Emilio's debasement by Luisa as she literally strips away his propriety.

Part of the genius and fun of the production results from the inventive set design by Gintautas Kažemėkas. An architect and photographer, Kažemėkas has an excellent eye for interiors. From the clear plastic oblong "closet" downstage right, to the line of chairs under the hanging noose, to the rectangular door and round "washing machine" window upstage left, the whole set is a playful grid of geometric figures, the garish, sterile, "contempo" living space as soulless as an advertising billboard: disposable, but interesting to look at. The costumes by Inga Kažemėkienės echoed the emptiness.

The play reflects what the cast considered the reality of Lithuania. Stampeded by cowboy capitalism, many of its citizens ill-equipped to handle the sudden influx of Western materialism, Kaunas suffers from an acute cultural schizophrenia. For many people, the humanistic sense of community has been traded in on cutthroat marketing strategies, enhanced buying power. Commodities have replaced relationships. As Baudrillard writes, "Advertising [...] is no longer the baroque, utopian scenario ecstatic over objects and consumption, but rather the effect of the omnipresent visibility of corporations, trade marks, PR men, social dialogue and the virtues of communication" (19). The production of *The Fourth Chair*, in a sense, is an act of catharsis, a purgation and an accusation, an apology for allowing conditions to deteriorate, in the spirit of progress and materialism, to a level where "the market is an ecstatic form of the circulation of goods, as prostitution and pornography are ecstatic forms of the circulation of sex" (23).

"People do not want to understand each other," explained Ieva Zelionkaitė, who, with a deft oxymoronic touch, plays Luisa as an advertising archetype: the vampish ingénue, the childish siren so prized by commercial retailers as the image of desire. "People are obsessed," she said. "Not with human relations but with things — cars, clothes, gadgets." Yet even Luisa, inured to emotional commitments, wrings sympathy from Zelionkaitė. "She believes in that world, the fake world of TV and radio and movies. She can't help it, so I can't blame her. She's a child playing in a world of make-up." But it is this inability to distinguish between human values and commercial imperatives — along with the seductive power of images — that Zelionkaitė finds dangerous. "As soon as Emilio discovers the value of a spiritual life, or at least the value of reality, she leads him back into the darkness, back to materialism."

Ramūnas Šimukauskas, who plays "Emilio," agrees that Emilio's debasement is self-inflicted, reflecting a loss of integrity in a crisis. Against Zelionkaitė's fawning flippancy, Šimukauskas tunes Emilio to just the right pitch, with a distracted intensity that creates a sympathetic if irritating portrait of a man who lives by the book, embraces the conventional stereotypes of his position, acts as expected, but still ends up with nothing of substance to justify his life. The difference in the characters' motivations and decisions underscores the ethical ambiguity of their individual situations. Luisa, convinced that her media-fabricated world is real, cannot in any strict sense be held accountable for her actions. Emilio, who realizes the error of his life, is so desperate for companionship that, in a crucial lapse, he consciously chooses the foppish, trendy, ephemeral, virtual world of popular imagery and empty sentiment, and so proves himself culpable. His ruin is of his own making, so all the more tragic. If the medium — Luisa — is the vehicle, Emilio is both victim and villain.

No one in Kaunas needs a telegram to "get" Baudrillard's message — that "[w]ith the disappearance of the public space, advertising invades everything (the street, the monument, the stage, language)" (19). The meaning resonates far beyond the tiny upstairs stage at Kaunas Little Theatre, certainly throughout much of the former "red camp," and especially along Freedom Street, from that St. Michael the Archangel Church at one end eclipsing the kiosks selling pirated CDs, to the green and white blinking neon Kalnapilis beer sign at the other end shimmering on the crumbling facade of a vacant factory. As Central and Eastern Europe look for the elusive "third way," Guerra's play reminds them (and us) that the road linking democracy and capitalism is often paved with fool's gold.

Lebeliūnas's passion for new forms and cross-genre productions results, he says, from an early involvement with experimental theatre and his visit to LaMama in New York City. (Given the option, he later moved to North America.) A graduate of Vilnius Conservatory, he majored in acting and cinema directing, crediting his teachers, directors Andre Tarkovsky, Larisa Sepitko and Vytautas Žalakevičius, with the most influence on his aesthetics. While his concentration was in acting and directing, Lebeliūnas worked in cinema and made short films for the commercial network Lithuanian TV. He directed programs for LNK, Lithuania public television. Typically, he cites Peter Brook, Steven Spielberg and Ingmar Bergman as directors whose work he most admires, the blend of diverse styles and the confluence of cinematic and dramaturgic techniques exemplifying the tenor of Lebeliūnas's approach.

Another theatre that illustrates the predicament of post–Soviet cultural relevance is The Kaunas State Academic Drama Theatre (Kauno Valstybinis Akademinis Dramas Teatras). The story of the Academic Theatre, the oldest and one of the most prestigious theatre companies in the country, encompasses the history of theatre in Lithuania. Beginning with Juozas Vaičkus, who invited his Flying Theatre to relocate from Petrograd to Kaunas in 1918, the company has been home to the most famous names in Lithuanian theatre, including Konstantinas Glinskis, Borisas Dauguvietis, and Antanas Sutkus.

In 1928, Andrius Oleka-Žilinskas, from Moscow Art Theatre, joined the group to implement reforms based on the teachings of Stanislavsky and Nemirovich-Danchenko. To accelerate the process he invited Michael Chekhov, Anton's nephew — a famous actor, director and teacher in his own right — to establish an actor's training school on the site. Vehemently opposed to Stalinism, and told he would be arrested, Chekhov had fled the Soviets by moving to Berlin, Paris and Prague, but dissatisfied with the Western theatre's emphasis on commercialism, he returned to the Baltics, settling in Kaunas until the Nazis forced him into exile again, this time to America. During his time with the company, he changed the direction of Lithuanian theatre, shifting its focus away from historical dramas to productions more aesthetically attuned to the sensibilities of modern drama.

Plagued first by Nazi manipulation, then again by the postwar renewal under strict socialist ideology, the theatre struggled to maintain its creative integrity. After Stalin's death, however, the situation became more favorable for artistic productions. In 1954, Henrikas Vancevičius, in order to promote Lithuanian playwrights, united the Young Spectator Theatre with the Drama Theatre and moved to its present location on Freedom Street.

From 1967 until 1990, the theatre endured a difficult period during which theatre throughout Lithuania was highly politicized, and many performances, especially of Western plays, took the form of political demonstrations. Jonas Jurašas, director from 1967 to 1972, championed this theatre of resistance, encouraging defiance of the Soviet authorities while seeking more autonomy for his productions, a position that eventually forced him from the country. In 1977, under Jonas Vaitkus, the theatre continued its resistance, but with a subtler approach which allowed them to maintain their political stance without jeopardizing their viability as a theatre.

Out of this hotbed of subversive activism, Gytis Padegimas became a transitional figure, overseeing the theatre's change from a politicized theatre during the Soviet era to a free theatre of aesthetics after independence. Padegimas, who served as Artistic Director from 1993 to 1999, has been active in Lithuanian drama since the 1970's, when theatre was the major stage for political demonstrations against the Soviet rule and a director's livelihood, no less his freedom, was precarious: it was a time when everything having to do with art and culture was by design intensely politicized.

A participant in the Sajūdis National Independence Movement[4] from 1988–1993, Padegimas recalls how, under the Soviet system, when he wanted to produce Western plays which the authorities deemed subversive, he found himself trying to convince them that the plays represented the isolation of the individual under a corrupt capitalist system, when, in truth, to Padegimas and his knowing audience, the plays depicted "simple people living without ideology, without propaganda" and a "celebration of individuality." He also enjoys telling the story of how, in the 1980's, he staged Pinter's *Old Times* on six occasions without any trouble from the Minister of Culture. But when Pinter, in a British newspaper, wrote that he did not believe in Gorbachev's *perestroika*, and the news hit the Russian press, the Minister cancelled the show. "It was a time," he says, "when the theatre was a place where you believed you could really challenge totalitarianism."

But not without a price. Because of his activism, and his refusal to stage any "propaganda revering Lenin and promising a bright socialist future," he was never allowed to head a theatre and was denied permission to travel abroad. But since independence, Padegimas, who trained as a director at the Moscow Theatre Art Institute, has staged dozens of productions on both stage and television. He also began to travel frequently, coordinating joint productions in various countries and lecturing on drama theory at both the Conservatory in Vilnius and Vytautas Magnus University in Kaunas.

Padegimas, almost defensively, points out that theatre, as a genre in Lithuania, is roughly a quarter-century old. The first plays were created for amateur theatre companies at the turn of the twentieth century. "Even then," he says, "the Czarist regime forbade literature in the Lithuanian language."

This is one of the main reasons for the late emergence of a Lithuanian national dramaturgy. The situation changed only when the Academic Theatre, the first professional theatre to play in Lithuanian, was established. He explains how the Academic Theatre was instrumental in developing the talent of what he considers the "classic" Lithuanian playwrights — Maironis, Vincas Krėvė-Mickevičius, Vincas Mykolaitis-Putinas, and Balys Sruoga — who mainly wrote tragedies and dramas in the 1920's and 1930's based on national history. He also cites Petras Vaičiūnas, an author of well-made plays based on actual events, as the most popular playwright of this period. According to Padegimas, in the fifteen years after World War II, the most interesting Lithuanian dramas were written by Antanas Škėma, Algirdas Landsbergis and Kostas Ostrauskas, all exiles in the U.S.A. These three very different playwrights had studied modern western drama, and were able to mix this experience with what Padegimas called "the painful experience of exile" to create what he considered the first truly modernist plays in Lithuanian.

Conceding that Lithuanian theatre has always been a theatre of resistance, geared to the soul of a country defined by wrenching historical events, Padegimas suggests that the renaissance of Lithuanian drama started in the Khrushchev era when Juozas Grušas wrote his historical play *Herkus Mantas* about the Prussian struggle against the Teutons. Written in 1957, it broke many Soviet taboos. From that time on Lithuanian drama became more influenced by a spiritual resistance against the totalitarian regime.

Padegimas admits that because Lithuanian theatre has always been so political, after "liberation" there was a loss of relevancy. But he quickly qualifies his remark. "Before," he says, "these playwrights were poets with the fists of boxers. Now ..." — he shrugs in that patented "new Lithuanian" gesture.

One thing is certain: Padegimas, through his past work at Academic Theatre, discovered, sustained, and promoted new talent as well as new venues. Besides the main hall, which seats over 500, the theatre has six performance spaces housed in a recently renovated adjacent factory. One room, seating only two dozen, consists of a resplendent table in what appears to be an actual dining room: the set for Thornton Wilder's *A Long Christmas Dinner*. It ran twice a week for years. Another space provides a shallow, oblong stage with bleacher seating for over 100, where innovative plays can be developed. The courtyard — similar to a college quad — is utilized for experimental performances, concerts, dances and performances pieces. Other spaces include a studio, a black box, galleries and rooms for installations. Padegimas also initiated an actors training course, a traveling theatre group to visit prisons and small towns, and a program designed to bring in visiting international directors and teachers for performances and workshops.

Padegimas acknowledges that fledgling Lithuanian playwrights often feel frustrated. Add to the isolation felt by the artists working in Lithuania the difficulty of competing for an audience against the ubiquitous din of Western entertainment — music, cinema and television — while stimulating theatre as both a vehicle for cultural ideas and a venue for entertainment, the task seems daunting. Nevertheless, Padegimas maintains his cautious, ironic optimism for the future of Lithuanian theatre. With a palms-up gesture of both faith and futility, he says, "It is very difficult to create fiction when everyday life in Lithuania is so much like theatre."

Another director from the State Academic Drama Theatre, Gintaras Varnas, is considered one of the most talented directors to emerge in post–Soviet Lithuania. Internationally recognized early in his career, Varnas continues to push the edge of theatre toward more challenging and avant-garde productions. Most critics agree that Varnas established his career with his 1998 production of Ibsen's *Hedda Gabler* at the Kaunas Academic Theatre (complemented with a stunning performance by Jūratė Onaitytė). According to Markeviciutė, "This performance was a start of his career and the greatest event of that theatre season. Now Gintaras Varnas is the real leader of Lithuanian Theatre, year after year awarded for the best performances." Bajorinienė, writing in *Krasnogruda*, a Polish cultural magazine, recognizes Varnas as "the epicenter of theatre artists of the younger generation." Bajorinienė distinguishes Varnas' work from that of his contemporaries, most immediately Koršunovas, in both style and content, describing their differences as a rivalry, "a direct confrontation between the theatres." Though she concedes that "Koršunovas sent a challenge to Lithuanian playwriting nurtured in the Romantic tradition, the ultimate goal of which has always been the preservation of national identity, often associated with the idea of statehood," and applauds Koršunovas for his attempts to foreground sociopolitical and historical issues — and by doing so reviving the relevancy of theatre — she complains that when he "transferred his 'off' theatre to the main stage," Koršunovas sacrificed his cutting-edge use of visual space and accepted the status of "professional." On the other hand, in her view, Varnas has not compromised his aesthetics in order to become a mainstream director. She writes, "Varnas chooses a different way: he makes capital out of consciously avoiding conventional performing spaces."

His production of *Hedda Gabler* (*Heda Gabler*) illustrates the virtues that Bajorinienė highlights. Set in the Long Hall of the Kaunas Academic Drama Theatre, the stage resembles a gymnastic room consisting of a maze of interconnected bars on which Hedda performs, keeping fit for her formidable challenge of navigating between her essential self and demands of the social life she inherits. Although the stage is stripped to its essence, Hedda's life is no less complex than if the play were set in a fully realistic mise en scène. The space poetically comments on Hedda's predicament and

Jūratė Onaitytė in Gintaras Varnas' ***Hedda Gabler*** at the Kaunas Academic Theatre. The stage resembles a gymnastic room consisting of a maze of interconnected bars on which Hedda performs, keeping fit for her formidable challenge of navigating between her essential self and demands of the social life she inherits. Although the stage is stripped to its essence, the space poetically comments on Hedda's predicament and illustrates her resolute spirit (photograph by Dmitrij Matvejev).

illustrates her resolute spirit. Bajorinienė notes also the meta-cinematic playfulness Varnas exploits in his work, especially evident at the premiere of *Hedda Gabler*:

> The director receives the audience coming to *Hedda Gabler* with a kind of installation: the lobby is full of portraits of various actresses of the world who played Hedda Gabler. Varnas finds it important that people would feel having come to theatre. He emphasizes the general theatre tradition rather than the concrete tradition of *Hedda Gabler*, as a cultural medium or micro-climate, which is so necessary and which has lately found itself in danger of extinction.

Another notorious — and this time epic — production, *Wasted Land* (*Nusiaubta Salis*), assured Varnas' success (in 2004 he became the Artistic Director of Kaunas State Academic Theatre). Staged in Vilnius at the former printing house of the Soviet newspaper *Pravda*, it has also been performed in an ex-shipyard in Klaipėda, a former fur factory in Kaunas, and in Gdańsk, Poland, the birthplace of Lech Walesa's Solidarity movement. Varnas' use of non-theatrical space–often called "environmental theatre" — is itself an act of antiestablishmentarianism, demonstrating hostility toward

Viktorija Kuodytė and Marius Jampolskis in *Wasted Land*, based on *Merlin* by Tankred Dorst and directed by Gintaras Varnas. Varnas uses "real" space to question the distinction between the theatre as representation and theatre as event. His use of shadow play, puppet theatre, physicality, irony and games creates an allegorical link between historical Lithuania and the particular cultural situation of Lithuania today (photograph by Dmitrij Matvejev).

Povilas Budrys and Viktorija Kuodytė in *Wasted Land* (photograph by Dmitrij Matvejev).

conventional theatre, yet the use of "real" space in which to stage a work of "fiction" allows Varnas to question the distinction between the theatre as representation and theatre as event, similar to his "installation" in the lobby of the Academic theatre in Kaunas before the performance of *Hedda Gabler*.[5] The set "inhabits a space of vanishing historical memory, an aggressive postindustrial landscape, between civilization and nature" (Salomonsson). As critic Ramunė Balevičiūtė points out, the play attempts to correct a collective amnesia regarding nostalgia and reality: "Each presentation of this play wandering in non-traditional post-industrial spaces is associated with places and cities having real historic memory."

Based on *Merlin* by the German playwright Tankred Dorst, the story deals with the classic theme of a young man's journey from innocence to experience, paralleling the myth of the Fall in Genesis. Perceval, naïve and wild, lives in a forest with his mother who, angry at having lost her husband to the chivalric code of knights, wishes to keep her son ignorant of the greater world beyond the woods. Perceval, however, has to go his own way. He must leave his mother (who then dies of grief) to experience life for himself. He meets a society full of destruction and despair, and in his quest for truth and beauty he becomes a murderer and a destructive force himself. In Dorst's play, the movement suggests an allegory: Perceval, accompanied by Merlin, the legendary sorcerer, is led out of the medieval forest and into the messy clearing of the modern world, connecting innocence with violence, wisdom with guilt, and the necessity of evil with the existential desire for self-awareness.

Balevičiūtė finds in this allegory both a general critique of contemporary society and the particular cultural situation in Lithuanian today:

> The concept of this performance project is related to the idea of a wasted land in the contemporary world: it is both a geographical and philosophical category in the space of declining historic memory or post-industrial landscape. It exists in between the past and the present, civilization and nature, which are the essential contradictions tearing our society today.

Most impressive is Varnas' eclectic mix of theatrical components — a *tour de force* involving shadow play, puppet theatre, physicality, irony and games linking the present with the past. Balevičiūtė notes how "the epic is connected to the lyric, the carnival to psychology, paraphrases of Middle Age genres to the extreme emotional expression characteristic of contemporary drama."

The principals at The Kaunas Youth Chamber Theatre (Kauno Jaunimo Kamerinis Teatras) also address this perceived Lithuanian twilight of relevance. Inconspicuously set at the end of an alley off a side street along Freedom Street, the non-descript L-shaped wooden structure looks like the equipment shed for the groundskeeper of the adjacent park, or one of those old-fashioned railway stations at the end of a rural line. But the rough facade masks a posh interior decorated with wall-to-wall gray carpet, plush living room style sofas and chairs and gauzy white curtains. A row of comfortable offices line the rear hall and one side of the foyer opens into a small bar-cafe painted in warm reds with rich wood trim, wooden tables and chairs. But, again, the neatness of the layout, with the middle-class trappings of the lobby — the mirror, the conservative decor, the carpet and furniture, the chic wall hangings — do not prepare a visitor for the perverse audacity of the productions.

A treatment by founder and Artistic Director Stanislovas Rubinovas of the French playwright Claude Magnier's *Blaise* turns a fairly straightforward farce into an expressionistic nightmare. The play chronicles the calamities of a foppish dilettante, a pretentious "artiste" plagued by a series of mishaps as he tries to complete a portrait of a teenage vixen commissioned by her wealthy parents. The clashing garish colors — bright primary reds and blues, poisonous pinks and greens — create a violent set peopled by equally scary comic misfits. The acting is stylized, alienating, the humor subverted by a psychological edginess that leaves the viewer laughing not so much at the hare-brained action as to suppress a creeping anxiety.

The edginess, the subversive subtext, is deliberate and essentially inevitable given Rubinovas's involvement with Lithuanian theatre during and after Soviet occupation. Candid about his disappointment with the direction Lithuanian theatre has taken since liberation, he criticizes the new capitalism and market society, and how they affect cultural establishments.

Rubinovas began his career as an opera singer, training at Vilnius Conservatory, singing in musicals and opera, and giving solo performances before moving to St. Petersburg to study acting. Citing Meyerhold and Michael Chekhov as early major influences, he soon became involved in studio theatres. At that time, during the late sixties and early seventies, in both Russian and the satellite states, studio theatres were recognized as non-official places where, according to Rubinovas, "freer thoughts could be developed without censorship." Those involved in the early studio theatre movement were aware of Artaud, Grotowski, Brook and others, but only in theory. The studios allowed them to put these ideas into action, to make them public, and to create, educate and sustain an audience that expected, thrived on and demanded these types of productions.

Looking back on this period, buffered by the safety of collective history and personal distance, Rubinovas can view the paranoia of the Soviets during the occupation as more comical than tragic. "It was forbidden," he says, "to advertise a play by Ionesco, or to present the ideas of Freud." Rubinovas claims he still cannot understand what the Soviets found so ideologically hostile in, for instance, the theatre of the absurd, when nothing on stage could compare to the absurdity of everyday life under the Soviet system. As a classic example of Soviet-style "double-speak" Rubinovas tells how the Party officials would not necessarily ban ideas, but they would explain to him that certain ideas were "not welcome." In the 1980s he staged Alexander Blok's *The Stranger*, a play that, if not officially banned, was officially "not welcome." And each time he produced it, he was called to the Party headquarters for questioning, and each time he told them the same thing: "if socialism is destroyed it will not be because of this play." To illustrate the absurdity of the commissars' thinking, and the extent of their paranoia, he said how, also during the 1980s, he managed to infuriate them by staging an adaptation of Hemingway's *A Farewell to Arms*. The culture czars condemned the play for being "too pacifistic."

In 1976 Rubinovas founded the Youth Theatre to continue in Lithuania the experimentalism and freethinking of the studio theatres he had explored in Russia. In 1986, the Youth Theatre was "confirmed" as an "official" theatre, and even though it had no independent site, housed as it was in a huge hall in the Kaunas Cultural Center, the productions, according to Rubinovas, were always crowded because at that time people were desperately hungry for ideas — ideas which Rubinovas says they could only get from theatre, not from newspapers or whatever popular entertainment was available. In fact, censorship legitimized theatre at a time when, as he puts it, "theatre was speaking Aesop's language," coded parables containing clever, politically critical commentary concealed within ironic allusions shared by the audience and players but lost on the Party bosses. Rubinovas explains this notion of the power of concealment is expressed in an old Lithuanian saying: the hand in the pocket is more powerful that the one that is shown. He delights in one of the central paradoxes of theatre during this period: with censorship, the officials had to attend the performances, but without it they quit coming.

The situation changed, however, during the "transition" between 1989 and 1991. The people, like the commissars, also quit coming to the theatre, but for different reasons. It was a time for direct action, and people were taking the ideas from the theatre into the street to protest. The theatre suddenly seemed tame, even irrelevant, so after "liberation" Rubinovas found the theatre in need of repair, and many directors were keen to recover its significance. During the transition, the focus had been so centered on message and resistance that talent suffered: theatre had become a political vehicle at the expense of aesthetics. Because the audience no longer felt the political necessity, theatres struggled to regain relevance.

One major complaint Rubinovas makes about the situation of the theatre after liberation, especially as it competes with the influx (or onslaught) of popular Western entertainment, is that the "educational level of the people is in jeopardy, it is slipping, and therefore theatre must help restore to both the audience and the productions a sense of some intellectual integrity."

In his attempt to revitalize the theatre and its audience in Kaunas, Rubinovas abandoned his studio theatre concept, and in 1991 established the "kamerinis" or "chamber theatre" as a repertory troupe. Utilizing all three performances spaces — a main stage with tiered seating for 100, a 30 seat studio space, and the 15 seat cafe in which actors and audience interact imaginatively (as in a performance of *Gargantua and Pantagruel* where actors in costume pour wine for the audience and relate stories from Rabelais) — the Youth Theatre offers a variety of plays with enough commercial appeal to attract a large audience without sacrificing the signature professionalism and often bizarre treatment of standards the loyal fans have come to expect.

Vilnius

The rivalry between Kaunas and Vilnius is striking. The Russian population, in any meaningful concentration, lives in Klaipėda and Vilnius, but the significance of this demographic constitutes the crux of the contentiousness between the cities. In Kaunas, a sense of patriotic nationalism continues to color any discussion of the post–World War II years, whereas in Vilnius, ideology seems less rigid, the historical past less immediate. In both cities, of course, many of the youth who never experienced Soviet style repression are often baffled at the attitude of the older crowd who remember vividly the "missing years" of the occupation.

But the past is never far from the present in Lithuania. The operative stereotypes the citizens of both cities use to define themselves and their "other" are succinctly summed up by a Russian Jewish businessman celebrating his Polish-Lithuanian wife's "name day." He condemned Kaunas, saying bitterly, "The money in Kaunas stinks" and accused the business community there — wholesale — of being unprincipled, even criminal. He speaks of the city as if it were a separate country, a nefarious backwater of hardheaded mafia and hapless students too poor to attend universities in Vilnius.

While it is true that Kaunas attracts people who cannot afford the more expensive, cosmopolitan environs of Vilnius, it is also true that Kaunas is in no danger of suffering a "brain drain" from its cultural clique. The city's universities, both technical and humanities, enjoy well-deserved reputations for excellence. But Vilnius has the stronger economy. One typical student from Kaunas, who admitted his fondness for watching young women stroll Freedom Street, confessed, "The clever girls go to Vilnius." By "clever girls" he means the women who want to make money — by whatever means, legitimate or otherwise. But escaping from Kaunas to Vilnius can be like jumping from the frying pan into the fire because the disparity between the haves and the have-nots in Vilnius is even more striking than in Kaunas. Along many of the "high streets," Bentleys, Mercedes limousines and American Corvettes line the streets alongside burned-out Škodas and busses crowded with commuters paying twenty-five cents a ride. Five star restaurants tower above shops selling "zeppelins" for a pittance and hotels charging several hundred dollars a night abut half-razed apartments housing decrepit pensioners.

If Kaunas, considered a "cow town" by many in Vilnius, suffers from an inferiority complex, its cultural scene proves relevant beyond its "second city" status. Still, the well-deserved reputation of economic superiority in Vilnius is replicated in its cultural arena, especially within its vibrant theatre scene. As one of the capitals of the emerging "new Europe," Vilnius hosts the best theatre talent Lithuania has to offer.

The literati are self-conscious about their now unique position in the middle of a triangle connecting Russia, Eastern Europe and Western Europe (including Scandinavia). This situation can be both a source of inspiration and confusion: on one hand, such a background provides a tradition of diverse influences and technical depth benefiting contemporary writers and directors. On the other hand, this confluence of disparate styles can lead to a dilution of, or deviation from, from what might be considered the traditional core of Lithuanian theatre. Whether Lithuania is on the verge of losing its "genuine" Lithuanian style of theatre or creating a new synthesis of styles provokes disagreement among critics. Nevertheless, Lithuania's integration into the European Union is significant beyond its emergence from political and commercial isolation from the West: the impact creates a cultural dilemma, that of a small country with a rich tradition of dynamic theatre hamstrung with a small language and a social milieu little understood outside its borders. With a population of only three and a half million, Lithuania is fairly limited in its choice of what might be called "universal dramatic situations," grist for the mill of social relevance that would not be lost on a wider, Western audience-at-large.

This cultural conundrum — of maintaining a national language and signature while attracting an international audience and the corresponding aesthetic recognition — seems to have been addressed, and solved (to some degree), by Marius Ivaškevičius, one of the most promising and popular of the young writer/directors working in Lithuania. In his play *Close City* (*Artimas Miestas*), staged at the Art Fort (Menos Fortas), the Vilnius theatre studio of Eimuntas Nekrošius, as part of Lithuania's 2005 New Drama Action festival (Naujosios Dramos Akcija), Ivaškevičius confronts both the particular circumstances facing local writers emerging in the new political and cultural landscape of contemporary Lithuania and the more universal themes of the human condition that transcend the borders of any nationality.

Airida Gintautaitė and Egidijus Bakas in Ivaškevičius's *Close City* at the Art Fort, Vilnius. Importing a hackneyed cultural contretemps from foreign (albeit nearby) countries represents a conscious effort on the part of Ivaškevičius to impose a broader referential frame on his play than any particular Lithuanian social situation can support. His purpose is simple: to allow his work to investigate universal themes of love, despair and betrayal in a context that otherwise might be lost on an international audience (photograph by Dmitrij Matvejev).

Located (appropriately and incongruously) behind the stately (and expensive) Shakespeare Hotel, the Art Fort offers a small upstairs performance space with a raised thrust stage and bleacher seating for fifty, quality sound effects, a professional fly and enough "distance" to create the necessary "performance illusion" without a loss of intimacy. The set for *Close City* consisted of a black floor bisected by a yellow stripe and two triangular yellow boxes that combine for various props — an efficient use of minimalist space testifying as much to the ingenuity of the staging as to the virtue of the acting and playwriting, and proving, as is so often the case in Lithuania's small theatres, that good performances are not based on props or the trappings of what some critics describe as American-style "living room dramas" inspired by sit-coms, talk shows and reality TV.

Significantly for a Lithuanian play, the core conceit is imported: Ivaškevičius borrows the stereotypical social friction and cultural differences shared in a common running joke between the staid, steady and relatively conservative city of Malmo, Sweden, and its more libertine, open and diverse neighbor across the Øresund, Copenhagen, Denmark. (The Swedes, for instance, refer to Copenhagen as "Little Paris," meaning a place to take a whore. The Danes explain why the Swedes come to Denmark to drink by pointing out that it is against the law to fall down in Sweden.)

Importing a hackneyed cultural contretemps from foreign, albeit nearby countries, represents a conscious effort on the part of Ivaškevičius to impose a broader referential frame on his play than any particular Lithuanian social situation can support. His purpose is simple: to allow his work to investigate universal themes of love, despair and betrayal in a context that otherwise may be lost on an international audience.

There are, of course, two ways to view this thematic scavenging by, in this case, a Lithuanian writing about a particularly Scandinavian phenomenon: cultural cross-breeding could well imply a corruption, a disavowal of a national dilemma as rich in the strife of the human condition as any other nation. (Imagine Chekhov writing about Franco-German animosity based on a squabble over the intrinsic superiority of Bordeaux or Riesling.) On the other hand, this borrowing might represent, metaphorically and realistically, the price of integration into a larger social unit, as Ivaškevičius confronts the assimilation of a small nation-state into an organization as vast, complex and, in some cases, impersonal and culturally effacing as the European Union. The question of national identity is foregrounded: the issue for states like Lithuania, Estonia and Latvia is more acute than, say, for France, Germany, Italy or

Britain, those stalwart members of the G-8 whose cultural histories and literature crowd the curricula of colleges and universities throughout the world.

But whether Ivaškevičius imported his dramatic situation out of "corrupt" motives — Europhilia — or for a geo-political illustration of the "new" Lithuania — integrated as a European constituency no longer relegated to the irrelevance of a so-called Baltic state — the style of the play is pure Lithuania exoticism. The staging offers a virtual smorgasbord of theatrical exercises incorporating symbolism, physical theatre, the mechanics of alienation, and mixed-media, as well as elements from Artaud's "theatre of cruelty" and Kantor's "theatre of death" all served up in a minimalist manner enhanced by a tastefully restrained exploitation of lights and music to create a showcase for actors hungry to stretch their limits within the demands of a small performance space.

A crucial aspect of the attempt by Ivaškevičius to "open" the play — that is, to transcend the dual Lithuanian dilemma of a small social milieu and an isolated language in order to appeal to an international audience — is the use of fragments of the dialog translated into English and projected onto the backdrop — a facsimile of a newspaper front page — *The Copenhagen Post* — the subtitle of which reads "The Danish News in English" and a headline declares "Love Theme for Amusement Poster" — meta-theatrical comments that by the end of the play become ironic notes on the action. Hardly serendipitously, in the subject column the word "news" is circled and the word "culture" is crossed out. Using a Danish newspaper, printed in English — stressing news over culture — as a backdrop for an English translation of a Lithuanian play about a Scandinavian cultural conflict — that in turn becomes a metaphor for the human condition — calls into question *and* acknowledges the necessity of English as a linguistic inevitability in the global market of commerce and culture, and also neatly illustrates the effects of globalization and the impact of Western cultural hegemony. (Staniškytė identifies this strategy as "a different kind of textuality, rooted in intertextual cross-references, collage, polyglossia and simultaneity, so that even 'traditional' staging of such plays will end up producing heterogeneous and open performance texts.")

Two other "stories" in the "newspaper" also reinforce both the political and social angle of the play: one warns of the Danish inclination to vote "no" on the European Constitution, a move that would limit further integration and assimilation into what many consider a homogenous European state; the other claims, "The time is ripe to take a fresh look at [...]

Airida Gintautaitė and Egidijus Bakas in *Close City*. The play represents, metaphorically and realistically, the price of integration into a larger social unit, as Ivaškevičius confronts the assimilation of a small nation-state into an organization as complex and culturally effacing as the European Union, foregrounding the question of national identity (photograph by Dmitrij Matvejev).

stereotypes," ostensibly referring to characters from the works of Hans Christian Andersen but in the context of the play suggesting a rethinking of the general concept of "national character" underscoring Europe's current ontological skepticism.

The play centers on Anika (whose name in Denmark means "grace") and her husband, Svante, a typical Swedish couple with three children and a house on the sea overlooking the straits between Malmo and Copenhagen. Svante has been making weekend trips alone to Copenhagen, leaving Anika to fret about the lack of intimacy in their marriage and her perceived inadequacies as a desirable woman. But even were she invited, she would hesitate to go, as she fears crossing the straits. Soon enough, however, she musters the courage to see for herself why her husband is so enchanted with Copenhagen. During the crossing she meets Birgit, a woman who advises Anika to find a male whore to satisfy her sexual hunger, to fill, as it were, her spiritual vacuum with physical abandonment. Both Svante and Anika, it seems, hope to transcend the loneliness of their life together by seeking in Copenhagen an ideal of anonymous gratification. In an attempt at reconciliation, the husband gives his wife a string of pearls for their fifteenth wedding anniversary, but the wife, now as obsessed with Copenhagen as her husband, has forgotten the occasion. Disappointed but not surprised, Svante confesses that his trips to Copenhagen were merely binges designed to alleviate the sorrow he has been experiencing since two of his best friends died, his drunken weekends nothing more than pathetic attempts to assuage his sense of despair — for the loss of youth, friendship, innocence and the promise of possibilities.

But Svante's confession comes too late to stop his wife's curiosity. So intense is her suffering, having endured the waning intimacy in their relationship for so long, she begins to fear that her legs are growing together. As if to compensate for years of sexual inaction, she has become, according to the male-prostitute she procures, an insatiable nymphomaniac who terrorizes him with her voracious energy. Another fear is that the two cities are moving towards each other, becoming, in essence, "close," in danger of colliding, like her and her husband's mutual desires (and like the disparate cultures at risk of homogeneity — not just Sweden and Denmark but all nations within Europe.) Even as Anika tries to cling to her sense of dignity, stressing to Birgit, the intractable reprobate who corrupts all she touches, that she lives in a respectable neighborhood with normal children, safe with all the comforts expected from a proper Swedish bourgeois existence, Birgit reminds her: "You're in Copenhagen now."

Svante tries to reclaim Anika, attempting to seduce her back into middle-class propriety by engaging her in skiing trips, scuba adventures and tennis, but Anika is too intrigued with the freedom she feels in Copenhagen, a freedom that soon enough metamorphoses into a prison of desire. She emerges from her Malmo cocoon as a notorious Copenhagen whore, and her spasmodic if perverse longing leads to inevitable violence and annihilation. Finally, in a subtle, oblique touch, Svante shoots her, although clearly Anika is a victim of her own perverted passion.

Paralleling the sordid tale of Anika's descent into mayhem and madness, Ivaškevičius creates another, even more visually aggressive mismatched relationship: that of an impish demiurge, Carlson, described in the program as "a comical personification of Swedish self-confidence and masculine desire," and his captured mermaid, "the symbol of Copenhagen [and] an example of the tragic desire to live a double life" (mirroring too the Janus-faced dilemma of Baltic playwrights yearning for acceptance in Western media). Their antics reflect, on a more subliminal, metaphorical level, the plight of Svante and Anika. In a series of crude phallic *double entendres*, Carlson obsessively brags about his huge propeller and his talent for flying over the sea, trolling for creatures to exploit in order to satisfy his innate and incorrigible selfish desire. The mermaid, explicitly reminiscent of Copenhagen's "Little Mermaid" as well as a trove of other mythological associations, suffers the tortuous burden of Carlson's relentless and insensitive machismo shenanigans. Having removed her from her natural element, he tries to remake her to suit his needs, until, as if incapable of understanding that she cannot live outside the sea, he kills her; in effect, by killing off the object of his desire by his desire, he essentially and symbolically kills himself.

The philosophical grounding of the action underscores without apology Kant's categorical imperative: to treat others not as objects but as subjective selves, recognizing their subjectivity, and never treating people as a means to an end but always as an end in themselves. Svante seems to have misunderstood the needs of his wife, whose fear of her legs growing together echoes the reality of the mermaid. (Carlson discounts her "lower half" as being of no use to him.) In perhaps the most unsettling scene in the play, Carlson tires to revive the dead mermaid by gyrating through a series of graphic, grotesque sexual positions — implying simultaneously bestiality and necrophilia — viciously unleashing the anti–Kantian motif permeating the action, a sequence hardly mitigated by his metaphorical rant expressing anger at her dying, as if her death were her fault, her abandonment intentional.

Understanding the parallels between Svante and Anika and Carlson and the mermaid is achieved less by cognition than by an intuitive sense of poetic intensity. Reinforcing this merging of the "real" life of Svante and Anika with the surreal world of Carlson and the mermaid is the overarching theme best summarized by Carlson, trying in his impish, inimitable, sadistic dialectics to explain his motives to his victim: the reason couples live together is to "use each other more efficiently."

One of the creative forces supporting the work of Ivaškevičius comes from the producer and impresario Audronis Liūgą, Director of the Theatre and Cinema Information Center in Vilnius. While Liūgą considers the political situation in Lithuania moot, settled and passé — at least as it relates to the travails during the transformation post–1991 — he identifies the new challenge facing those involved in theatre as financial viability. Because the shift to a market economy had a negative impact on the funding process (he complains, for instance, that the only money he can secure from the Lithuanian government supports specific individual projects), his operating budget now relies almost exclusively on international grants. But the quality of the talent he promotes, and the success of many of the writers he has launched, keeps his organization afloat in the precarious seas of private theatre where salaries and royalties depend almost exclusively on ticket sales. Among the writers from former Soviet Bloc he has nurtured or worked with who have gone on to achieve international recognition include (along with Ivaškevičius) Grezegorz Jarzyna from Poland, Arpad Schilling from Hungary, Alvis Hermanis from Latvia, and Yevgeniy Grishkovets from Russia. He staged the Baltic premiere of Mark Ravenhill's *Shopping and Fucking*, has worked with several international production companies (like the Dutch troupe ZT Hollandia) and collaborates frequently with Chris Torch, Artistic Director of the Stockholm based Intercult.

In 1999, dissatisfied with the direction of Lithuanian theatre, Liūgą founded New Drama Action to invigorate and integrate Lithuanian and Baltic theatre. By developing his own company, Liūgą sidestepped the need to collaborate with traditional theatres that, in his view, were not interested in supporting the development of new talent. The established theatres merely poached new writers *after* they became successful by garnering international recognition, eliciting critical praise or — especially — securing proven box office returns, all at no risk either to the budget or reputation of any theatre seeking to siphon off the talent. Liūgą decided to produce new writers himself, starting with new play development, then sustaining and touring artists outside "the system."

That system includes theatres still imposing a director-based authority on the text, an approach Liūgą finds anathema to his aesthetic. According to him, the theatre system is plagued by a monopoly of directors that use texts and actors as tools to make the performance theirs. For Liūgą, this approach does not reflect the possibilities of a theatre that must respond to a new reality: pop culture, mass media, and the erasure of national identities. Liūgą defines the self-reflexive nature of recent performances directed by Eimuntas Nekrošius, Rimas Tuminas and Jonas Vaitkus as introversive play with the director's own concepts, methods and themes from past performances. "In this way [...] theatre doubles back upon itself and avoids its socio-cultural function. It projects only an authorial self-image, concerned entirely with 'theatre about theatre'" (Staniškytė). Liūgą looks to the past to revive the future, seeking in Grotowski and Brook the virtues of "poor" theatre without the paraphernalia associated with the traditional theatre-house and the dictatorial inclinations of director-based methods.

Many theatres respond to the challenge presented by the influx of mass media on the public by a return to "realism." ("A lot of talking," in Liūgą's words.) New Drama Action responds by critiquing electronic media, dramatically appropriating and exploiting elements to create a new experience that the mass media cannot duplicate. The questions Liūgą poses are: How can art on stage reflect the new reality of pop culture and its impact on the situation of theatre? What is a play? What potential for discovery is in the text *outside* the limitations of the director's vision? How can theatre transcend the overly sophisticated productions that Liūgą thinks sap the vitality out of performances?

Liūgą sees a play as a negation, in the way Hegel and Heidegger understand the term, the staging an impersonation of experience (as in the pejorative use of the term "staged," meaning artificial). His aim is to create or restore immediacy to the experience, to erase the mediation between spectator and action, representation and meaning, so that the act of being at the play becomes enjoined in the performance. In a Nietzschean sense, Liūgą wants to fuse the secular with the performative. As problematic as this praxeological alchemy sounds, it recalls the same idealistic rhetoric and intent of the post–World War II writers who wanted to rehabilitate the introspective novel (e.g., Michel Leiris, in *Manhood*, wondering if a book can become an act). Liūgą comes uncomfortably close in his musings to the now trite "death of the author" vogue popular in the 1960s, although his ideas also reverberate with the more theoretical notions De Man attributes to Mallarmé, conceiving of drama (in Liūgą's case) as a privileged action that negates, as it were, representational negation systemic in visual — indeed, any — art.

Liūgą's remedy, as well as those espoused by other young Lithuanian critics (including especially Balevičiūtė), is for directors to appropriate non-theatrical space in their productions to close the gap between spectator and performance, creating, instead of a play staged for an audience, a raw, "innocent" performance that becomes authentic in its autonomous purity: an aspect for which theatre, unlike film or prose, is intrinsically suited, as if these directors create an unmediated experience through their performance. The problem lies in the intentionality and the constitutive function of "directing" itself. No matter how you dice it, a performance, by the nature of the act, usually lacks the aleatory suspense of life. But according to Staniškytė, many critics "have been slow to recognize the critical importance of self-reflective techniques, discussing them as formalistic exercises, rather than ideological/critical responses to the crisis of credibility suffered by the theatre in the last two decades."

The directors working with Liūgą have made impressive, if not always original inroads into the nature of theatre and how space can be used not as a set but as the actual location of an event traditionally labeled a "play." The effect is an attack, essentially, on the stage as a "sacred" space, reduced to an announcement of a performance more than a rendering of a "set," shifting the focus from theme to form — ideally exposing both simultaneously, where the action becomes a critique of the play while presenting "the play." The traditional demarcations between "in here" and "out there" are erased, plot is superseded by performance, and the spectator, according to Liūgą, is left to create "meaning" alone.

At the very least, Liūgą hopes to provoke a dialog exploring the nature of European theatre and its relevance in an age of mass culture and the seduction of cinema, MTV, raves, video games and soporific classical theatre catering to a worn-out aesthetic. To initiate this dialog, Liūgą says he first traveled to the cultural capitals of Europe — London, Berlin, Edinburgh, et al.— seeking contemporary, avant-garde texts that might otherwise be ignored by the run of the mill festivals which have for years offered a predictable menu of performances. He was looking for plays that do not privilege the director-as-auteur, that lend themselves to new ways of making theatre in which the text is only a concept, shaped by a collaborating ensemble into a fluid experience, representing, according to Liūgą, an event unto itself, a style he calls "post-dramatic." The performances he envisions resemble "happenings" more than the tightly choreographed well-made plays that litter the junkyard of mainstream theatre. In Liūgą's view, the possibilities of modern theatre have been exhausted.

"The stereotypes," he says, "the methods of expression have been finished and there is no more discovery, only repetition."

The sense of redundancy in method and expression is a textbook recipe for decadence, and it is Liūgą's mission — he seems evangelically inspired — to remedy this aesthetic malady. Staniškytė acknowledges this trend, noting how "the text and the homogeneity of the audience are central assumptions on which traditional literary theatre is based [...] the drama text is only a pretext for an already predetermined compositional structure, determined by the director's concept." Now, however, due to the efforts of a new generation of directors, "the situation has changed, as visuality (sic) as a means of expression [has replaced] the traditionally dominant position of text in performance." Staniškytė identifies "two kinds of 'visual dramaturgy'" in contemporary Lithuanian theatre: performances where visual expression is clearly dominant and the meaning is produced by means of visual narration and performance, where all the structural elements are placed in nonhierarchical, equal position.

The solution to this conundrum signifies not only an aesthetic dilemma but ontological, existential and socio-political complications too. Still, Liūgą's ideas preclude any attempt to compete with pop culture; instead, he insists that theatre should establish a new approach that cannot be achieved by other media, a sort of fusion of traditional styles into a new hybrid. His formula is both reductive and complex. Simply put, he wants theatrical performances to exploit space, time, and what he defines as "presence in the moment."

But the ease of the phrase belies the difficulty of the practice. Liūgą believes that his new way implies a play cannot simply be a vehicle for a director's vision, the text no longer the authoritative source for a character's motivation. The text presents a challenge, not a solution, a conflict reconciled not by a director's interpretation but by a collusion among the writer, director and actors that basically neutralizes the authority of the director, that fuses the writer and director into a moment of expression, allowing for improvisation and discovery — a sort of aleatory theatre, instinctual, poetical, adaptable, utilizing, in Brook's phrase, "space as tool."

Staniškytė, to a degree, agrees:

> [...] the text is no longer the center and it is no longer perceived as the authoritative force that governs and structures meaning in performance. [...] The playwright's intentions are not irrelevant, but rather this

intentionality is perceived within a more complex matrix of interpretation. Once the textual space — which used to be the exclusive communicator of meaning — is opened, it calls upon the spectator to synthesize the elements presented.

Liūgą's theories naturally provoke controversy, especially among the professionals at the mainstream repertory theatres that he accuses of promoting decadent bourgeois productions while now and then posing as innovators by pinching new talent fomented by the smaller alternative companies.

One such theatre is The Lithuanian National Drama Theatre (Lietuvos Nacionalinis Dramos Teatras). This vast complex, housed in an imposing Soviet era building established in 1940 (reconstructed in 1983), originally served as both a theatre and a meeting hall for the Communist Party. The baroque exterior facing trendy Gedimino Street is dominated by the theatre's trademark three muses framed in black cowls jutting their mask-like luminescent faces over the portico. The main reception area resembles an elegant four-star hotel lobby, with a sunken central floor lined by sumptuous sofas; an entranceway off one side leads to a darkly lit cocktail lounge. The theatre offers two stages, one a full scale production facility featuring 15 performances a year, the other a small black box for developing more experimental work.

The National maintains a stable of 35 actors and a slew of the most celebrated directors in Lithuania, including Jonas Vaitkus, Saulius Mykolaitis and Gytis Padegimas. Funded by the state, the National features mainly classics by Shakespeare, Chekhov and Dostoyevsky, as well as an eclectic mix of modern plays by writers like Samuel Beckett, Howard Barker and Joe Orton, plus some plays by traditional Lithuanian writers like Jonas Mekas. Two spin-off theatres closely associated with the National provide even more experimental possibilities: the Vilnius Little Theatre led by Rimas Tuminas and the Oskaras Koršunovas Theatre. The National also encourages and supports new directors, tyros like Rokas Ramanauskas and Agnius Jankevičius.

But it is the directors, according to the National's Artistic Director Egmontas Georgas Jansonas, that are the heart of Lithuanian theatre. Jansonas studied at the Theatre Institute in Moscow and worked on the Board of Culture there for six years after graduating. He remembers the Khrushchev years (1958–1963) as a time when Russia was experiencing more freedom than Lithuania, and it was his good fortune, he says, to be working in Moscow during that period. He was the first student allowed to write a thesis on Meyerhold, a director who at that time had not been "rehabilitated" and whose work students had been forbidden to study. Jansonas managed to find some of Meyerhold's secret letters, and he attributes this covert exposure to Meyerhold's writing as the most significant influence on his career — along with, of course, adopting strategies from Stanislavsky and Nemirovich-Danchenko. His affinity for theory and theatre criticism accounts for his bias against Lithuanian writers and his dogmatic enthusiasm for Lithuanian directors. As to what factors explain why Lithuania, in his opinion, produces great directors but no good writers, Jansonas is equivocal. He suggests that there are no good schools at the moment for teaching playwriting. The focus, he complains, is on information systems and marketing. He also thinks too many young writers try to emulate "Western writers" instead of writing honestly about their own experience. There is, according to Jansonas, no lack of scripts; the problem is, in his opinion, they are not interesting.

"It is better," he says, "to stage Western writers instead of Lithuanians pretending to be Western writers."

As to why Lithuania turns out so many exceptional directors, he becomes enigmatic, almost mystical. He turns his palms up in a typically ambivalent Lithuanian gesture and says it is simply a "combination," but of what he is not exactly sure. Lithuania, he says, has excellent poets and novelists, but playwrights — at least the current contemporary breed — have been irreparably corrupted by mass culture and are more interested in emulating formulaic writing than originating new styles. This attitude makes clear why Jansonas prefers to adopt novels like *Madame Bovary* and *Crime and Punishment* to the stage than to encourage new writing for theatre.

Jansonas is equally equivocal discussing changes in the theatre after 1991. Yes, he says, the Soviet censors created difficulties for artistic expression, but in Lithuania, many of the commissars were Lithuanian and so sympathetic to artistic directors who were trying to open up their offerings to include modern Western productions. He also speaks of the "speech of Aesop" — the codified language of "hidden truths" — with a mischievous nostalgia that mitigates (if not contradicts) the reality of the harsh repression enforced by the Soviets during the occupation. The directors, as Jansonas remembers, were too clever for the censors, and he seems to miss playing the game that all parties — the audience, the directors, the censors — seemed to tolerate with a conspiratorial wink and nod. Jansonas' account seems more benign than other accounts — by Padegimas, for instance — but all the veterans of the Soviet period remember those days with mixed emotions: as another well-established director from the old school, Stanislovas Rubinovas, says, at least people in those days seriously cared about theatre.

Jansonas also plays down any significant change in the nature of the theatre from before 1991 to the present. The changes, in his view, are more economical than ideological. After all, he says, the same directors were able to work both before and after what he refers to as "the Soviet times." The major issue for him was how in the 1990s people stopped coming to the theatre because they had no money. In the final years before liberation, direct action in the streets — political activism — replaced the more passive political act-in-theory promoted by theatres, as the audience lost interest in passive-aggressive resistance and turned more frequently to mere aggression (culminating in the now famous shooting of thirteen students in 1991 by the Soviet army around the Vilnius television tower that precipitated the Soviet withdrawal and hastened independence). Jansonas acknowledges that the recovering economy has revived attendance, yet the costs of seeing a production can be prohibitive. And with so many theatres competing for punters, the audience base is thin at best. (A young bartender who identified himself as part of the Lithuanian Polish minority living in Vilnius claimed that attending the theatre is more expensive now than going to the cinema, and he confessed that he feels no immediacy — no relevant connection — between his life and what theatre offers, so he opts instead for DVDs, cinema and television.)

Predictably, Jansonas prefers Realism to other styles, and he cites this difference in aesthetic sensibility as another difficulty in attracting young people to the theatre. Pop culture and TV are cheaper, more accessible, perceived to be more exciting, and seem to speak more directly to the desires of young people than the work of Flaubert and Dostoyevsky — the two novelists he prefers to adapt to the stage (as opposed to acknowledged playwrights like Chekov, whose work he considers "ready-made" for theatre and therefore too limiting for his vision). He does believe, in any case, that the kind of classic theatre offered by the National will always appeal to the intelligentsia, and Jansonas exhibits nearly a disciple's faith in the discretion of those in Vilnius who demand traditional quality in theatre performances, and it is to that audience that Jansonas has pledged his allegiance.

Both Liūgą and Jansonas agree that the crisis in Lithuanian theatre is existential. After independence, the people were free politically, but they were encumbered with the baggage of the discredited Soviet social and financial system while suddenly confronting the influx of a new economic model and its concomitant cultural influences. This drastic shift in everyday living overwhelmed many ordinary Lithuanians that felt, in a sense, displaced in their own country. This paradoxical feeling of indigenous displacement — a phenomenon without parallel in most parts of the contemporary West — explains why Jansonas appreciates classical works over local talent. For years, Lithuanian writers concentrated on plays that reflected narrow national issues, while what the directors wanted — as well as, presumably, the theatre-going audiences — was grand stories illustrating eternal values, so the homegrown writers were usually summarily dismissed as too parochial. Jansonas insists that this is still the case, but, of course, the younger generation, many represented by Liūgą, disagree.

Another one of the "old school" directors to take issue with Liūgą's ideas of liberating theatre from the authoritarian hand of the director-as-auteur is Jonas Vaitkus. He compliments Liūgą for his efforts, especially in nurturing and supporting new writers by providing them with a venue — at some economic risk — but he dismisses Liūgą's theory of establishing a "post-dramatic" approach to new performances as "nonsense." Vaitkus laments in Lithuanian theatre — and, for that matter, in Baltic theatre generally — a turn away from what he defines as human values to what he sees as a decadent sort of aestheticism in which the focus is primarily on form at the expense of content. He, too, is supported by Staniškytė: "the visual performances in contemporary Lithuanian theatre can be conceptualized as examples of an attempt to abolish the absolute dominance of the text, but they do not try to eliminate text from the theatrical performance."

Skendelienė notes that Vaitkus "was one of the most outstanding directors in Lithuania in the 1970s and 1980s" and credits him with "breaking the link with psychological realism." Trained in the tradition of strong directors at the St. Petersburg University of Dramatic Arts and the Film Academy in Moscow, under the tutelage of Tarkovsky and Vytautas Žalakevičius, it is to his credit that early in his career he embraced innovation, early on "inclined toward Brechtian concepts [in which] there is no illusion on the stage [...] structure and sight dominate, where the role is minimized, cleansed of psychological features [and] a generalized constructive space [...] is devoid of everyday associations and realism" (Skendelienė). Bajorinienė insists that his early work in experimental styles explains his interest in characters that "confront the hypocritical society and leave it in search of another, metaphysical reality. This farewell of the characters to

[...] the depraved material world and their journey toward God constitutes the essence of Vaitkus' theatre today."

As a proponent of the tradition of the director's theatre, it is not so unusual for Vaitkus to cite Ivaškevičius' *Close City* as a prime example of the mistake new writers make when they try to democratize a theatrical production by diminishing the role of directors in controlling the performers. He considers the performance at Art Fort an "amateur" production, objecting not to the play itself but to the fact that Ivaškevičius chose to direct the play himself. He compared the work to primitive staging — "like a club production by my uncle," he says, "in a Lithuanian country village" — in which the scenes are presented as loosely interconnected skits. A good director, he says, would have been able to bring more coherence to the performance by facilitating the transitions between scenes, connecting the fragments smoothly and creating the necessary sense of inevitability needed for unity and meaning — especially in a play like *Close City*, composed of a series of vignettes that can easily devolve into a disjointed fiasco, or what Vaitkus describes as "old fashioned sentimental theatre disguised as new."

Vaitkus does not discount the value of a play that addresses the contemporary situation in Lithuania — its integration, for instance, into the larger cultural entity of the European Union and the influx of new influences threatening the unique cultural fabric defining the country — but he thinks the best way forward for Lithuanian theatre is through a sort of benevolent nationalism. Convinced that reform of a nation is only possible through a sense of strong national pride — "You must love your country," he says, "if you want to change it." — he stresses simple values — family, religion, respect for nature — and believes that much of the new European theatre — including imported adaptations and much of the new Lithuanian writing intended for export — is too limited, or shallow, lacking core values. The new writers, he insists, are more interested in recognition than substance. He complains about a "new aestheticism" — all form without significant themes — and attributes this deficit to the relative youth of the new writers, their lack of life experience, and to the fact that they must contend with the new media for audiences. In the case of *Close City*, he complains that the ideas of the play are sound and worthy of investigation, but the myopic attention to aesthetic values dilutes the moral value of the work, illustrating, in his view, how young writers are not sufficiently trained in dramaturgy to properly stage their own work. This combination of good writing and "bad taste" in directing creates an impotent theatre incapable of lasting value.

True to form, Vaitkus asserts that the director is the key to any successful production and challenges Liūgą's scheme to remove the director. "A good play," Vaitkus says, "needs no language." He compares the director with a surgeon who cannot divide up the body, working on one part as if it were separate from the whole, but who must address the entire system holistically, understanding how the parts operate independently *and* as a single unit. His romantic view of the director stems from his training and experience as a Lithuanian studying in Russia during the 1970s. According to Vaitkus, directors at that time were forbidden to study their craft in Lithuania because directing was considered too ideological, and the Soviets believed they could condition the sensibility of fledgling directors by educating them in what they considered a politically correct environment — that is, in an approved institution at the center of the state apparatus outside of any nationalistic tendencies fostered within the cultural community of a satellite state.[6] The best Lithuanian directors absorbed the aesthetic virtues of their Russian education while ignoring or, often, exploiting the enforced political ideology to serve their own artistic ends. Few became "true believers." When the first artistic directing school opened in the Music Academy in Vilnius, Vaitkus was the instructor, which explains why many critics consider him "the initiator of the Lithuanian school of artistic directing" (Skendelienė).

Unlike many of his compatriots who remember the Soviet times either with irony or wistfulness, Vaitkus gives the account of the transition a more insidious spin. Even though he admits that he would not want to go back to the old system, the new capitalist model created, in his view, an even "more dangerous" situation. Paraphrasing Marx, Vaitkus says flatly, "Capitalism is bad for art." As he sees it, a new form of censorship has been created by the need for theatres to raise private funds for operating expenses. Given how the price of theatre tickets, which must be high enough to sustain the theatre, alienates a large percentage of a frugal public who cannot afford the price of admission, combined with how the need for operating capital affects the kind of plays a theatre decides to produce — especially at the National, the main venue for Vaitkus — Marx's observation that art cannot be produced without absolute freedom — which includes freedom from economic determinism — does not seem so far-fetched, absurd, theoretical or wrong. Vaitkus recalls how, after independence, while serving as Artistic Director at the National, he wanted to shake up the old system, to hire young, new actors and directors to change the venue, which in his view offered only old-fashioned, clichéd productions. The resident actors and directors threatened by Vaitkus demonstrated outside the front door of the theatre — beneath the three jutting faces of the muses — by polishing the shoes of the surprised, intrigued and finally sympathetic pedestrians shopping along Gedimino Street. The directors of the theatre sided with the old actors and directors, and Vaitkus became, in his words, "a free agent."

"Money is the object now," he says. "During the Soviet period, we could get around the censors, but now the need for money is insurmountable."

In addition to the new emphasis on private funding, and the superficiality of the new productions, Vaitkus cites a third problem: the "old friends" network. For Vaitkus, many of the political changes in the country are as superficial as the new theatre. "The old Communists are still in charge," he says. He is skeptical, given this centralized control even in the theatre system, that any significant reform at the National is possible. He wants a "real revolution" fueled by students versed in Dostoyevsky, not dulled by the ephemera of pop writers and directors more involved in flash reputations than art and poetry. But the theatre will only be reformed, says Vaitkus, when the system is reformed, and the intelligentsia demand from theatre the "traditional values" so poetically expressed, according to Vaitkus, by his beloved Dostoyevsky.

A strong advocate for Vaitkus's call for a theatre that reflects traditional values associated with the classical tradition is Daiva Šabasevičinė, a theatre critic based at the National. About Vaitkus, she has written:

> These days, when ever more frequently the creative renewal is merely imitated by directorial shallows intermixed with new playwrights' names, this process is reversed in J. Vaitkus's theatre. [...] For Vaitkus, the moral imperatives of a production are holy. For their sake the director often sacrifices rather substantial motifs of a play. Actually, morality is an unquestionable companion of both the earlier and the present productions directed by J. Vaitkus. But this does not mean his work is prudish: by choosing no less brutal, shocking means, by bringing them to the surface and turning them into theatrical language tools, the director thus attempts to shake up everyday existence, and so to restore the lost values of both theatre and life itself [79].

Šabasevičinė, who describes herself as a "conservative" critic, worries along with Vaitkus that much of the new drama in Lithuania is overly concerned with formal qualities at the expense of character and content. She applauds, for instance, Koršunovas' approach to the raunchy and (to some) shocking material in Ravenhill's *Shopping and Fucking*, suggesting that it was the director who made the play enjoyable in spite of its subject matter, describing it as Koršunovas' "most tender, poetic and lyrical work." For Šabasevičinė, too often the new style of theatre finds value only in presentation: theatre as aesthetic experience only. But in Koršunovas' performance — not necessarily Ravenhill's text — she finds a quality that harmonizes the harshness of the material with the expectations of the contemporary Lithuanian theatre-going public. "The director does not search of newness in itself," she says. "But by using new stylistics, he tries to convey the contradictions of life with the help of philosophy, theatrical expression, the play itself, different manners of speech, contemporary art, poetry, technical means and platitude."

Her focus on the director's "stylistics" explains why her reaction to *Close City* is mixed. While Šabasevičinė appreciates the writing for its incisive psychological insight and its progressive mode, she agrees with Vaitkus that Ivaškevičius' directing does not do the play justice. "Content should produce form," she says, and in the performance of *Close City* she complains that Ivaškevičius tires too hard to impose a form on the disparate scenes. The result, which Šabasevičinė describes as appealing to a "culture of surfaces," reminds her of a comic book, a series of animated skits that tend to illustrate emotional encounters instead of rendering them with any subjective depth.

Paradoxically, given Liūgą's priorities, Šabasevičinė attributes this (in her opinion) unfortunate trend of writers directing their own work to the pervasive cult-of-the-director dominating Lithuanian theatre. She agrees with Jansonas that Lithuania has no real history of playwrights, so the new dramatists have been bred from a tradition of a theatre that privileges directors, so it is only natural that the writers want to extend the same control over their material that strong directors exert over other writers' material. "The director is king in Lithuania," Šabasevičinė says, "and the new writers are hoping to change this situation."

Šabasevičinė also recognizes the changing nature of theatre, but she sees no threat to its necessity or popularity. She remembers the years immediately after independence as a time when Lithuanian theatre lost its audience because of the benefits of independence. Art thrives, she says, during periods of strife. Before independence, the theatre served to speak metaphorically to the people, creating a community of resistance to authoritarian Soviet rule. Now, the transition is over, and the theatre once again functions as a critical forum for social issues: in the new Lithuania, those issues deal with the dehumanizing, spiritually debilitating effects of crass consumerism that threaten not just Lithuania's national identity but the health of individual dignity everywhere. Theatre, she says, can respond in two ways. On one hand, it can succumb to the trends and become "fast food theatre," experimenting only to attract an audience, seducing them with the charms of "surface life." She cites the work of Sarah Kane as an example of theatre pandering to the base instincts of a de-aestheticized audience, her material "politically correct" but offering "no inner life."

"Her subjects," she says, "lead people to despair."

On the other hand, theatre can reject commercialization and become a counter-force to pop culture, thriving by its very resistance to it. True theatre, she says, is more intense, more intimate, more faithful to experience, using its formal qualities to enhance, not destroy, the values humans share.

Regardless of the subjects of contemporary theatre, Šabasevičinė insists that the themes need historical context, and she worries that many young Lithuanian writers are trying to write about situations in Europe they only half-understand. She suggests that, for themes and subjects, the writers need to look closer to home to maintain authenticity. But as for aesthetic values, she points out that during a European theatre festival the productions from the small, struggling countries were aesthetically far superior, in her opinion, to the productions from the larger, more successful Western countries. But often the esoteric themes embraced by writers from small countries were lost on the general audience. To "reform" Lithuanian theatre (and by implication, the theatre in all of the Baltics), playwrights are caught in a paradox: they must stick to dramatic works by classical writers, which denies or ignores their local situation, or they must find a way to express the existential core within their cultural uniqueness that transcends their particular situation in order to expresses universal truths.

Part of this reform seems well underway at the State Youth Theatre (Jaunimo Teatras) under the directorship of Ingrida Daunoraviciutė. The Youth Theatre is situated — along with Lėlė (the puppet theatre) — between the Bix Baras and the Old Town Strip Club, a juxtaposition that neatly illustrates the cultural dilemma in Lithuanian theatre: How do theatres compete with topless waitresses, lap dancers, cheap beer and rock'n'roll? (Not that there is anything inherently wrong with erotica and inebriety.) But forced to operate within a system now financially dependent on "bums in seats," what is the attraction for theatre?

Like Liūgą, Daunoraviciutė believes that the quality of the theatre experience creates the "draw," attracting an audience tired of the easy fix of pop culture, interested instead in a more complete, satisfying cultural experience than what pop culture offers. She feels no threat from mass media; in fact, she sees a rejuvenated interest in theatre as evidence of a resurrection in aesthetic values. What Vaitkus sees as a creeping decadence — his derision of the contemporary "theatre of aestheticism" — Daunoraviciutė interprets as a virtue.

"Pop culture," she says, "is not a problem because the theatre of today retains elements of quality from the old theatre, but the issues addressed in mass media are more relevant to the new reality," a new reality that she defines as an exploration of what it means to live not as a Lithuanian but as a European. She is much more comfortable with the issue of Lithuanian integration into the European Union than, say, Vaitkus or Jansonas and feels less threatened by the encroachment of pop culture on the traditional Lithuanian theatre. In a subversive move, she admits she frequently appropriates the star power of television celebrities to enhance attendance at the Youth Theatre performances. Instead of rejecting the appeal of pop culture she utilizes it and celebrates the best of both worlds.

According to Daunoraviciutė, the purpose of the Youth Theatre is to promote new Lithuanian playwrights, although the program also develops new directors and actors. But the primary focus is on new Lithuanian writing. Daunoraviciutė explains: "In Soviet times, Lithuanian writers were as strong as the directors, but today the economic situation discourages writers from pursuing their craft." Because directors can still get jobs in their fields, Lithuania remains a powerhouse for talented directors. But the Youth Theatre emphasizes writers, offering them prime opportunities to get their work on the boards, so to speak. A student of Jansonas, Daunoraviciutė agrees that Lithuania continues to produce many of the most important directors in Europe, but she is optimistic that her apprenticeship program will reestablish Lithuanian writers as also among the strongest in Europe. As to what sets off Lithuanian directors from the rest of the Baltics (and Europe), Daunoraviciutė suggests that the history of people living in a small country surrounded by powerful nations creates an intensity of life that directors translate into a vision that transcends the particulars of a local community to express an acute sense of the human experience.

Daunoraviciutė reinforces the complaint by Vaitkus and others about the economic predicament discouraging new writers while agreeing with Jansonas that part of the problems with developing new work is the lack of interest and training in the contemporary education system. She says things are changing, however, due to a collective sense of guilt on the part of the Ministry of Culture. After years of neglect or, at least, inaction on the part of Lithuania, during which time the Latvian Theatre Institute, for instance (thanks to Lauris Gundars), created programs specifically to support new Latvian writers, Lithuania finally began to offer state support to promote new writing — programs which channel the talent to the Youth Theatre for further professional development. Most of the students range from sixteen to eighteen, but some older students may well find a home for their projects here as well (Laura Sintija Černiauskaitė, for example).

Though Daunoraviciutė, like most artists in Lithuania, confesses that she does not miss the Soviet system, she thinks the theatre has lost much of its poetry, "ruined" (in her words) by a "realism and naturalism" she defines as a "new brutality." Even given Šabasevičinė's qualified blessing to the sensitive and mitigating directing by Koršunovas, she fingers the Lithuanian production of *Shopping and Fucking* as a sign of Lithuanian theatre "importing violence" in an attempt to exploit sensationalism to generate attendance. And though the play was a major commercial success, she and many others were uncomfortable with the performance.

Daunoraviciutė feels the same about Ivaškevičius' *Close City*, but her complaint in that case is more personal. Whereas *Shopping and Fucking* represents the reality of a jaded Western sensibility — a truth about life in England, and by extension Germany, France and the United States — she fears that playwrights like Ivaškevičius who try to emulate this style are not reflecting the truth of life in Lithuania, regardless of its new national status as a member of the European Union. She worries about a loss of national identity, and, as an antidote, focuses in her work at the Youth Theatre on plays about the specific truths of the Lithuanian situation.

But defining exactly what that situation is in its twenty-first century guise is problematic. Baudrillard argues that our cultural imagination has been sapped by the deluge of immediate flat imagery, constantly looped through our senses to the degree that "[t]here is no longer any transcendence or depth, but only the immanent surface of operations unfolding, the smooth and functional surface of communication" (12). Ironically, it is our inescapable interconnectedness — "where all terms must remain in perpetual contact with one another" (14) — that estranges us from the essential particularity of the objects by which we maintain our innate subjectivity. According to Baudrillard, a plague of "multiple networks" (16) simultaneously connects and divorces us from reality as we telegraph desire from within our "private living space" (16) or "operating area" (16). Public space collapses into a mirage, an "ephemeral connecting space" (20).

Likewise, as our private space becomes fodder for reality TV, our domestic theatre is rendered transparent by an overload of imagery. We have lost the "symbolic benefit of alienation" (21).

This phenomenon — of collapsing the boundary between object and self, of public and private space, "this forced extraversion of interiority, from this forced introjection of all exteriority" (26) — is acutely evident when the entire culture of a country, ripped from its political alienation, is paradoxically erased at the very moment of its emergence as a restored national identity: having lost "the obscenity of the hidden" (22) it becomes "entirely soluble in information and communication" (22). The seduction of communication in all its pervasive forms is absolute, irresistible: "Pleasure is no longer that of the scenic or aesthetic manifestation (seductio) but that of pure fascination, aleatory and psychotropic (subductio)" (25). In this sense, Lithuania (and the Baltics in general) is a testing ground for Baudrillard's thesis: the cultural, social and psychological effects of this sudden overload of powerful, all-pervasive imagery.

This confluence of influences that informs contemporary Lithuanian drama is perhaps best exemplified by Cezaris Graužinis's staging of the British playwright Martin Crimp's *Attempts on Her Life*. Crimp's play is a shrewd choice at this particular time in Lithuania's transitional period. As Lyn Gardner notes in her review in *The Guardian*, the play is a "chillingly well observed consideration of the soullessness of modern human existence in a consumerist culture." But given the situation in Lithuania, where the traditional Catholic concerns over spiritual values clash with the new ethos of its fledgling consumerist society, the polemics of the play are compounded by the urgency and immediacy of the critique. The play also suits the prevailing style of directing in Lithuania today that privileges texts written for a strong director — for instance, work that is already nebulous on the page, so the performance mirrors as much the director's input as the writer's. The script, composed of 17 scenes only tangentially correlative, specifies no props and provides no guidelines as to the number of actors, their appearance, their names or who is speaking. The shape of the play is left up to the director. As Gardner says, the play is "not an easy tool."

The play can be viewed as a morality play denouncing hedonism, materialism, and a loss of spiritual values, delivered, however, in a surreal style of Grotowskian minimalism overlaid by a Western-theatre-inspired mixed-media techno-expressionism. Most conservative critics in Lithuania look East, the progressives West. But this dichotomy simplifies and dis-

The "suits" in Cezaris Graužinis's staging of *Attempts on Her Life* imaginatively create Anne to fit their own emotional needs. The play can be viewed as a morality play denouncing hedonism, materialism, and a loss of spiritual values in a surreal style of Grotowskian minimalism overlaid by a Western-theatre-inspired mixed-media techno-expressionism. Graužinis explodes the "new situation" in Lithuania — that sudden virulent outbreak of liberal capitalism that erases and supplants ethnic cultures (photograph by Dmitrij Matvejev).

torts the rich hybrid emerging in a performance like Graužinis's that explodes the "new situation" — that sudden virulent outbreak of liberal capitalism that erases and supplants ethnic cultures.

Performed on the small stage at the Youth Theatre, with its black box stage and bleacher seating for seventy five, the play opens with the black floor bare except for a huge white projection screen dominating the upstage space and black cushioned desk chairs on rollers scattered against the far wall. The lights come up on three men and two women entering in business suits while heavy Gothic music creates a strange sense of angst and suspense. The anonymous corporate types pose arrogantly before the audience, but having difficulty maintaining their posture of ceremonial self-importance, they arrange themselves in the chairs and begin eavesdropping on a series of phone messages all directed to a woman named Anne — recordings from what would appear to be her husband, her lover, her mother, an assassin, a man who threatens to sexually abuse her. Clearly Anne is the object of many people's diverse desires. At the end of the messages, a final generic voice declares: "messages deleted." Along with the messages, any determinable identity of Anne is deleted too.

The uniformly dressed corporate types begin their conference by filling in the blanks, attempting to solve the mystery of Anne's identity. From within their virtual world of vicarious passion, they express their own various versions of her, creating her according to their individual needs, as if desperate to experience at least some facsimile of life. They act out their fantasies like an exercise in improvisation, as if life has been exchanged for a critique. The bare black stage implies the sterility of their lifeless, loveless world where one of the women, describing actions attributable to Anne, violently grinds her chair in a paroxysm of frottage and masturbation. The others analyze her story and performance, offering critical summaries, arguing, defending various possibilities and points-of-view — conducting, in effect, a parody of the post modern critical tendency to privilege the art of criticism over the creative process (as well as the plasticity of art over the vicissitudes of life). Each participant offers his or her different interpretation for the actions of the others as they assume Anne's role, devolving from innocuous tales of everyday life to sordid descriptions of violence and suffering and acts of inhumanity delivered in cold, philosophical tones — the difference between their delivery and the gruesome truth of the accounts evidence of the protective buffer of impersonal distance they have designed as a prerequisite to their existence. They have sanctified Anne; she serves as their last-ditch Madonna for desensitized souls trying to imagine a "natural" life. But because they are locked into a private, solipsistic version of Anne, no variant personal image can be reconciled by an appeal to any authentic model.

Julius Žalakevičius in *Attempts on Her Life* (photograph by Dmitrij Matvejev).

As if aware of this ontological trap they have created for themselves, the executives turn fearful and hostile, accusing Anne of being the lifeless one, trying to turn the tables on their own creation, blaming Anne for their antibiotic reality. By this time in the performance the irony of the title is clear. The "attempts on her life" are the executives' efforts to create a life for themselves by imagining Anne's life, literally projecting their desires on to that huge white screen upstage, investing in an ideal image they cannot necessarily control. But because they naturally fear what they desire, they must conspire to kill her — an action illustrated obliquely on the set by eerie shadow play rendered from behind the white screen.

The suits, suffering from their acute Frankenstein complex, try to assuage their guilt by a series of disturbing, personal confessions, but no matter how earnest they pretend to be in atonement, their attempts at exculpation are stripped from any semblance of sincerity by the ballad-like chords of a lone figure strumming along with their apologies on an electric guitar. Theirs is a world that turns even the most heart-felt truths into pop songs, as the artificial sentimentality of the market economy transforms the most intimate and violent sentiments into a radio sing-along. The executives, seduced by the bottom line, exploit all values, even, maybe especially, their own.

In a note made public through the media, Anne confesses that she has killed herself, but the executives will not let her die. They regroup in another board meeting. Because Anne exists only in the collective corporate imagination, she can be neither killed nor restricted: she is a nightmare product of a debased world, the blank screen onto which everyone projects a vision, but, significantly, nothing ever appears on the screen but shadows, as if Plato's cave has become a shopping mall, his allegory an advertisement for a runaway consumerist society.

The suits resurrect Anne as a disco diva, selling "the new Annie" like a car, shouting sales homilies in Lithuanian — Electric windows! Air-conditioning! Available in diesel! — while a man to one side repeats the pitch in deadpan English through a megaphone. The bi-lingual effect is disconcerting, with the hyperventilating Lithuanian sales screed finally degenerating into a Fascist rant reminiscent of Nazi hyperbole selling its "Aryan" ideals.

When the executives regroup again, they reassess their product — "the new Annie!" — like critics who reduce the vitality of art to fit their own clever concepts, their arrogance wrapped in rationalizations, explication and critical jargon, psychological cant and self-referential speculation — all proving nothing by demonstrating that the search for meaning destroys meaning: the search — the process — *is* the meaning. Cryptically, one suit finally admits: "Theatre has nothing to do with this," a statement pregnant with irony, yet as tautologically empty as the sardonic world of the boardroom itself.

The executives are soon reduced to spooky secret agents in a totalitarian state providing "security" through fear, having created an Orwellian world where idealism is reduced to a cliché and sold with empty phrases cooked-up by corporate sponsors. As the end product of a world infected by a language disconnected from emotion, Anne has become a packaged, corporate piece of pornography. In the ad-speak of her creators, pornography is her ticket to success, allowing her to achieve the virtuous life available to those capable of realizing economic freedom. By dehumanizing her, the purveyors of porn claim exploitation as a virtue. The action ends with the executives applauding the blank screen, returning to their board meeting, resorting again to the safety of critical evaluation — a.k.a. market strategies — fearful that, after all, "she could be any one of us."

The target of the barbs in Graužinis' eviscerating production of Crimp's admittedly acerbic piece — the desecration of art by soulless critics, the spiritual vacuity of corporate marketing — dovetails in the streets of the "new situation" in Lithuania. The first issue, at least in the Western experience, is almost quaint. The assault on art by the post-structuralists invites a critical dispute best settled in other quarters more suitable for academic mud wrestling. But the latter issue, the perversity of marketing imagery and language, and the corrupt ethos driving the unprincipled exploitation of global capitalism, is very real, acute and ripe in the experience of the locals. Along Piles, Gedimino, Vokiecu or any number of pedestrian streets through the maze of the Old Town section of the city, advertisements create a lifeless tableau projecting from billboards and the sides of buildings a vision of potential life guaranteed to deaden the sensibilities of the most resilient citizens.

The change from the Soviet centralized state economy might have been inevitable, and the Western style of private capitalism does not come without certain benefits, including career possibilities and accelerated personal freedom, but the luxuries — no matter how trivial — do come with a price, and the concerns about cultural homogeneity are valid, especially given the delicate sensibility of emerging markets in which the consumers until recently were unaccustomed to the impact of mass marketing, on both the landscape and the spirit of the people. In this sense, as a frontal assault on corporate vampirism, performing *Attempts on Her Life* indicates the ability of Lithuanian directors to import work from the West — in this case, Britain, the black-heart of the Anglo-Saxon economic model the French so vehemently resist — yet stamp the performance with the indelible imprimatur of the particular situation on the streets of Lithuania, showcasing the talent of Lithuanian directors in whose hands the foreign material becomes theirs.

Along with the Youth Theatre, another institution dedicated to developing new talent in Lithuania is the Theatre Laboratory, part of the Lithuanian Musical and Theatre Academy. A good example of their work is *The Open Circle*, directed by Aidas Giniotis. Conceived as a dramatic exercise of autobiographical improvisations (what the British call "playback theatre"), the piece exceeds its function as an interesting theatre game and becomes an outright riveting performance. The structure is based on twelve actors telling stories of their lives, beginning with their earliest reminiscences of childhood, working through experiences in school and traveling, culminating in significant moments of their young adulthood, recalling escapades involving romance, the rituals of experimenting with drugs and alcohol, and the deaths of friends or parents. As the players begin to elaborate on specific episodes, they choose fellow members of the circle to act out their narratives, spontaneously creating, from separate memories, a sort of psychotherapeutic exploration of the collective creative process — individuals coalescing into a productive ensemble unit.

One production is staged in an adopted space — a black room where the students sit in a circle of metal chairs. A young man plays a mesmerizing two-chord riff before one of the actors begins talking. The improvisations start tentatively — like any other group of friends swapping stories — the music providing a rhythm to the oral versions of events. But then the guitarist speaks, breaking — or punctuating — the mood, surrendering the guitar. The silence reinforces the intimacy of the group — as if they are now even more isolated from the audience in a bond of mutual purpose. The recollections grow more animated, and more intimate, then more expressive and elaborate, until the story-tellers began to employ the others, assigning them seemingly random roles, some comic, some violent, each episode becoming a means by which the individual actors explore singularly and collectively a wide range of emotions as members must adopt new strategies for their assignments, including sound effects, word games, parodies, dance, stage combat, tenderness, violence, playing children, adults, animals, sundry inanimate objects, building to a strange paean to

Kurt Cobain that returns the guitar player to his two-chord riff, then silence before the prompt for applause.

The virtue of the exercise, according to Giniotis, is "to refresh in one's memory all reminiscence from everybody's individual past and using theatrical means to create a performance." The actors must rely on their ingenuity, as the element of surprise forces them to discover — spontaneously — new means of expression. This way, says Giniotis, "theatre becomes the way to share and to heal collectively."

This notion of using theatre as an instrument for healing resonates with Lithuanian directors young and old, from Vaitkus to Graužinis, no matter how disparate their approaches or contradictory their intentions. Some critics disagree, suggesting that too many of the young, stimulated by what they consider avant-garde presumptions, produce meaningless, onanistic art — "the new aestheticism." But the Catholic vein of amelioration runs deep in Lithuanian theatre, and even the generational differences seemed to be reconciled by the consensus of concern for social rejuvenation. Where the older generation focuses on spiritual values from within the tradition of humanism, the younger directors concentrate on the soulless entropy caused by the shock of naked consumerism — the same themes, actually, explored from different perspectives. A watermark for contemporary critiques of the "new situation" seems to have been the performance of Ravenhill's *Shopping and Fucking*, celebrated by Liūgą, decried by Daunoraviciutė, and seen by about every theatre-going patron in Vilnius. Included in the National Theatre's repertory, the directorial interpretation by Koršunovas unapologetically addresses the paradox of how independence and democracy create the sort of blood-sucking conspicuous consumption that drains the spirit out of a nation. As Skendelienė notes, "Koršunovas has taken up the most pressing problems of contemporary society and reflected these problems in his performances."

Audra Zukaitytė, a spokesperson for The Oskaras Koršunovas Theatre, admits that Koršunovas decided to perform *Shopping and Fucking* "to reflect the new reality for Lithuania, the materialism, the spiritual loss, the corrupting influence of capitalism." She thinks this "new reality" requires a "new language," especially for directors. She disagrees with Liūgą that the theatre can be revitalized only by diminishing the role of the auteur-director, although she does stress the need for close collaboration between writers and directors. "The situation in Lithuania is different from Britain and the United States," she says. "In what we still consider 'Western theatre' the writer is considered the key to the work. In Lithuania, playwrights defer to the director." This deference of the writers to the directors reflects the tradition of strong directors (underscoring Vaitkus's observations) but it also creates a problem for writers because they see the cult of the director as their best chance at working and getting performances on stage — the same problems Daunoraviciutė tries to address at the Youth Theatre. In addition to the lack of recognition, young writers are frequently not interested in the social issues facing ordinary Lithuanians and tend to seek their material elsewhere, evidenced by Ivaškevičius in *Close City*. That play, for Zukaitytė, demonstrates the problem of writers who do not defer to strong directors — e.g. Ivaškevičius, who directed his play himself— yet she argues that it is a landmark play marking the transition for the old Soviet style of theatre to a new style that she identifies as "Lithuanian": the physicality, the use of mixed-media, the intense minimalism, metaphor and poetic irony.

Of the big three directors in Lithuania — Nekrošius, Tuminas and Koršunovas — Koršunovas was one of the first directors internationally recognized to graduate from the director's department at the Lithuanian Music Academy, so he did not need "to change his language," as Zukaitytė puts it. According to Ramunė Marcinkevičiūtė, theatre critic and lecturer at the Department of History and Theory of Art, "Even Eimuntas Nekrošius and Rimas Tuminas did not have the debut that Koršunovas did" mainly because, according to Marcinkevičiūtė, Nekrošius and Tuminas "had to work under the rigours of the communist regime." Koršunovas, on the other hand, was never part of the Soviet controlled, ideologically centralized system, so his approach appeals more directly to young audiences than the work of more traditional, Russian-trained directors like Vaitkus, even though he studied under Vaitkus at the academy. In the tradition of Nekrošius, who during Gorbachev's experiments with openness (*glasnost*) was allowed to direct throughout Europe, the first, so to speak, to put Lithuanian directors on the map, Koršunovas is considered, like Nekrošius, a "European" director too. Because he was allowed to move freely during his formative years in the early 1990s "between the two Europes" (Marcinkevičiūtė), he was able to incorporate from his broad international exposure new stylistic trends into his work, creating a truly influential theatre that initiated the first contemporary style-"theatre as confrontation" (Marcinkevičiūtė) — initiating "artistic projects facilitating the cultural integration between East and West" (Marcinkevičiūtė). But even though he is more "international" than other less seasoned or well-traveled directors in Lithuania, Zukaitytė considers his work the best example of authentically new contemporary Lithuanian theatre.

What seems to set Koršunovas apart from his mentors and contemporaries is his focus on creating a seamless connection between the historical and the contemporary, staging classics as if they were current and contemporary pieces as if they were classics. For instance, his provocative production of *Shopping and Fucking* evokes Shakespeare, while his raucous *A Midsummer's Night's Dream* plays eerily across a contemporary landscape. This ahistorical confluence, in Marcinkevičiūtė's view, appeals to an "interdisciplinary public not over-attached to purity of genre." She notes how early on in his career Koršunovas began "expanding the concept of dramatic performance by confronting the public with means of expression taken from music, the cinema, video and the visual arts."

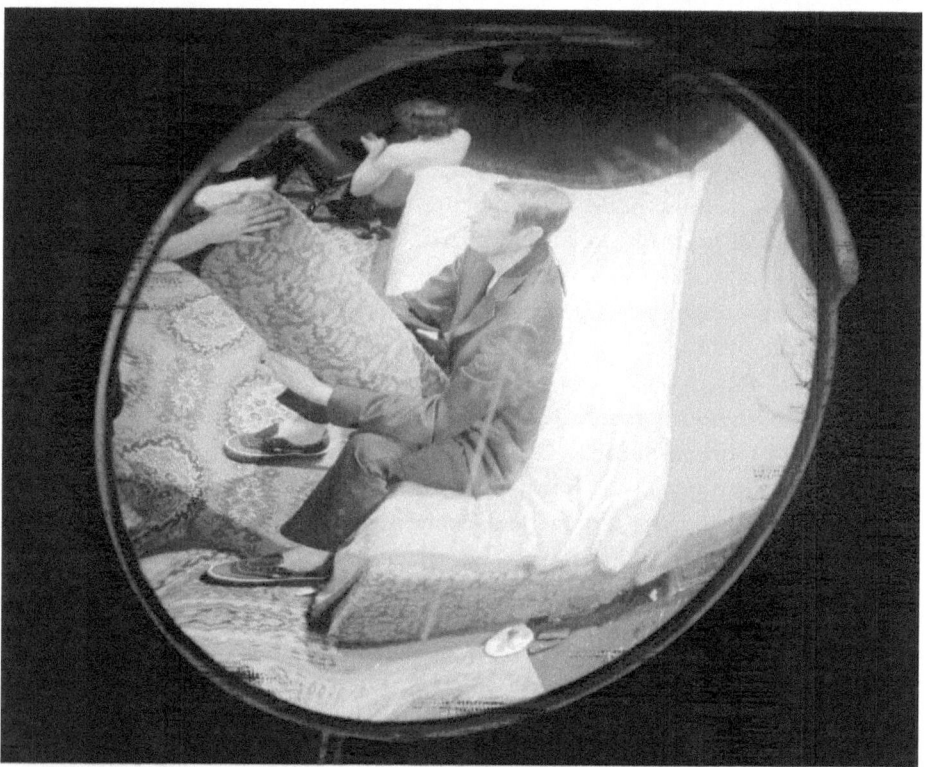

Arūnas Sakalauskas in *Shopping and Fucking*, directed by Oskaras Koršunovas at the Lithuanian National Drama Theatre. Many mainstream Lithuanian critics accuse Koršunovas of "importing violence" in an attempt to exploit sensationalism to generate attendance. For these critics, the play may represent jaded Western sensibility, but it does not reflect the truth of life in Lithuania (photograph by Dmitrij Matvejev).

This mélange of media styles perhaps explains his instant success with young audiences; in fact, some critics credit Koršunovas as being singlehandedly the one director to reinvigorate theatre after its stagnation in the early nineties, when after liberation it lost its relevance and power to express cultural, political and psychological truths. Rasa Vasinauskaitė, author of *The Theatre of Oskaras Koršunovas: Interviews and Articles*, claims, "At the end of the Nineties, when older artists were painfully shocked by value crisis, Koršunovas was the first to get audiences back to the theatre." In often messianic language, Vasinauskaitė describes his work as achieving a "synthesis of various branches of culture and art [...] a new theatrical reality [...] a new mythology for Lithuanian theatre." Skendelienė concurs. She views the experiments of directors like Koršunovas as reconnecting with the historical roots of Lithuanian theatre, explaining that these new directors who are confirming and challenging Lithuanian traditions manage to "keep their distance from literary theatre and psychological realism while at the same time maintaining a strong connection with an archaic Lithuania world-outlook, its signs and symbols."

Dissatisfied with the repertory theatre bureaucracy, Koršunovas split

In his production of *Romeo and Juliet*, Koršunovas challenges what he considers the stale aesthetics of the repertory system, in this case setting the action for *Romeo and Juliet* in a pizzeria, reducing the aristocratic elements and foregrounding the human tragedy in more colloquial and humanistic terms. Typical of his generation, Koršunovas treats any text abstractly (photograph by Dmitrij Matvejev).

from the National Theatre in 1998 to form an independent company in which he could challenge what he considered the stale aesthetics of the repertory system. For instance, he set the action for *Romeo and Juliet* in pizzerias, reducing the aristocratic elements and foregrounding the human tragedy in more colloquial and humanistic terms. And though some critics grouse, suggesting his reframing classics in contemporary contexts is nothing more than "a puerile attempt to modernize the Bard" or "cultural sabotage" (Marcinkevičiūtė), others view his approach as a revival, "a joyful playfulness of the old anarchic dramatic spirit" (Vasinauskaitė). Typical of his generation, Koršunovas treats any text abstractly, be it Shakespeare's or Ravenhill's, synthesizing the words into action. "No matter what the play is, every one of his productions has the same structure, peculiar to the dream and paradoxical thinking, which suggests a special combination of the abstract and verbal levels" (Vasinauskaitė). This formula, which Vasinauskaitė describes as the Word giving way to Action, expresses the Catholic-inspired visual element so predominant in Lithuanian theatre and underscores the notion of Lithuanian theatre being a director's theatre. As Vasinauskaitė notes: "Koršunovas is an essentially theatrical director; [...] simple situations become metaphorically meaningful, theatrically transformed realism becomes almost symbolic romanticism, and the social definition of performance is a new poetic, or mythological, space."

In an interview with the Goethe Institute, Koršunovas explains his reasons for setting *Oedipus Rex* in a children's playground, saying, "If children play, they create a real situation" (qtd. in Kessing). This enigmatic response is not as coy as it may first appear. The reality of the nightmare Oedipus lives through may be expressed best by the childhood experience of believing imaginative contexts without the intrusion of a reality principle interrupting the dream work of the play. The oversized teddy bear, the swings and random detritus of the playground enhance the notion of threatened innocence and compound the impact of Oedipus' terrible revelation: he moves from innocence to experience, from blindness (ironically) to enlightenment, as the spectator moves from "reality" to "fiction," and yet the gap between those two antipodes shrinks perilously within the context of child's play. "The spectator who comes to the theatre," he says, "should not come as into another, unreal world" (qtd. in Kessing). Very much in line with Liūgą's theories, Staniškytė identifies this approach in terms of "what Umberto Eco has called the 'open' text, in which audience interpretation is demanded by the text in order to complete understanding. In these performances, the text is opened up to the perception of the audience in such a way that a specific theatrical situation is created that enables a variety of interpretations and a plurality of meanings."

Koršunovas defines himself by his ability to distill the essence from even the most antique material, then recasting it — reinvigorating it — to parallel (and appeal to) a contemporary audience's expectations. In *Oedipus*, he claims to have realized "the possibility of reading a 2,500 years old piece [...] contemporarily. With this production I had today's spectator in the head, its conceptions of power, fate property ..." (qtd. in Kessing). Like many Lithuanian directors who want to export their performances, Koršunovas seeks the universal — values that transcend language — as a survival strategy, and usually it works, gauging from the positive response from international audiences (though he confesses that his plays often contain the same Aesopian language playwrights and directors used during the Soviet years — in the case of *Oedipus*, a coded critique on the politics of the then current mayor of Vilnius).

Zukaitytė admits that before independence theatre in Lithuania enjoyed a status missing in the contemporary scene. During the Soviet period, theatre in Lithuania was "like a church," she says. She recalls how, when plays were metaphors that critiqued the Soviet system, one line from Alfred Jarry's *Ubu Roi*—"There are too many Russians around"— created a new context of meaning that — given the circumstances — eluded the censors and made the Lithuanian audience feel "connected." (Almost all artistic forms exploited this "speech of Aesop," including popular singers from the 1970s like Wysockij, whose romantic double entendres primed couples with lines like: "I can't get to you, my love, because the border is closed.")

Like others, Zukaitytė agrees that after independence, street life became more interesting than theatre. But in her opinion, the shift in cultural appreciation did not swing toward pop culture, which she says was always available at some level, but to social events that seemed to offer more relevance than the metaphor of theatre. During the Soviet period people would line up for tickets — often standing all night — but after independence theatre seemed redundant, unnecessary and irrelevant. People at first were idealistic, uncritically embracing the new capitalist system, but Zukaitytė looks back at this initial ideological optimism as naiveté. The new system, while better than the old, is not a "paradise." The sudden change to a market economy requires personal responsibility, and this is disorienting for the people who cannot change from the Soviet style where bureaucrats made decisions for people and individual career choices were basically non-existent. The existential crisis brought on by changing from the centralized system to one offering personal freedom created a "victim complex." For their personal failures, the people who could not navigate the new society first blamed the Russians; then "Western influence" became the boogey man responsible for their predicament.

According to Zukaitytė, the new generation represented by Koršunovas does not suffer from this Lithuanian "victim complex," and this is why what she calls the "new language" of theatre is so important. The old issues are no longer issues. Even the label "Eastern Europe" is problematic. The young writers and directors consider themselves European — no less Lithuanian but unaffected by issues of national identity, not incensed or bitter or even ironically nostalgic about Soviet censorship. They have never experienced the "clash of ideology" of the older directors and consider many of the "classic" productions "museum theatre." Directors like Koršunovas grapple with their own generational problems — the mass-market mentality, for instance, and globalization. They are no longer insecure about integrating into the European Union, understanding perfectly well that preserving a small culture is impossible in the new paradigm. Classical texts for them are considered rich sources for eternal values, but their transformations of these texts, their interpretations of them into performances, represent a new vision — that "new language" — that transcends regionalism.

This new language is the essence of Rimas Tuminas' theatre. As resident director of the Little Theatre of Vilnius (Vilnius Mažasis Teatras), his deft touch is his signature, blending metaphor with realism, physical theatre with poetry, romanticism with biting irony. His productions, simple and open on the surface, generate a subterfuge of motifs that seduce the audience into a complex of dramatic tensions. His staging of Lermontov's *The Masquerade* (*Maskaradas*) exemplifies this approach. The controlling metaphor of snow — beautiful and deadly, inspiring and numbing, itself a mask and a natural "truth" — sums up the passions paradoxically dueling at the center of the play. The ease with which he transcends the "historical" moment of the play, yet sustains the charm of a nostalgic period piece, testifies to his ability to connect with contemporary audiences, creating an aesthetic approach that nevertheless avoids diminishing the intimate human tragedy the play depicts.

Staniškytė identifies two forms of what she calls "self-reflexivity in contemporary Lithuanian performances: the critical, executing the ideological function and the playful, executing the aesthetic function." She cites Tuminas' production of *The Masquerade* as a prime example of "the playful," exploiting both ancient and contemporary myths (i.e., archetypal systems of identification) while "subverting or rewriting them, exposing their underlying power structures by giving voice to 'unrepresented' marginal subjects."

Because *The Masquerade* is basically *Othello* rewritten in a nineteenth century context, the story is familiar and disarming, predictable and suspenseful, but instead of opting for the easy "update" approach so common in contemporary attempts to contemporize dated material — borrowing various mixed-media strategies, sampling pop cultural references from Hollywood to hip-hop — (a charge that, indeed, Koršunovas is open to) — Tuminas manages to both exploit and deconstruct the essence of sentimentality. The overall impact of his use of space and props is stunning — enchanting fish, the ubiquitous snow, the "postcard" tableau: everything is at once symbolic and natural.

Ramunė Balevičiūtė, theatre critic and dramaturge at the Little Theatre, explains Tuminas' move away form the elaborate theatricality of Vaitkus in terms of what Tuminas calls "Fantastic Minimalism." The old style epitomized by Vaitkus and his generation relied on spectacle, actual stage space and theatrical effects. The new directors like Tuminas, Varnas, Graužinis, Jankevičius and Koršunovas tend to seek out non-traditional theatre spaces for their performances, to undermine intentionally the expectations of both actor and audience as to what a theatre experience essentially entails. Even though an "old school" director like Vaitkus, steeped in Russian precision — both psychologically and visually — often tries to incorporate new technology into his productions — video, for instance, and elements of "alienation" in his production of Dostoyevsky's *Demons* (*Demonai*) — the results still reflect the old approach, the performances relying on the traditional trappings of theatre: dramatic space, elaborate sets, props, lighting: relying on theatre "as theatre."

Balevičiūtė cites the performance of French playwright Natacha de Pontcharra's *Rats* (*Les Ratés*) directed by Jankevičius and Graužinis's production of Crimp's *Attempts on Her Life* as prime examples of the new approach of Lithuanian directors who are looking to "transform the inner space of a performance." This transformation of non-theatrical space allows the director, she says, "to find a 'spatial image' for a certain production which encompasses its meanings, so the form itself can be conceived as the form of the creation born within it." Jankevičius staged *Rats* in a bleak cell-like space of an abandoned blackened room with no fly, no sound, no lighting effects, using only four chairs, an empty beer can and a soccer ball for props, the scarcity reinforcing the exclusionary lives — both imaginatively and literally — of the twins Jef and Jeffy, born with rats' heads, physically and existentially withdrawn from society, impossibly isolated yet yearning to connect with the world of men. The claustrophobic room is not a set, necessarily: the space is an actual representation of the metaphorical space of the play. Likewise, the sterility of the executives' imaginations in *Attempts on Her Life* is expressed by the emptiness of the stage: a barren space dominated by a large white projection screen onto which only shadows are projected. Other examples abound. Tuminas staged Beckett's *Waiting for Godot* (*Belaukiant Godo*) in a partially razed building that was subsequently torn down, the space of the production as ephemeral as the production itself. Varnas intentionally set Dorst's *Wasted Land* in "disposable" locations, compounding the ironic context peculiar to each production.

According to Balevičiūtė, "a non-theatrical space in which a performance is born always affects its language and its form." This emphasis on

Inga Filipovič (*top*) and with Sergejus Ivanovas and Leonardas Pobedonoscevas (*following page*) in Agnius Jankevičius' production of *Rats* in Vilnius. Illustrating what Rimas Tuminas calls "Fantastic Minimalism," Jankevičius tends to seek out non-traditional theatre spaces for performances to undermine intentionally the expectations of both actor and audience as to what a theatre experience essentially entails. The claustrophobic room is not a set, necessarily: the space is an actual representation of the metaphorical space of the play (photographs by Dmitrij Matvejev).

space and form represents the turn from Vaitkus's generation to the approach of the new generation. The key, says Balevičiūtė, is to understand that "the 'real' performance is in the spectator's imagination — an especially important concept for directors when they begin to work with actors: no sets, no audience, only the connections between the actors and their characters."

Hers is the philosophy of Tuminas, who describes his approach as "open theatre" — that is, he expects his actors (and the audience) to be open to possibilities throughout the creative process of bringing the text to life. Tuminas wants actors who are experienced and naïve: they should know how to create an image and character but should also remain open to chance, alert to serendipity, and willing to violate the boundaries implied by theatre space. In his production of *The Masquerade*, for instance, Tuminas does not stage the melodramatic lifestory at the heart of the traditionally romantic play; instead, he creates a pastiche, combing elements of Broadway and *commedia dell' arte* with the self-referential absurdism of Fellini's films. The effect casts the play into a wider context than the one for which it was originally intended, using the

Valda Bičkutė in *Madagascar*, written by Marius Ivaškevičius and directed by Rimas Tuminas at the Little Theatre of Vilnius. In his subtle directing, Tuminas humanizes Lithuanian stereotypes but maintains a formalist, stylized distance that enhances the metaphorical significance of the action. His technique employs paradoxes that are never merely contradictions (photograph by Dmitrij Matvejev).

original as a springboard to explore not what *is* there but what *could* be there, making discoveries within the process the central concern of the performance. His playfulness is evident in small venues too, as in his production of Ivaškevičius' *Madagascar (Madagaskaras)*. This comical and imaginative retelling of the exploits of Kazy Pokštas, a famous Lithuanian explorer and utopian, "explores the phenomenon of what the 'Lithuanian' is, analyses problems of the Lithuanian mentality and describes the ambitions of Lithuanian people [...] they are a little bit nitwits, but very delightful by their childish naivety ..." (Atėnai). In his subtle directing, Tuminas humanizes the stereotypes, but maintains a formalist, stylized distance that enhances the metaphorical significance of the action. In one scene, when a striking woman — a prototypical feminist — tries to seduce a young poetess, the irony is never destructive: it serves more like an accelerant in a chemical process that brews a tasty mix of comedy and passion, tenderness and violence, absurdity and willful logic. The vulnerable poetess is never a victim, the sultry seductress not wholly a villain. Tuminas' technique employs paradoxes that are never merely contradictions: choreographed spontaneity, dramatic clowning, a slapstick Stanislavsky method continuously undercut by improvisation.

With its focus on experimentation, the Little Theatre of Vilnius offers Tuminas just the sort of venue he needs to continue producing distinctive performances, allowing him to explore new ways of thinking, new ways of staging, especially through cooperation with international sponsors like the British Council and the Goethe Institute. In their newly renovated building off Gedimino Street, situated among icons of crass consumerism — across the way from the Olympic Casino, squeezed between Faberge and Galezya boutiques — the Little Theatre of Vilnius is strategically positioned — literally and figuratively — to keep Lithuanian culture anchored in its innovative tradition.

Tuminas jokes that for all his "sense of the new," he is an old-fashioned director who, he says in ironic deadpan, does not understand the contemporary world. Because we all "come from the past," the theatre must "look to the past" for its essence, not necessarily to a particular historical context, but to "archaic values," the timeless concerns that bind humanity. And though this approach sounds heavy-handed and traditional in the worst sense (in the reactionary or nationalist use of the term), his affinity for theatre as a genre, a self-referential "play" of images and tropes, sets him apart from the generation preceding him. Old-fashioned to Tuminas means keeping in mind that we are products of the past, a construct of cultural memories, and in his performances he seeks images that evoke these memories, these deep, collective emotions. He believes theatre can most effectively express these shared human values only when they are freed from any rigid cultural context. To this end, Tuminas teaches his actors to withhold their personal histories, to keep them inside, as it were, so their characters develop through the actor's exploration of these memories.

Balevičiūtė thinks directors like Tuminas, though popular throughout Europe and therefore exposed to international trends, remain righteously indigenous. They still work within the Lithuanian tradition of a director's theatre, defined by Balevičiūtė (slightly contradicting Vaitkus and Jansonas) as practitioners more interested in formal qualities than themes, true to their own visions rather than in involving themselves in political or social commentary, though Balevičiūtė is quick to argue that separating form from context may be a necessary component of literary criticism but in the creative process of bringing a text off the page to the stage, it is impossible to separate the two if the intent is to produce serious, mature dramatic art. This attention to formal qualities and the insistence on synthesizing form and content distinguishes the new Lithuanian directors from their elders whose work, especially during the Soviet period, tended to focus obliquely but pointedly on issue-oriented work that stressed political and social values.

Balevičiūtė points out that the Western influence, reworked by the strong directors in the Lithuanian tradition, has transformed Lithuanian theatre. For her, the integration of Lithuania into the European Union is not a corrupting force working to dilute the essence of Lithuanian culture; on the contrary, she sees the sudden availability of new material as a chance for rejuvenation. During the 1990s, she says, there were no new texts; theatre was stagnate. When access to the West opened up, the new plays allowed directors to rethink their craft.

3

Estonia: The Lutheran Narrative — Writers' Theatre

Determining the historical nature of Estonian theatre depends on which Estonia a particular critic identifies with. Romantics associate logic and linearity with a Germanic tradition associated with the professional repertory theatre, implying that the dominant style throughout the modern Estonian period is derivative, an import, a corruption of the pagan environmental theatre based on fertility rituals and intuitive performances. Others unapologetically suggest that Estonian theatre is indeed a product of the Baltic-German occupation, modified to reflect the reality of Estonian culture: a reform of peasant sensibility essentially "taken over from the conquerors" (Rähesoo, *Estonian Theatre* 70). Even so, Rähesoo underscores the importance for Estonians developing a vernacular theatre that could, through its language and social circumstances, be considered Estonian. Ironically, he cites the work of "'Estophiles'" (25) — Baltic-Germans enamored with Estonian folklore who compiled traditional stories — as a seminal feature in the evolution of an indigenous literature. The national epic *Kalev's Son* (*Kalevipoeg*), for instance, was created by Germans in the same condescending mode: collecting and preserving a small country's heritage.[7] But Rähesoo attributes the "real birth of Estonian theatre" (27) to Lydia Koidula and her Estonian language play *The Cousin of Saaremaa* (*Saaremaa onupoeg*) that fueled an already intensifying nationalist feeling among the newly emerging middle-class Estonians.

The ensuing generation, intoxicated with a new freedom of expression, soon experienced its first taste of things to come from the Russians. In the late nineteenth century, the Czarist rulers began a series of repressive measures, including abolishing the Estonian language in educational institutions. But according to Rähesoo, Estonian nationalism proved too resilient, and though the developments in the theatre are ineluctably tied to Estonia's historical relationship with the power struggles between Russia and Germany, Estonia slowly nurtured an independent intelligentsia that embraced Modernist trends then sweeping across Europe, a spirit of artistic creativity best embodied by the Young Estonians (Noor-Eesti) who self-consciously began to develop a national culture. As part of this mission, the Young Estonians encouraged the development of a professional theatre capable of staging performances dealing specifically with Estonian issues in a homegrown context. But even with these reforms, including the influences of radical new literary movements in Scandinavia and Paris, most productions remained true to the German and Russian styles.

During the years 1918–1940, as a result of the growth of professional and institutionalized theatres supported by the newly independent state, a growing number of new plays were written and produced by Estonians, especially A. H. Tammsaare and Hugo Raudsepp. But in Rähesoo's account, this nationalism led to a rejection of the experimental styles still being explored around greater Europe, and creeping conservatism let to a notable return to Realism, an ominous sign of the power that the middle-class audiences still exercise in determining the shape of Estonian theatre.

The years of occupation began in 1940 when the Soviets annexed the country, continued under war-time Nazi domination, resumed when the Soviets returned in 1944, and lasted until 1991 when Estonia was recognized again as an independent state. As in the other Baltic countries, while occupation and repression led to a rise in exile literature, indigenous talent was all but eliminated. The only local writer of importance Rähesoo mentions in the pre-Khrushchev era is August Jackobson, cited because he could "easily accommodate Stalinist formulas" (57). In the 1960s and 1970s, however, Estonian theatre (and culture in general, most notably literature) began a process of renewal, fueled in part by the events of 1968 that both depressed and stimulated the artistic community. (For example, the Soviet army crushing the Czech liberalization movement was definitely a negative, but the success and optimism embodied by the student movements in Paris and elsewhere in the West was encouraging.) The psychological fragility of the period, with society vacillating between optimism and pessimism, created a fertile dynamism in the theatre, inspiring two stage directors most often cited by contemporary aficionados as true avant-gardes: Evald Hermaküla and Jaan Tooming. Their physical and metaphorical performances became the most influential style for a whole generation. Some critics suggest that what many young playwrights consider new now is merely a reworking of what Hermaküla and Tooming were doing in the early 1970s. In the history of Estonian theatre, and especially after World War II, the creative focus centers mostly on directors, as playwrights have never enjoyed the sort of prestige and importance in Estonia that they do in United States or Britain. Still, their attempts were naturally a part of wider cultural context, supported by new generation of authors (e.g., Paul-Eerik Rummo, Mati Unt) often working in tandem with these directors.

More serious, perhaps, was the Soviet threat to eliminate Estonian cultural identity altogether. Because Estonians have had their own country infrequently, and in the modern period only from 1918–1940, Estonian identity, like many nationalities throughout the Soviet Bloc, including the Balkans, Hungary and the Black Sea nations, was based on language. Sensing this as a source of resistance to assimilation, the Soviets devised a plan to prohibit teaching in the Estonian language, substituting Russian instead. Even though this linguistic purification was never actually enforced, the very suggestion caused a crisis in the cultural community (indeed, among the general population). As universities began, in some disciplines, to switch to instruction in Russian, the theatre was suddenly thrust into the vanguard of a cultural preservation movement; because the productions were in Estonian, the theatre kept the language (and therefore the culture) alive. Theatre critic Andres Laasik suggests that keeping the language alive is the primary role of theatre: "In small countries theatre has a task to serve the language [...] in order to protect it" ("Nomadism"). This function alone, of preserving the language and unique cultural qualities of Estonian life contributed in no small way to the romantic status of the theatre as a mythical force of resistance in the face of Soviet oppression, and given the very real threat to their linguistic heritage, the reputation is deserved.

Tallinn

Some of the most dynamic theatre talent in Estonia resides at the Tallinn City Theatre (Tallinna Linnateater). Located off a cobblestone street in the Old Town section, the complex itself, a maze of five interconnected houses attached to the original core of a small medieval merchant's house, offers an impressive array of performance spaces, none of which is a classical Italian-style theatre. Begun as the Estonian Youth Theatre, established in 1966, it was renamed Tallinn City Theatre in 1994, and the renovated houses became theatre spaces in 1999. The small stage, seating 100, in use since 1975, is a black box space with a balcony to one side. The so-called "Hell Space," inaugurated in 1997 with, appropriately, Brecht's *Threepenny Opera*, is a basement space with an unusual triangular shape, a wooden floor and professional fly that seats 160. The "Heaven Space," the main performing area, seats 200 in the large former attic of the original fifteenth century mansion. Other unusual spaces include the open air stage consisting of a huge performance area in the center of the courtyard among the surrounding buildings, seating 600, although plans are in place for a renovation eliminating the open air aspect of the area and creating a new main performance stage for year-round, large-scale productions; the "Chamber Theatre," a small performance room; several intimate and versatile rehearsal spaces; and even the lobby of the main building, the "Deilei," where the theatre staged *Romeo and Juliet* with the balcony scene set on the staircase of the medieval merchant's house.

It is no wonder why, offering such exotic, challenging yet professional performance spaces, Tallinn City Theatre draws such serious talent, employing 25 resident actors, two set designers and four directors. The theatre's repertory features world classics by Chekhov and Dostoyevsky, but also features new work by the young Estonian playwright Jaan Tätte (also an actor in the theatre) whose plays *The Bridge* and *Happy Everyday!* are included in the repertory, along with modern pieces by David Storey, Samuel Beckett and David Mamet.

The variety of performance spaces and strong talent allow Tallinn City Theatre the versatility to stage several performances — classics, modern, avant-garde — often simultaneously, satisfying a diverse audience that remains faithful to the vision of the theatre, averaging over 400 performances a year for 70,000 spectators.

A performance of Tätte's *Meeletu* (loosely translated as "mindless"), directed by Eva Klemets, youngest of the resident directors, is evidence of Tallinn City Theatre's dedication to new work and challenging performances. The set, below the A-frame ceiling of the Heaven Space, consists only of a huge wooden asymmetrical bench resembling a picnic table at least six feet high and fourteen feet long, with two parallel planks running beneath and connecting the base. As the audience files in, the lights stay up while everyone is seated, but they stay up until the audience begins to stir, impatient, even uncomfortable with expectation, then finally a man stands in the audience and explains that he is waiting for someone at a bus station. He walks onto the stage and begins to explain why he is there. The ensuing play depicts the series of events that have led him to this moment: waiting for a woman at the bus stop.

A play that seems not to start, that just happens, as if being in that theatre space is an excuse for this man to relate his existential confession, does not incorporate a new or necessarily innovative technique. The tradition of anti-theatre and alienation effects is well-established. But in this case the approach effectively frames the conflict, the collision between the man's past and his present, as soon enough the characters from his memory enter and begin to reenact the significant moments the man narrates directly to the audience, interrupting the line between the stage reality and the reality of the audience. By attempting to erase this theatrical demarcation, Klemets fuses the two experiences to create immediacy for the audience that a more traditional staging may not achieve.

In the course of the narrative, punctuated by the dramatic scenes, the audience learns that the man made millions selling Nokia telephones (a joke the Estonians share with the Finns), but at some point he came to realize that he was not living the life he had hoped he would, that even with all his money he feels unfulfilled. When he decides to take a year off, he is surprised that his wife, son and business partner are actually indifferent, so he rents a primitive cottage in the country — no electricity, no running water — and begins his sabbatical, rethinking his life and wondering about the lack of authentic affection between him and his family — his wife and son — and any genuine respect between him and his partner in business. Soon he begins experiencing visions, ideas that he claims are strange, or not his own. Villagers visit him, saying they have heard he is a good, wise man, and that maybe he can give them advice, but the visits only further the man's confusion.

One night a mysterious girl comes to him and convinces him that the ideas he is having are a calling, as if announcing him as a new messiah. He follows her advice, and as if beyond his will, he begins to preach through a series of rituals, telling the villagers that money is not the answer to their quest for meaning in their lives. On cue, his wife shows up asking for a divorce and his partner demands that he relinquish the rights to his business. The man agrees, giving his wife the house and all his material goods, and signing over his business to his partner. But the next time he performs his rituals, no one shows. Later, one of the villagers explains that when the man first came there, the people thought he was wise and good because he was wealthy, but now that he has given away all his possessions, they consider him a fool. Distraught at the villagers' utter misunderstanding of his message, he withdraws into his cabin until one day, near death, he discovers a secret drawer with an old photo album and finds out the mysterious girl is the granddaughter of the former tenant of the cabin who was also considered a shamanistic preacher. Because he has idealized the girl, considering her the key to his future happiness, he contacts her — she is a student at university — and reveals that, in fact, he has not given away all his assets, that he is still as wealthy as before. Not surprisingly, she agrees to meet him, but when she arrives at the bus stop, not noticing the man waiting for her, she is accompanied by her boyfriend, both hoping to further exploit the man as a pliable benefactor. The narrator then returns to the present — his waiting is over, his illusions destroyed — and he now understands that waiting for others to bring him happiness and fulfillment is a mistake. He finds himself free, as it were, "meeletu," in the moment where one thought — his former life — ends and yet the other — his future — has not yet begun.

Rain Simmul (*top*) and with Hele Kõre (*following page*) in Jaan Tätte's *Meeletu*, directed by Eva Klemets at Tallinn City Theatre. The tradition of anti-theatre and alienation effects is well established. But in Klemet's approach the conflict, the collision between the man's past and his present, interrupts the line between the stage reality and the reality of the audience. By attempting to erase this theatrical demarcation, Klemets fuses the two experiences to create immediacy for the audience that a more traditional staging might not achieve (photographs by Siim Vahur).

The set, that huge wooden bench that doubles below as the interior of his cabin, neatly illustrates the man's feelings of being diminished, overwhelmed by "things." According to director Klemets, the bench was intended to give the effect of a child's wonderment at the simplicity of nature, reinforcing the idea in the play that what is needed to counter the polluting influence of materialism is a return to innocence and the purity inherent in a child's perception of the world. The man confesses how he likes to sit on the bench and watch the lake in the distance, but the effect of how small he appears as he sits, legs dangling, gazing into the forest visually underscores a central theme of the play: man's diminutive state before the awesome power of nature, and how petty his materialism seems set against the eternal values of love, spirituality and self-respect. Contrasted with his former life, where his materialism created a hunger that fed only empty desire — and that drove his wife into crass consumerism and vulgar affairs, his son into a zombie-like addiction to pop culture and monosyllabic responses to his father's attempts to communicate — the bench implies a reverential innocence that even the villagers, denizens of the forest themselves, misapprehend. The idea seems to be that the value of life is best understood only by those who have experienced both sides — the extremes of wealth and poverty — and can strike a balance between the two: a chiasmatic journey resolved in a transcendental synthesis available to those alert enough — and lucky enough — to take advantage of their privilege.

Tätte's focus on universal themes and generic dramatic situations reflects a deliberate strategy to make his plays accessible to audiences outside any strictly specific "Baltic" or

Eva Klemets (photograph by Kaliju Orro).

Jaan Tätte (photograph by Siim Vahur).

Estonian social or political context. The situation of a wealthy businessman discovering that money is not the key to happiness, though trite, could represent the same conflict in any culture, and for that matter, almost any historical period in the post-Enlightenment world. However, Tätte's plays also illustrate the difference between the director-based theatre of Lithuanian drama and the more social/realistic/psychological approach of the writer-based Estonian theatre. Granted, Klemets' staging toyed with the conventions of theatre, but the play is text-based, relying on, as it were, the voice-over narrative to connect the individual dramatic scenes, and though the set is minimal, the space itself is not integrated into the action — is instead imposed, and therefore lacks the metaphysical integrity, for instance, of Graužinis's *Attempts on Her Life*.

Tätte is well on his way to earning this status of "European" writer, mainly because in his plays he manages to mirror situations that connect with audiences cross-culturally. An excellent example of this "universality" is evident in his plays *The Highway Crossing, or the Tale of the Golden Fish* and *Happy Everyday!* Both illustrate Tätte's strategy to internationalize his work and to address what he considers the overriding concerns of the new Estonian socio-political situation: spiritual consciousness, commitment, love, benevolence and personal integrity threatened by crass materialism (a more prosaic treatment of the same themes in Graužinis' *Attempts on Her Life*). The play focuses on Laura and Roland, two young professionals who, having met at university and afterward moved in together, planned to marry, but they seem more committed to the idea than the act. She is "doing a bit of translating" (22) and he "has a finger in the advertising pie" (22), and though both are convinced that their love for each other is unconditional, their relationship is sorely tested when they meet Oswald, a recluse who "has been living alone for a long time" (11)

The plot, which borders on magic realism, turns frequently on inexplicable (and implausible) coincidences. Because Roland wanted to imbibe at a friend's party, he and Laura, to be safe, nostalgically decided to hitchhike. The man who offered them a ride suddenly discovered "he had left all his papers and his driving license at home and turned back" (17), stranding the couple deep in the woods on a wet, freezing night. They stumble upon Oswald's cabin and ask for shelter. Oswald invites Laura to stay, but on the condition that Roland must "come back in the morning" (13). Roland offers to pay, though he confesses he had always assumed "that money had no value here in the woods" (13), but when Oswald persists, Roland agrees, and Laura settles in for a night alone with Oswald in the cabin. Oswald explains that he saw her photograph in a magazine, and he proves she is the girl of his dreams when he identifies her "thin gold chain with a tiny golden fish" (17) that in fact she does wear around her neck. While Laura resists, understandably confused, claiming, "I love him, and he loves me" (15), Roland barges in, complaining that it is too cold and miserable to stay outside.

Oswald shifts tactics, humoring the couple and allowing them both to stay. After Laura falls asleep, Roland summarizes their life together in a materialistic context, describing how they "finished university two years ago, lived in a hostel, now [...] have a flat, furniture, a car — what else do you need?" (21). As if taking his cue from Roland's recitation, Oswald suddenly offers to buy Laura. Roland is indignant, saying, "Laura is not an object to be passed from hand to hand" (28). Oswald counters Roland's condescending pretense: "We're not talking about Laura, not even about you. We are talking about your habit of thinking that Laura is yours" (28). Roland checks himself only when Oswald offers him a billion dollars. Incredulous, Roland continues to profess his inviolable love for Laura and self-righteously assert the sanctity of their relationship. But when Oswald shows him the money hidden around the shack in brown cardboard boxes, Roland reconsiders his position. Realizing that by momentarily entertaining the idea he has irreversibly compromised him, Roland acquiesces to Oswald's wacky plan and abandons Laura.

When she awakens, she finds money scattered around the room. Oswald tells her, "It's not money. It's a fairy tale" (37). He relates an allegorical history of his life, culminating one day when he caught a "small bright fish" (38) that, in exchange for Oswald returning it to the water, granted him his wish for money — four billion dollars. Oswald claims he found the money as soon as he returned home, except it was not the money he really wanted; his true desire was for a young woman wearing a chain with a golden fish who would be delivered to him "one autumn evening with a young man" (39). Laura then understands that Roland has basically sold her to Oswald. Instead of being shocked or angry, she is calculated and cautiously expectant, selfishly plotting how she and Oswald should handle the cash.

Roland returns to collect his payoff but plagued by guilt, shame and self-recrimination he soon reneges. Laura is contemptuous and suggests they should simply kill Oswald and keep all the money with their relationship intact. After a knife-fight, during which Laura is stabbed in the ass, the couple continues to scheme. Laura offers to live with Oswald for a year, even while professing that she still loves Roland. But Roland is uncomfortable with this plan. Oswald first humiliates them — asking them to jump like a bunny or preen like a stork — then renounces the money. Roland, seeing an opening in Oswald's demurral, ties him to a chair so that he and Laura can escape with the loot. Before they can get away an armed gangster interrupts, explaining that the money is his.[8] He records their identification information and leaves with the money. Laura and Roland are left even more destitute than before, having lost their dignity, self-worth and respect for each other.

This Faustian tale is not unfamiliar. (Terry Southern's *The Magic Christian* is only the first example of the genre that comes readily to mind.) Everyone has a price. But for Tätte, the scenario serves a more immediate purpose than merely offering another contemporary take on a classic moral fable. By removing the dramatic situation from a specific identifiably local circumstance to a more ambiguous universal situation, the play as Tätte has conceived it is easily exportable. The cabin could be anywhere. Laura and Roland could be any professional couple. Oswald plays a typical disillusioned foil.

The play also questions the veneer of values created by a system that equates existential success with acquisitions. Laura and Roland seem less like free human agents than victims whose motives are governed by conspicuous consumption, their identities conditioned by superfluous icons of an artificial status. Roland first extols the virtues of hard work and thrift, but the only pay-off for his tenacity seems to be his five year old Mazda — "a decent car, not an old banger" (21). Laura professes to "love Roland as much as it's possible to love anyone" (17) while complaining, "I earn next to nothing" (21). When Roland tells her he has bought wedding rings, she asks, "Were they expensive?" (25) and Roland, contemplating his sudden wealth, says, "The first thing I'll buy is a mobile phone" (34). He operates on the assumption that "Everybody wants money" (33) to justify selling his wife. She readily accepts the deal, essentially playing the prostitute to Roland's pimp, her value system rooted in economics: "We want our money, admire our bank cards, the fridge is empty, we don't eat in restaurants, we don't go out, I have nothing to wear, and our home looks like an exhibition of second hand goods" (49).

Only Oswald has learned the lesson of how to measure human worth, having "dreamed of happiness all his life, and when it was within his grasp he had asked for money" (38).

Though the critique of the "new" Estonian situation is more oblique in *Happy Everyday!*, dealing as it does with middle-class marital ennui, the play is designed in plot, theme and setting to be as exportable as *The Highway Crossing*. Not unlike a Joe Orton farce flavored with Pinteresque cosmic ambiguities, the dialog gyrates through an absurdist exercise in sophistry, debat-

Anu Lamp and Jaan Tätte in Tätte's *Happy Everyday!* at Tallinn City Theatre. The play depicts Estonia as a culture that no longer faces the kind of geopolitical, economic and ontological threats incurred by a hostile occupation and instead enjoys the luxury of anomie, despondency and disillusionment nurtured by the expectations of a democratic, stable and relatively affluent community. This tendency of prosperity to create generic, homogeneous lives, where individual identities are lost in comfortable routines, is underscored by the interchangeable names of the characters: Fred, Manfred, Anna and Annette (photograph by Priit Grepp).

ing the question: How does a couple, enjoying — or cursed by — the security — or fatal mundanity — of normal conjugal habits maintain a sense of romance, eros and self-fulfillment to keep their marriage vital and exciting?

The play illustrates the changing nature of art, too, as it reflects a shift in the concerns of a society — exemplified by the Baltics — from a national existential crisis to a more personal one. It is the product of a culture that no longer faces the kind of geo-political, economic and ontological threats incurred by a hostile occupation and instead enjoys the luxury of anomie, despondency and disillusionment nurtured by the expectations of a democratic, stable and relatively affluent community. In this regard, *Happy Everyday!* can be considered Tätte's most Scandinavian play, reminiscent of the couple in Ivaškevičius' *Close City*. This tendency — or syndrome — to create as a result of prosperity generic, homogeneous lives, where individual identities are lost in comfortable routines, is underscored by the interchangeable names of the characters: Fred, Manfred, Anna and Annette.

Fred, an elected official, and Annette, a translator, have been married for seventeen years. One night Annette returns from a conference in France and announces that she is now in love with Manfred, whom she met on the flight and with whom she spent "a very beautiful and happy couple of days" (153). Flabbergasted, Fred tries to reason through what he considers her aberrant, emotionally charged lapse in logic. The refrain he relies on, that seems to reassure him most, is "in what sense" (147, 148, 151, 152, 157, 199, 205), employed whenever he is confronted by an ambiguous phrase or double entendre, until Annette turns it back on him in a piquant, devastating reversal:

> FRED: You haven't had anybody?
> ANNETTE: You know that.
> FRED: I meant — later?
> ANNETTE: In what sense? [173]

Fred also relies on the routine of his domestic life and insists that the solution to his wife's "bad joke" (159) must be "written down somewhere" (174).

Annette, however, complains that every "day is exactly the same as the one before" (163) and that even though they have "a beautiful home, there's no life in it" (163). For her, the passion has gone from their marriage. She explains, "I didn't marry a politician. I married a student who proposed to me on his knees" (194). To remedy her boredom and to offset her fear that she will never again "light a fire, once, before it all goes dark"

(173), she plans for Manfred to move in and become, in effect, her second husband. She does not want a divorce; instead, she looks forward to the "competition" (185) and having the two men wonder "who gets to come to bed with me" (185). Her proposal, she says, will be "compensation for my idiotic life" (192).

Annette's motives, though, are not as romantic or curative as they first appear. Before she introduces Fred to Manfred, she claims that she is "madly in love" (16), even if she and Manfred have yet to sleep together sexually. Following her new philosophy that to maintain desire a "man has to be tortured all the time" (193), she delights in describing to Fred the intimacies she and Manfred have shared during their brief stint at the conference, culminating in their having dedicated parts of their bodies to each other (her arm, the hairy part of his chest). She brags that the most important factor in her attraction to Manfred is "mental compatibility" (153, 157, 171, 178, 186, 196, 202, 203), which she explains as the ability not "to talk at all and [...] still enjoy each other's company" (171).

The truth of her affair is less subtle. For years, she has been jealous of Anna, a long-time neighbor who has been secretly longing to make a play for Fred, but he has remained naively oblivious to her advances. Even she admits that Fred "doesn't see me at all as a woman. [...] I just come and go around here like some kind of repairman" (195).

Annette's revenge is aimed at Anna as much as Fred. Anna blames Annette for her dissatisfying marriage, accusing her of not appreciating Fred's faithfulness, sobriety and generosity. She tells Annette, "if you had loved him the way you should, I wouldn't have moved here" (194). In her opinion, Fred is an ideal who "doesn't deserve this" (192). She allows herself to believe that she has "lived my whole life for him" (193). She makes a play for Fred, but he rejects her, even while Annette is entertaining the idea of having Manfred move in (with full benefits). Anna first vows to kill herself, then, reconsidering—"Fate has given me all the right cards" (208)—she tries seducing Fred. Again she is rebuffed, Fred explaining, "You're a beautiful woman [...] like an airline hostess [...] nothing more [...] you're not Annette" (208).

Like Anna's failure to impassion Fred, Annette's plan to engage Manfred as a vehicle of vengeance goes awry when Manfred is exposed as an imposter. He claims to be involved in a scientific experiment studying extreme consumption—"no eating for twenty five days" (187); "Hamburger and cocoa cola. For one month" (187)—but he lacks the discipline and restraint to complete the study, succumbing to his voracious appetite, at one point "eating like crazy" (189). When Annette offers to have sex with him, he dismisses her flatly: "I'm really not into sex" (202), explaining, "When two people have mental compatibility like ours, anything physical is absolutely unthinkable" (202). Annette's response is equally blunt: "Screw mental compatibility" (203).

In a dramatically inconsistent twist, Manfred becomes childish, petulant and insecure, then, as if to alleviate being "afraid when I'm alone" (205), he tries to initiate a homosexual encounter with Fred. When Fred denies him, Manfred allows Anna to satisfy her "growing desire" (210) with his assistance until suddenly, in a crescendo of "Loud music. Crazy Lights" (210), Anna and Manfred disappear. Annette and Fred are left to confront their situation. With no more secrets, the couple considers the events of the evening cathartic, clearing the ground, as it were, for renewal. Reconciliation begins with understanding. Annette confesses, "I don't think I really take care of you any more" (212).

Unlike, say, Lebeliūnas' staging of Mrożek's *Charlie!*, which explores the absurdity of life under forced occupation, or Tuminas' direction of Ivaškevičius' *Madagascar*, which profiles Lithuanian stereotypes, Tätte's plays overtly ignore any contextual reference to the particular cultural situation of Estonia as a former Soviet satellite state, the ramifications of liberation or the impact of joining the European Union. *Happy Everyday!* incorporates no obvious allusions to politics — national, international, or local.[9] The dramatic situation is patently personal, investigating the dynamics of relationships, the nature of commitment, the conflict between individual happiness and mutual respect. This elision allows his plays to appear ethnocentrically neutral, thereby widening their appeal to audiences more interested in the human situation than the particularities of Estonian cultural and/or geo-political history.

Still, the underlying subtext, covertly framing the larger thematic considerations, acknowledges how prosperity creates pettiness and exposes a fundamental skepticism challenging the value systems emerging in incipient capitalist countries that have yet to develop the innate checks and balances that come after years of experience, including legislation and social conditioning. These systems in some permutations promote selfishness and greed at the expense of family and community, and in this context Tätte's plays provide evidence of a sensibility bred within a culture wrenched from deprivation into affluence with no buffering, mitigating period of adjustment.

This difference in both text and staging illustrates aesthetic, philosophical, political and social distinctions between the Scandinavian sensibility and the two other Baltic states to the south. Two factors account for this: the virtual isolation of Lithuania (and to nearly the same degree, Latvia) and the relative openness of Estonia during the Soviet period, and the historical connection of Lithuania with Poland and its strong ties to Catholicism contrasting with Estonia's connections to Finland and Sweden and the Lutheran Church. Because Estonia, even during the Soviet period, had ferry access to Helsinki — albeit extremely limited and controlled — and exposure to Swedish and Finnish television, the new consumerism after 1991 was not so unusual and did not create the social shock in Estonia that it did in the insular and seriously segregated Lithuania. Estonia, already more familiar with Western-style marketing, adapted relatively easily, living, after the transition, as many people say, the way they always wanted to. Also, the more liberal attitudes associated with Lutheranism and its orientation toward material wealth, which taught that financial success was not necessarily evil — indeed, in Calvin's view a sign of God's benevolence and approval — combined with its relaxed approach to the typical bourgeois market philosophy made it easy for Estonia to assimilate the capitalist model, whereas the introspection associated with Catholicism, with its stress on the virtues of poverty and its distrust of material values (except, of course, in the service of the church, resplendent in its piety), often equating secular success with sin, created during the transition period a spiritual crisis in Lithuania, fueled by the guilt of competition in a free-market economy. This depth of feeling in Lithuania and its ties with the introspective theatres in Russia and Poland, still haunt many of the writers and directors — as Vaitkus notes — but in Estonia, with its historical and cultural ties to Scandinavia and Germany, the writers use a lighter touch, as it were, reflecting an optimism (or, more likely, self-irony) that separates Estonia from its neighbors to the south and east.

In the Estonian critique of the capitalist model, there is less finger pointing, less evidence of a "victim complex," which may again reflect the difference between the Lutheran and Catholic approach to personal responsibility and communal will. The stress on national identity — that fear of losing a cultural uniqueness — is also more muted in Estonia than in Lithuania, so the concerns of the writers tend to stress universal values, a strategy that also allows the plays to be translated, exported, and relevant outside any specific Estonian context.

One writer like Tätte that addresses the topic of identity, cultural uniqueness and the Estonian dilemma of adapting to the values of the new consumerism, while also providing a sharply ironical depiction of the process, is the popular and influential Andrus Kivirähk. Best known as a journalist, primarily for his humorous, iconoclastic satirical newspaper columns, Kivirähk's play *The Estonian Funeral* (*Eesti matus*) offers a comical yet scathing view of the clash between traditional values and the new consumerist ethos changing the cultural landscape in Estonia. The play, grounded in the particulars of Estonian history, manages to critique the immediate cultural calamities of contemporary Estonian society while creating an exportable comedic context that a general audience can appreciate without being privy to the internecine conflicts peculiar to the Estonian situation.

The Estonian Funeral operates within a classic dyad pitting the country, a place of perceived traditional Calvinist principles — virtue through industry, respect for tradition — against the city, an unprincipled place of tedious careers, compromised standards, and a disregard for family values. Ostensibly, the play is a story about an Estonian family and their neighbors gathering at a farm for a funeral, the implication being that given the transitory and peripatetic nature of contemporary human relationships, funerals are the only events where relatives and friends meet to share common memories. In this case, the action involves the children, friends and a few strangers who congregate for the burial and the traditional funeral feast for Andres, a grandfather who died chopping wood on the farm he has lived on and run for 100 years. Depicting contemporary Estonia within the framework of common national stereotypes, and much like Ivaškevičius in *Madagascar*, Kivirähk's ironical treatment explores the current cultural dilemma facing Estonians caught in an ethical conundrum: lamenting the loss of traditional values while embracing the new consumerism blamed for destroying those values.

The play is typically Calvinist, in structure and theme. Although Kivirähk's irony intentionally undercuts (while celebrating) the critique of the Puritan work ethic, cleverly exposing both the pride and the dismay of the characters trying to measure up to the overarching Estonian peasant ethos that equates hard work with virtue, the style of the text resembles Tätte's: preachy, long-winded, and narrative-based, like a novel told through dialog, with little dramatic action and even less physicality or metaphorical layering. The characters align into camps representing the "new way" (the city) and the "old way" (the country), with the grandfather obviously one of a dying breed, as it were (literally), of Estonians who prefer to die with a hatchet in hand and who, for instance, continue to can preserves, whether they can be consumed or not, until the "cellars are like catacombs, where many generations of fruit and berries are in their eternal sleep" (Kivirähk). Their old fashioned need to stay busy — working for the sake of working — extends even to the perfunctory rituals of interment, when the "grief of the funeral made way for the joy of working."

Andres, the deceased grandson and namesake, represents the new Estonian, both appreciative and embarrassed by the stereotypical response of, on one hand, the city dwellers' disrespect for the deep-seated conventions of country life and the equally dismissive attitudes of the country folk towards the careerists living in the city. He is a paradox: a pragmatist who refuses to live in the past but who dreams of a romantic escape from his present. He wants his poetical wife Lee to "take me so far away that I simply can't go back." Though Andres understands the predicament, he feels incapable of changing it. He is the only one to admit, correctly, that the surviving family members are too busy to dedicate the time and energy to maintaining Grandpa's house, but when he suggests they sell the house, his father Sass, a country-bred stalwart who has relocated to the city for business opportunities, objects: "Each log here could give you a lecture on Estonian history." Andres replies: "I've heard that story a hundred times, but I don't care." Exasperated by his family's insistence on not just preserving but wallowing in their tragic past, he finally accuses the others of exploiting in their collective memory "a huge amount of nightmares, and now we're stuck with them, and we worship them like an altar [...] promising redemption through hard work and labour."

For Indrek, Grandpa's son, Andres' uncle and a self-described "city slicker" nostalgic for a past he reveres but from which he is hopelessly divorced, life in the city has reduced him to "a rat in the wheel." An idle idealist, he describes Grandpa without irony or criticism, but with dogged respect, as "a real Estonia [...] Working until his very last breath," even as he considers his grandfather's death an imposition and objects that he is too busy to join the others in mourning. He refuses to consider selling the house, calling it an "amazing place, a real home," but claims he has no time actually to make the necessary repairs. Likewise, his nationalistic fealty, embodied in empty slogans like "Estonia remains, and lives, as long as lives the Estonian farm" exists only in his imagination. He admires his sister Maret because she is "the real sturdy country stock, like an Estonian woman ought to be." In a foolish attempt to prove "you can't escape your roots [and that] once a peasant, always a peasant," he walks around barefoot, sermonizing while being stung by wasps yet claiming the sting "to a country boy's feet [...] gives more vigor."

His wife Tiina (his third, which the elders see as a sign of the times) is no less delusional and schizophrenic, cramming her life full of activity to the point of exhaustion while complaining constantly about being so busy. She compares her job to working in a "madhouse" but is "sick and tired of sitting at work." She cannot relax, even on her days off, and on vacation strives to "pick up the pace" because "no one can be spared from work." As anxious as Indrek to maintain Grandpa's farm, but equally inept for the job, she claims that even she, "a city girl" ill-suited for farm work, has started "longing for a garden" and, as harried as she is, will volunteer for the work anyway, careful to "wear gloves and later put lotion on my hands."

Grandpa's daughter Maret and her husband Sass, Andres' parents, born in the country but now living in the city, also embody the contradictions of displacement: they are faithful in their hearts to the farm but their pragmatism (and sense of necessity) keeps them economically bound to their urban careers. Maret, a fatalist who is no less duty-bound to staying busy as the others, is upset that her father died on Friday because "now the funeral will have to be on a working day." She not only cares for her own home, but looks after Sass's father's house and is now determined to keep her father's farm operating too. Like the others, she enthuses about how the family must save the farm but cannot commit to the project herself because she is already stressed-out and over-obligated. Nevertheless she competes with the others in a contest to see whose life has been the hardest. She delivers a litany of complaints: "I've never had a chance to rest [...] no vacation in the country [...] I don't know how we'll find the time [we're up to our necks." Comparing herself to delicate Tiina, she sounds as if she is bragging when she describes how hard her work is on the farm: "It's no joke, you know. My hands are completely ruined from all this digging in the ground. The skin cracks and the nails get broken." Most troubling for her, however, is the fact that Andres and Lee have gotten married without telling her or without having a wedding, and now the couple is leaving for an exotic locale where "orange trees grow." Her son's non-traditional lifestyle distresses her even more than her father's death.

Sass also competes with the others, especially Karl, to determine who is more authentically Estonian. Karl has laid claim to the mantle because he never abandoned the country life. He equates Sass's move to the city as treasonous, accusing him of selling out, denying his roots and becoming "fashionable." His resentment, however, is less chauvinistic than personal. Karl's anger results from his not having the chance to marry Maret because he had to stay on the farm harvesting potatoes while Maret and Sass went off on a college field trip which led to their marriage. In his parochial view, "no countryman can travel around the world during the harvesting of potatoes, only a townie has so much time on his hands," although he conveniently ignores the fact that Sass was born and raised in the country and had not exactly traveled "around the world" with Maret but had only gone on a hike. Karl's hyperbolic harangue ends with, "you city slickers [...] stealing our women." Sass's remonstrations are no less over-zealous, adding to the absurdity of the argument and undermining his skewed romantic notions about tradition, nationalistic piety and devotion to the work ethic. When he first hears of Grandpa's death, he responds, "These things always happen at the busiest of times" and he later complains, "I'm so busy that I hardly have time to go to the loo." Yet he, too, adamantly refuses to sell the house, reiterating his veneration of what Andres refers to as the "bloody talking logs again!"

The other two members of the funeral party, Karl's wife Iida, a brawny termagant, and Tiit, a doddering old-timer, are as eager as the others to prove their authenticity by the degree of their respective families' past suffering and their dedication to work. While berating Karl for his drinking, Iida revels in the travails of Estonia's past, trying to trump the others' tragic stories by stating flatly: "My mother and father were eaten by wolves." She tells a horrendous story about having her head shaved and being sent to an orphanage, concluding, "That's what the life of an Estonian is like." Tiit, of all the mourners, relates his personal tragedies as if they were emblematic of a national character. And though he offers perhaps the most sobering tale, describing how he and his family were deported to Siberia where every member of his family but him died, and provides the most sincere assessment of the lack of respect for tradition in contemporary society, like Karl lamenting how "ancient Estonian farms" are being bought by "holiday-makers [...] just lying there belly up all summer," his complaints are couched in platitudes that flatten the emotional intensity. True to form, he worships pessimism, suffering, fatalism and work, stipulating for instance: "As long as there is life one must live; there's enough time to rest in the grave. [...] How could I live without work? [...] You can never have the things you want." Fulfilling his fate, his last act is to grab a hatchet and declare, "A human being must live and work [...] I'm not used to being idle! I really want to exert myself!" before dropping dead. With tragedy again at hand, Sass can only whine, "What a mess ... And tomorrow's a working day too!"

Lee, Andres' wife, emerges as the most curious character. Whereas Andres acts as a normative value against which to measure the eccentricities of the others, Lee's amused detachment more accurately resembles the attitude of contemporary young Estonians towards their elders' reification of tradition. Andres recognizes the foibles of his family, decrying them as stereotypical slaves to outmoded ideals who cannot take a break from hard work, who believe sacrifice and penury are the only values to live by and working until the last breath, either on a farm or in the city, represents a life well-lived, but he cannot separate his past from theirs so neatly. He sees the funeral ritual as "more a habit than real sorrow" and views his grandfather's house as "greedy and stingy [with] an insatiable appetite." He sums up the situation in a self-evident quip, "It's downright horrible, what a gruesome past we all have!" But his summary is not self-pitying, and that is what distinguishes his perspective from the rest of the mourners.

Lee is not so invested in the past. She gravitates towards water, suggesting an image of life, of renewal and nurturing. When at the funeral "everyone was so serious [...] I wanted to laugh," she retreats to the river. Similarly, she met Andres by a lake, recalling how, referring to Andres, "not only sun was reflected in the water, but you too." She notices that Grandpa's house is not reflected in the river: "The clouds and treetops were [...] but your house wasn't," implying that the house—an image of the Estonian historical past—is as dead as the last occupant. Most of her descriptions are metaphorical—for instance, in the cellar the jars' "glass tummies shone in the glow of the pale light bulb like armour"—suggesting that redemption through an imaginative engagement with the world is more possible (and preferable) than the stalwart, conventionally medieval ethos of hard work, suffering and allegiance to the past.

Another writer concerned with the history and identity of the Estonian national character is Triin Sinissaar, a translator and dramaturge at Tallinn City Theatre. She sets her play *Ship in the Swamp* (*Soolaev*) in a fairytale world connecting the contemporary situation in Estonia with the twelfth century, in part to show how issues relevant in the Middle Ages are still reflected in the events of today. Though her play ostensibly deals with women living without men, their husbands or sons either dead or at war, the position of women in society has not changed, at least regarding what Sinissaar considers the eternal values of women's strength and nurturing natures in times of crises.

There is an element of nationalism in *Ship in the Swamp* that

Sinissaar readily admits borders on chauvinism: trying to counter the perception — to some degree self-perpetuated — of Estonians as "slave people," that is, people that have been historically identified as an underclass, occupied by Swedes, Russians, Germans. Of course, Estonia is a small country that experienced independence only once before 1991, after World War I, when the Russians drove the Germans out and had not yet begun their Leninist expansionism. (Ironically, when the Germans returned in 1940, they were seen by most Estonians as the preferable alternative to the Soviet experiment.) After 1945, when the Allies divided-up Europe, the Stalin-era deportations began: the violent relocation of whole swaths of the population. Sinissaar draws on this historical data to remind the Estonians, she says, of their "glorious past," to inspire anyone plagued by self-doubt about independence — those who might question whether the Estonians have the capacity for self-rule, given their history of subjugation. She thinks of Estonia as a mighty tiny kingdom, often occupied but never daunted, and though she insists that *Ship in the Swamp*— as well as her other work — transcends local topics, her intent clearly is to magnify the contemporary Estonian situation through the lens of a benign, nationalistic point of view.

Sinissaar admits that, by its nature, theatre is a local art, and that dramatic works by Estonian writers must be written for Estonian audiences, but she is confident that plays written by Estonians that manage to deal with universal themes will elevate domestic writers and give them the wider audiences they deserve, as well as a reputation for being a "European" writer as much as "Estonian."

Although the Russian influence in Estonian theatre is undeniable, the Estonians by nature do not identify with what Sinissaar calls the "culture of the Slavs." The people, outside of special dramaturgical considerations, identify linguistically as well as by temperament with the Finns and Swedes. But the German influence, in the structure of society and the cultural development of theatre is pervasive. The sense of the Estonians suffering form a "peasant complex" — that is, in a medieval mindset, believing that they deserve occupation, or poverty, as if their underclass status were simply the natural order of things — is evident throughout Tallinn, exemplified dramatically by the preserved areas atop Toompea Hill, where the German bourgeoisie lived in splendor in an area topped by Toompea Castle. The hierarchic design of the Old Town — with the wealthy Germans living above the poor Estonian peasantry below, typical of medieval villages — resonates with special meaning for Estonians even today. In the new capitalist market, for instance, which has evolved to resemble more closely the

Anglo-Saxon American-British style than the French socialist model, many Estonians still consider their social status, no longer based on nationality (e.g., in relation to German or Russian occupiers), as a natural reward for either their hard work, their ingenuity, or both. This insensitivity to the less fortunate by those well up the ladder of economic success, and the resignation of those who either choose not to play the economic game — whether by career choice, bad luck or sheer incompetence — has created what many consider the inevitable gap between the "haves" and the "have-nots" that has in turn fueled a new social tension — a questioning of values — highlighting the inequities of the new system that were not so evident during the Soviet period, and the expected problems brought on by the transition from the state-centered model to the free market, though mitigated in Estonia (compared to the other two Baltic states), are emerging as legitimate issues driving much of the new theatre.

Even with this new awareness of social issues, theatre in Estonia, as it does elsewhere in the world, serves as a source of escape from the drudgery of everyday life, into fantasy and romance as much as into aesthetic spectacles of tradition and classical works. And though the Estonian Drama Theatre has in the past been associated with a traditional, less confrontational approach to contemporary issues, it is now moving towards edgier drama, featuring work by Hendrik Toompere, Jr., Tiit Ojasoo and other young, more experimental writers. Ironically, the theatre is housed in the renovated art nouveau building built in 1910 for the German Theatre Union (designed by Russian architects), a graphic reminder of both their past cultural segregation and their new status as an independent, unique, national cultural entity.

According to Ene Paaver, Literary Manager, the Estonian Drama Theatre developed from the Drama Studio, the first professional drama school in Estonia, under the guidance of Paul Sepp. The Drama Studio Theatre, formed by the first graduating class in 1924, evolved into the Estonian Drama Theatre in 1937, and in 1939, after Hitler called the Estonian Germans "home," the company moved into its present home at the German Theatre Union building.

The vast interior, completely renovated in 2003, provides a huge main stage in the Italian opera-house style, with plush tiered seating for 360, loges, balconies, carpeted halls, chandeliers, a reception area — all the trappings of a Victorian theatre in the grand tradition. A repertory company, the Estonian Drama Theatre employs 38 actors, a slew of directors including Priit Pedajas and Toompere, and offers 15 plays averaging 500 performances a season for more than 100,000 spectators. An attic space is used for readings and rehearsals, and an upstairs small stage with a professional fly and bleacher seating for 150 provides an intimate space for more experimental performances. Paaver notes that "producing Estonian dramaturgy, both classics and new writing, is an important part of our identity. We are regularly staging contemporary authors of different generations, and we are the only theatre in Estonia offering staged readings of new Estonian plays every month. We also publish new Estonian play texts which have had premieres in the theatre."

Pille Jänes, a freelance set designer closely associated with the theatre (who was for ten years employed as the house set designer), admits that working in the auditorium with the "Italian box" space is often uninspiring. She prefers, she says, "to create a sense of reality opposed to creating a 'set.'" In the manner of the young, aggressive Lithuanian directors, she views theatre space as a possibility for metaphor, in which the "stage" and the action mesh to tease out meaning from the text. To illustrate her point, she

(*Above and right*): In Mart Koldits' *The Metamorphosis* at Tallinn City Theatre, the walls prevent the audience from seeing what is happening except when the actors invade the audience's space or a door opens to allow them to witness a scene. The viewers are forced to experience "reality" from Gregor's perspective, closed off from the external world, shut away in his room, isolated from the events going on around him yet acutely aware of them too, leaving the audience, like Gregor, often literally in the dark (photographs by Priit Grepp).

cites work directed by Mart Koldits, one of the directors now working at Tallinn City Theatre, where Jänes staged two of Koldits' pieces in that theatre's "hell space," *Tschapajev and Pustota* by the Russian Viktor Pelevin and *The Metamorphosis* by Kafka. The first piece tells the story based on an old Russian hero whose name Pustota means both "emptiness" and "desert."

To depict his descent into madness, she created three spaces separated by black translucent drapes so that the three scenes, played simultaneously, gave the audience a subjective sense of being in a madhouse, trying to decipher the stories told by four men (four being a magic number in Russia). The effect, for Jänes, intentionally violates the boundary between stage and audience, but it also collapses the distance between observing a scene and becoming a part of it.

"Which is the illusion?" Jänes asks, rhetorically. "Theatre is as 'real' as life."

The Metamorphosis is a compilation of scenes from Kafka's work but centered on the point of view of Gregor Samsa, the man who wakes one morning to find himself transformed into an insect. Jänes created a set consisting of a walled-in center space for the audience around which, and outside of, the action plays, so that the walls prevent the audience from seeing what is happening except when the actors invade the audience's space or a door opens to allow them to witness a scene. The viewers are forced to experience "reality" from Gregor's perspective, closed off from the external world, shut away in his room, isolated from the events going on around him yet acutely aware of them too. Every so often a door will open and a fully lit scene will be presented, then the door slams shut, leaving the audience, like Gregor, in the dark. The actors dehumanize the audience in the same way Gregor's family treats him. In one scene, when Gregor's mother and sister enter his room, the actors regard the audience as if they were merely furniture.

"The impulse comes from outside," Jänes explains, a process that reverses the traditional expectation of theatre for spectators, locating them not outside the action but within it, frustrating their innate desire to understand what is happening, just as life must seem to Gregor. The response from the audience was mixed. "Too claustrophobic," she says, indicating that was the point.

Jänes defines new theatre — as opposed to the classics, even modern plays, staged for large audiences in the "fourth wall" tradition — as a performance that incorporates mixed media, combining music, video and extreme physicality with an experimental use of space. Whether Estonian theatre has been writer-based or director-based in the past, she says, is problematic, but citing work by Koldits and other young directors, she is convinced that the new direction is definitely toward director-based productions. In her experience, the new breed of directors do not revere the text the way, for instance, other (the implication is "Western") directors might remain faithful to a play script written specifically for the stage; in fact, the new directors tend to ignore textual works in favor of creating fresh, new "visual experiences" free from a textual anchor.

"They hate stories," she says. "The physical world is more intuitive. It speaks more directly to young people. It's a language they understand." Jänes is confident that this new, vital theatre of mixed-media and physicality will recover the attention of young audiences, holding their interests in a way neither pop culture nor traditional theatre can.

Jänes notes the similarities of the new style of young directors throughout Estonia, citing their affinity for Tadeusz Kantor (a strong influence in her own work). These directors tend to fuse Kantor's approach (which Kantor describes as a "theatre of death," working away from the more subtle, sensitive, classical psychological Russian style) with Grotowski's "poor theatre," mixing in loud, thriving, visually and physically vibrant trends imported from Western media to create a perverse amalgam.

"Artists like him," Jänes says. "Directors like him. But actors hate him. He treats them like tools."

As for the Scandinavian influence that many Estonian critics claim separates Estonia from the other Baltic states, citing its Lutheranism, its history of Western consumerism, its theatre tradition of precise realism, of Ibsen, Strindberg and Bergman (who epitomizes the Russian style), Jänes is unequivocally dismissive of any contemporary relevance. In her opinion, life in Scandinavia is so comfortable that much of the situational material the Scandinavians think is ripe for drama is boring to Estonians. "They may be perfect technically," she says. "But they tend to emote, to overdo it." She complains that when the Scandinavians visit Estonia, "a poor post-Soviet country, they want to talk about totalitarian regimes, but they don't know it from the inside, so they miss the truth, don't recognize the tenderness the people have for life who were actually living daily under the occupation."

She also suggests, like many others throughout the Baltics, that although the same communal feeling people shared during the Soviet times no longer exists, the theatre still offers a vital critique of the new consumerist society—in the style of *Meeletu*—asking the ironic question: "What have you done with your freedom?" Some people, she says, cannot let go of "the old fear, that dread of the next train leaving for Siberia." But she agrees, too, with Vaitkus, that the new, even possibly more insidious censorship is money, the secret forces of economics operating on the quality and essential viability of a theatre of free ideas. That market pressures will contaminate theatre as an institution, she thinks, is a very real threat. Nevertheless, she has faith in the conservative nature of the Estonians and their ability to resist corruption. In the early years of independence the exuberance sometimes crossed over into crassness and exploitation, but now, after things have settled down and the possibilities of the new market economy have become routine, she sees the younger generations "turning back to basic things," demonstrating an authentic respect for human values that, too often, their parents, thrown into the system after liberation, sacrificed for money, success, and what they thought, at that moment, was the pay-off of freedom, not the price of it.

About this Scandinavian influence on Estonian theatre, Hilda Hellwig can speak with some authority. A resident director at Bergman's theatre in Stockholm, she has directed two plays at the Estonian Drama Theatre: Ibsen's *Ghosts* in 2003 and Shakespeare's *Othello* in 2005 (with set designs by Jänes). She sees Estonia suffering a sort of cultural inferiority complex, having had to compare itself with Russia, and living under the intimidating influences of Stanislavsky and Meyerhold whose teachings still, in their different ways, dominate the traditional approach to theatre. In Hellwig's experience, students trying to break free from the authoritarian "method" tend to introduce stereotypes into their acting style — what she calls "Ken and Barbie" characters. This attempt to empty a role of psychological depth can only be effective, she says, when combined with the anti-realistic acrobatics in the style of Nekrošius. In her opinion the Estonian actors she has worked with have not successfully gone beyond "the method" to the "new physical" theatre. The Russian tradition is still too entrenched in the Estonian acting academies, ingrained even in the collective cultural psyche. Hellwig suggests that Meyerhold, not Stanislavsky, is now the dominant influence. "The epical style," she says, "is still the most popular theatre in all the former satellite states."

Besides the obvious connection to Russia, a relationship that often resembles a Freudian "family romance" bordering on Oedipal obsessions — with Estonia playing the rebellious but guilt-ridden wayward child to the overbearing, authoritative Russian father — Hellwig notes the influence of what she calls Finnish workers' theatre, an amateur theatre promoting powerful males — "sweaty guys" — not beautiful but strong, she says, appealing to an audience she compares to soccer fans, a burly bunch of country bumpkins, as she describes them, for whom theatre satisfies atavistic, primitive urges, the expressions of which are otherwise muted or socially discouraged. In another chiasmatic trope, Hellwig connects the physicality of this so-called workers' theatre with the Russian nuance of psychological realism to explain why (in her opinion) so many Finnish directors work in Estonia directing Verdi style opera that still appeals to theatregoing Estonians (noting in a pointed aside that Shakespeare is essentially not suitable for opera and that treating his material as such is a bizarre nineteenth century invention).

Hellwig predicts that the future of Estonian theatre rests in the vision of the new writers and directors who are moving away from realism. "What more," she asks, "can be done with this kind of theatre?" Instead, she finds faith in plays that create "eye pictures" and rejects what she calls "the New York City School of Inwardness"— a product, she is convinced, of a misunderstanding of Stanislavsky's method that for her implies more the significance of action than the static, moody introspection that has degenerated into characters on stage merely talking about themselves that passes for drama off Broadway.

Hellwig and others mention the Finnish influence on Estonian culture in benign, if critical terms, but others are less generous. Ene Paaver acknowledges the corrosive impact of the Germans' domination and their pernicious sense of intrinsic superiority over the occupied Estonian people, and she reserves much of her bitterness for the Soviets. But she also resents what she identifies as the unwillingness on the part of the Finns to admit the truth about the "real politik" association they established with the Soviets that severed for fifty years the natural cultural connections between Scandinavia and Estonia.

"We often wonder," she muses, "what is the real price to pay for being two-faced like Finland regarding their relations with the Soviet Union, or to be realistic about the occupation, as in Estonia."

Anneli Saro attributes the popularity of theatre during the Soviet era — especially in the turbulent 1990s — to a need for the people to escape the pressures of life. She compares the 1990s to the 1920s, when Schiller's escapist dramas were popular, offering the people the palliative illusion of romance in a time of severe financial crises and the emergence of new economic elites. With Estonia peaceful, stable and relatively prosperous, the situation is now different, and the issue confronting contemporary playwrights is paradoxical: In times of peace and prosperity, what topics might again engage an audience, intellectually as well as viscerally, without degenerating into pure aestheticism?

For Saro, the answer lies in the sort of issues Tätte raises in *Meeletu* and *The Highway Crossing*: the corrupting power of money and how people strike a balance between the need for financial success and security and the correlative need to maintain a sense of humanism and dignity in a world spiraling towards generic homogeneity and dehumanization. Of course, in the 1990s, no one (basically) would have thought to question the transition. In the popular imagination (romanticized by the self-interested parties in the West) the theatre had worked is magic. The Soviet system had been defeated. Estonian sovereignty (and Latvian and Lithuanian) had been restored. The ensuing honeymoon overlooked, or at least played down, the innate problems associated with Western capitalism.

But the honeymoon is over. The new generation of writers and directors view the struggle for independence as distant history with little impact on their present or future. Saro can cite only one play produced in the last few years that deals with the issue of Soviet occupation (unlike in Germany, where issues of unification and East German assimilation remain contentious topics). Whereas the directors who graduated in the 1990s were steeped in productions of Shakespeare and Chekhov in the traditional styles, the new breed does not shy away from confronting contemporary social issues, though to be fair they, too, are open to criticism: quick to find fault in the new social model, they are slow to offer solutions. And even if the new generation might too easily adopt historical amnesia when it comes to the atrocities of the Soviet occupation, that era is quickly becoming blotted by an acute historical blindness.

Saro worries that the new theatre could come to resemble American soap operas — Hellwig's "New York City School of Inwardness." Even Tätte's plays rely too much on discourse, in her opinion, at the expense of spectacle. Saro has noticed how in many international play festivals she sees plays set in kitchens or shopping malls, generic locations — international spaces — representing everywhere and nowhere — that could be written by anyone, and so no one. Her concern underscores the problem particular to small countries with limited opportunities for exportation: How do they retain a national character in the theatre while engaging an international audience?

Without offering a pat resolution, Saro stresses the appeal and the power of the visual component in theatre as a potential means to retain a cultural identity while speaking directly to a cross-cultural audience. But this approach is also culturally more complex than it might appear. Echoing others (including Jänes), Saro points out that the Lutheran tradition in Estonia historically stressed a pedestrian piety, focusing not, as in

Catholicism, on sensual rites with Gothic overtones, incense, luxurious iconography and splendor, but on Protestant simplicity, plain sermons — harangues, really — emphasizing sinfulness and the need to work hard: in short, the Catholic tradition is steeped in imagery; the Lutheran rooted in language. This, in part, explains the universal appeal of theatre produced by Lithuanian directors who operate from within a Catholic tradition of visual intensity. Saro notes how mesmerized Estonians were by the television coverage of the death of Pope John Paul II and the selection process of Benedict XVI and how many young people have switched from Protestantism to Catholicism, not so much for ideological or theological considerations as for a fascination with the mysteries embodied in Catholic rituals. Although Catholicism is not widespread, and many of its new "converts" in Estonia tend to appreciate the spectacles and rituals much the way they do any trendy movement in popular culture, Saro suggests that this new appreciation of the sensual, elitist appeal of Catholicism, as opposed to the democratic, straightforward pulpit pounding of the Protestants, might account for the appeal of the new visual and physical theatre preferred by so many of the new directors.

Still, the statistics regarding Estonian theatre are impressive. Out of a population of 1.4 million in 2004, 1.1 million people attended a theatre production. Forty percent of Estonians regularly go to the theatre. Positive sources for funding also stabilize Estonian theatre and distinguish it from the cash-strapped theatres in Latvia and Lithuania where funding remains precarious and the movement towards privatization in many cases has been disastrous.

Andres Laasik, cultural editor at *The Estonia Daily* (*Eesti Päevaleht*), agrees that, at least in part, the reason for the seemingly universal popularity of the strong directors' theatre in Lithuania can be traced back to its Catholic roots, especially in the Church's tradition of proselytizing via liturgical drama, a theatrical form especially attractive to illiterate peasants during the Middle Ages. He draws a parallel between the Latin American countries and Lithuania, connecting them through their expertise with puppet theatres and the predominance of that art within their cultures. Laasik sees a direct link between the bread and puppet festivals still popular in Latin countries — including Italy and Spain — and the theatre-of-spectacle that dominates contemporary Lithuanian theatre. (During the New Drama Action Festival in Vilnius, children and adults alike stared in rapt fascination at the Corpus Christi processional, an event that stimulated more popular interest and emotional power, it seemed, than any theatre performance on the venue.) Laasik believes that the relative lack of interest in puppet theatre in Estonia stems from the Northern Reformation and the zealous "purification" movements that trashed the images, monuments and relics of Catholic iconography.

Laasik also suggests that the early disavowal of imagery in religion, and the subsequent privileging of "the word," explains why Estonian theatre has been labeled, by its own practitioners, "text-based."

"Estonia has good writers, the best in all the Baltics," he says, without a trace of hyperbole. But he admits that performances in Estonia tend to be less visual and more storied. He cites Tätte as a good example, a talented writer whose work is "situated on the edge of theatre. Next stop," he says, "is the novel." In his opinion, Tätte, coming as he does from an acting background, creates plays for actors, character-based pieces that retain a psychological quirkiness that keeps them free from stereotypes but on the verge of the absurd, a difficult trick.

As to whether Tätte is writing as an Estonian or a European, if he trades-in his Estonian roots for a generic, transportable style, Laasik is politic, suggesting that Tätte's themes and situations are universal enough to survive translations and transpositions without losing their essence. But "he is still very Estonian," Laasik insists, "because it is the personality that makes the writer." Laasik notes the idiosyncrasies, the "marks" in the play that signal Tätte's origin as strictly Estonian, though Laasik confesses these signs denoting his national identity are lost on international audiences. As a theatre critic, however, Laasik is not troubled by this threatened loss of identity of writers from small countries seeking an expanded audience base and more wide-spread recognition by creating pieces that transcend their particular local social contexts.

"Theatre, by its nature," he says, "must talk about mankind." Besides, he adds, Estonia is only 100 years old, a new society that has built a truly multi-cultural modern theatre culture from a strange mix of German, Russian and Scandinavian influences evolving out of a nation that, until recently, found itself in a perpetual state of crisis.

To explain his ambivalence about issues of "national identity" and the assimilation of the unique character of what it means to be Estonian into the larger cultural entity of the European Union, Laasik suggests that many of the new Baltic theatre companies have adopted a "nomadic philosophy" of traveling from festival to festival, transgressing, as it were, to erase boundaries, so they often intentionally establish no permanent connections with any particular audience. He worries that Estonian theatre will become a medium "without any roots [...] theatre that is not interested in roots, either" ("Nomadism").[11] Tätte's plays, in this sense, could be considered "nomadic." Laasik also names the Von Krahl theatre as an early nomadic Estonian company, designing performances that would be played in different countries in various venues with no real consideration for audience expectations. The beauty of Von Krahl — and, for that matter, Tätte — is that they create their own audience, successfully exporting their style of performance on an international circuit.

Laasik admits that the tradition of Estonian theatre is local. "Perhaps too local," he cautions. Because all the important actors, writers and directors know each other, and the audiences are partial to one theatre or another, or to one style or another, the theatre community risks creating an unhealthy laziness that can stifle creativity. Laasik (among others) describes the Estonian theatre audience as "very conservative"— to the degree that it is risky to stage a production that might run counter to what the audience expects — plays, for instance, without a recognizable storyline, like absurdist drama or anti-realism.

Yet Laasik is convinced that contemporary audiences are shedding this parochialism without diminishing their enthusiasm for theatre productions. He notes that two decades ago, staging a new play seriously risked alienating audiences. If a theatre announced it was staging a work by a new Estonian writer, the audience automatically assumed it would be boring: an Estonian writer could not be expected to have the humanistic range and dramatic depth to compete with the classical writers from the world stage. Now, the announcement of a new work by an Estonian writer generates an authentic buzz because audiences know the play will reflect their new situation, that of a small country working out is particular problems while, of course, connecting Estonian life with the eternal values shared by people everywhere. This, says Laasik, is the key to Tätte's success. As Monika Laanesaar writes in the Introduction to Tätte's *Plays* (*Näidendid*):

> The best original Estonian drama of the last few years mainly treats topics that can best be understood by those who are familiar with the local situation. [...] Against this background the plays of [...] Tätte stand out. It is not important whether the world of Tätte's characters is located in Tallinn, New York or Berlin, because when it comes to dreams and love we are more similar than the geographical distances may at first let us believe. This is proved by the fact that Tätte's plays have already found their way onto the international landscape, and with great success.

His critique of the new consumerism is obliquely overlaying his main themes of love, life, loss and death that elevate his plays beyond the merely topical. Tätte's plays are certainly political, but not overtly so, combining Estonian roots — especially the strong story element — with transnational themes.

Regarding the historical role of theatre as a political force during the Soviet era, Laasik agrees with Saro that the reductive, clear demarcation between the forces of good — the citizens of the occupied countries — and the bad — the Soviets — has been mythologized by the West for their own ideological and propagandistic purposes, perpetuated even today in a sort of retro-reification of cold war Western policy decisions. While this Manichean certainty may be good for domestic consumption, especially in the United States where the evils implied by the Iron Curtain have been used to justify everything from US support of Latin American dictators, to the Vietnam War and the revanchist policies of Ronald Reagan, the truth, according to Laasik, is not so tidy or convenient. There were no such clear, distinctions between Russians and citizens of satellite countries, or between Communists and dissidents. Even Russian playwrights were writing plays critical of the Communist policies.

"We were all gray," Laasik says. "Some lighter, some darker."

Applying an abstract either/or fallacy to the situation on the ground is facile and misleading. Even the censorship was inconsistent and, especially in the theatre, easily circumvented. That was why the theatre was so important, he says: the censors could only cut words, so theatre allowed for what Laasik calls "visual solutions" in a context beyond their control.

Visual solutions inspire Mart Koldits, one of the resident directors at Tallinn City Theatre, to work in an entirely different direction form Tätte, not that he is trying to outwit government censors or catholicize Estonian theatre, but true to Pille Jänes's precepts — non-linear narratives that challenge the traditional "space" of the performance and the relationship of the actors to the audience — Koldits wants to "free" himself from the text. In the two plays he did in collaboration with Jänes, *Tschapajev and Pustota* and *The Metamorphosis*, Koldits complains that he did not allow himself to get "far enough away" from the texts to create the effect he was seeking.

Nevertheless, his production of *The Metamorphosis* offers ample evidence of his approach: minimizing textual language while maximizing the visual. The play opens in a performance space designed like Grotowski's "anti-theatre" stage, marrying the idea of Grotowski's "poor theatre" with a poetic-grotesque absurdism that, while providing a subjective component to Kafka's nightmarish vision, creates a fresh intensity by breaking down dramatic conventions, foregrounding the structure of the action, and integrating the audience into the performance.

Enclosed in a room around which and through which the action occurs, the audience is mixed in with the actors, creating zero distance between the viewer and the action. The mechanics of the play are exposed: there is no disconnect, no seam. As the scenes develop, the audience, sitting literally inside the acting space, painfully close to the actors, participates in the emotional context of the characters. For the audience, the proximity is unsettling. The effect is to have the audience experience subjectively Gregor's perspective — isolated in a room, literally in the dark about what is transpiring outside — while convincingly visualizing his emotional state: curious but frightened, aware but incapable of understanding. The tension is heightened by Koldits' startling, caustic use of chiaroscuro in which the stage is often kept totally dark until a sudden incursion or excursion violently sprays the space with light, action is glimpsed, a door is shut and the space plunged back into total darkness. Windows open abruptly from the side panel, framing busy clerks mechanically reading accounting sheets that at one point literally begin to choke Gregor. His metamorphosis into an insect is rendered though another clever chiaroscuro effect: he struggles to escape the vivid white sheets of his bed only to emerge trapped in a dehumanizing black skein he cannot shed. Each scene seems to play inside out, with the action outside the audience's view, until — like with Gregor — characters intrude on their — and his — space. The family interrupts, as when his sister and mother conspire to remove his furniture, immersed momentarily in Gregor's reality, before exiting, shutting out the light and leaving Gregor and the audience behind, sharing a dark incomprehensible world.

For his adaptation of Orwell's *Animal Farm*, Koldits abandons the storyline for a mélange of techniques — dance, parody, mixed media, farce, live performances of original music as well as songs by The Doors and Radiohead — in a performance that combines pure entertainment, social relevance and psychological acuity with strong physicality and epical spectacle. Played in the huge outside space at Tallinn City Theatre on a sloped wooden stage mined with trap doors and an opening jaw out of which emerges at one point truly threatening German Shepherds leashed by black clad figures in balaclavas torturing hapless victims in a Bosch-like nightmare that is as funny as it is disturbing, Koldits creates a total theatre experience, closer, perhaps, to Von Krahl's approach yet maintaining a sense of an "authentic" theatre.

Mart Koldits on the set of *Animal Farm*, the outside stage, Tallinn City Theatre (photograph by Siim Vahur).

The choice of *Animal Farm* was a shrewd gesture by Koldits, as if to answer another complaint often voiced by critics of contemporary work — namely, that Estonian theatre, especially since liberation, no longer concerns itself with social issues. *Animal Farm* is a political treatise, but Koldits manages to transform the context into entertainment without diminishing the social or ideological critique. He does not try to solve any political issue but rather cleverly manages to expose the subtext without becoming preachy, pointed or particularly didactic.

Not all of the young Estonian directors share Koldits' disdain for narrative. Eva Klemets, the director of Tätte's *Meeletu*, for instance, admits that she likes stories. Further differentiating her style from the "total theatre" of Koldits, Klemets works more within the tradition of minimalism. "In theory," she says, "to apply Grotowski's ideas would be nice, but in reality it's not possible."

Klemets eschews elaborate staging, preferring a spare set and a simple, text-based style that, she says, sticks to the writer's intentions. She rejects formal *mise-en-scènes*, props and theatrical effects, opting instead for a lean psychological realism she levitates with a buoyant touch of alienation that keeps the process from sinking under the weight of Stanislavsky interiority. Her appreciation for a sparse, story-driven work explains her

For his adaptation of Orwell's *Animal Farm*, Koldits abandons the storyline for a mélange of techniques: dance, parody, mixed media, farce, and live musical performances. Played in the huge outside space at Tallinn City Theatre on a sloped wooden stage mined with trap doors, the performance combines pure entertainment, social relevance and psychological acuity with strong physicality and epic spectacle (photograph by Siim Vahur).

enthusiasm for Frank McGuinness's *Someone Who'll Watch Over Me* (*Et Keegi Mind Valvaks*), which she staged in Köismäe Tower on the edge of the Old Town in Tallinn. What began as her final degree performance has become a successful, if not signature work for her, selected for the 2005 Estonian Drama Festival in Tartu. The story, based on kidnappings in Lebanon during the 1980s, recounts the ordeal of, according to the program notes, "Three men — three nationalities — a single cell." The set is necessarily sparse; the only props are bottled water, the Bible and three chains.

The circumstances — both the story and the space — immediately universalize the play: the cell could be anywhere, and the ordeal could happen to anyone. McGuinness has taken what could have been a particularly political situation and stripped it down to an examination of what happens to people when they are forced into close confinement against their will. Klemets renders the captivity of the men, and their strategies of survival — the word games, the alternating moods of hostility and sympathy, the acting out of their former ordinary lives — with excruciating restraint and intensity. By setting the piece in an actual place of confinement instead of in a traditional theatre space — at least, in a room not dissimilar to that in which the hostages were held, with seating for only sixty — Klemets is able to exploit the audience's apprehension, that feeling of being in the play, not just watching it from a distance, to create a mood and identity with the characters that applies Grotowski's ideas with eviscerating honesty.

Klemets and Koldits, who graduated in 2004 from the Higher Drama School of the Estonian Music Academy, both question whether there is value in discussing a national identity, of Estonia or any country.

"The idea of nationality is threatened everywhere," Koldits says. "The term 'nationality' may vanish."

(Events like the French and Dutch rejection of the European Constitution bode otherwise, but Klemets' and Koldits' idealism, their belief in the benefits of trans-nationalism, remains unvarnished.)

They agree that Estonian theatre is historically a product of German occupation, when the Estonian language was not acceptable for cultural expression and was considered a language of peasants and "simple folk." Soon, however, inevitably, the Russian influence — mainly, of course, Stanislavsky — began reshaping the Estonian theatre about the time the Estonians began to develop their own "mainstream" theatre. This confluence of the German grand style and the Russian psychological precision created a rich breeding ground for producing talented actors. But this hybrid, mainstream theatre soon became predictable, stale and uninspiring. Worse, an audience base emerged that expected this singular, Chekhovian style, and any deviation from the program was met with suspicion, even hostility.

With a few exceptions, mainly in the late 1960s and early 1970s, this traditional theatre remained *de rigueur*, satisfying the apparatus of the state theatre system as well as keeping the critics and audiences (who were for the most part aesthetically identical and symbiotic) satisfied. Still, even with this decadent system and redundant productions, theatre thrived until the transition period, when the theatre seemed irrelevant and unnecessary. Because life on the streets was more interesting than the vicarious life on stage, the people, suddenly free and inundated with colorfully packaged goods, advertising blitzes, mass-market consumerism and rampant pop culture, in Koldits words, "went mad."

If the national identity of Estonia had been threatened by the Soviet occupation and the imposition of Communist ideology — not to mention the threat of linguistic eradication — after liberation, according to Koldits, the identity of Estonia was even more insecure.

"In the old days," he says, "people went abroad for adventure, and if they stayed it was because they wanted to, because they found something interesting. Now people leave Estonian to work. They plan their lives outside Estonia. Even the language is again under threat," this time by marketing slogans, MTV, and a sort of reductive, generic Mc-language.

Koldits thinks theatre is in a position, however, to help recover not just Estonian identity — by keeping the language vital, resilient and relevant — but also the original roots of what he considers authentic Estonian culture. Koldits theorizes that the German imposition of a rational, linear, eschatological cultural paradigm (basically Western and Christian) does not reflect the nature of indigenous Estonians. The early Estonians, he says, were "forest people," shamanistic pagans whose rhythms were more in tune with the cycles of nature.

"The Germans," he explains, "gave us 'high culture,'" which the bourgeoisie emulated and equated with sophistication, refinement and a cosmopolitan ethos. "Even the so-called official Estonian epic *Kalevipoeg*— our *Iliad*— was written by a German," he says.[10] "He collected the stories into a system" that Koldits identifies as alien to the pre-Enlightenment cosmology of the native Estonians. Koldits believes that even the contemporary mainstream theatre still relies on German values, especially, on one hand, its sentimentality, and on the other, its earnest sincerity: that is, easy comedic entertainments and psychological realism *a la* Stanislavsky.

This affinity for Teutonic kitsch might explain the Estonian theatregoing audience's fascination — and demand for — Irish culture: Irish folklore, dance, music and plays. Klemets suggests that the Estonian interest in the Irish experience indicates a sympathetic identification with Irish history: a small country, frequently occupied, oppressed, discriminated against, stereotypically fixed as an "essential" underclass that has nevertheless maintained its identity and emerged as a thriving member of the new economy within the European Union.

But cultural and historical identity is one thing. Aesthetics is another, and Klemets's major concern is not that the Estonians are so interested per se in the Irish experience; what she objects to is the presentation of that experience. She notes that Tallinn City Theatre chose the relatively tame and family-friendly play by the Irish playwright Martin McDonagh *The Cripple of Innishmaan* and contrasts that decision and production with the more avant-garde Tiit Ojasoo's choice of McDonagh's *The Lieutenant of Inishmore* (staged at the Estonian Drama Theatre), a riveting, violent and funny expose on terrorism. Klemets sums up the difference economically but effectively: "The City Theatre provided the audience with what it wanted: sweetness. Ojasoo's production was, 'No mercy.'"

This anecdote illustrates just how conservative the mainstream theatre audience can be in Estonia. Yet, the young directors are keen to work against the grain. Klemets and Koldits, in different ways, are deliberately moving away from the tradition of Meyerhold, Stanislavsky, Grotowski and others who tend to see theatre as a vehicle to express their theories instead of the aesthetics of life.

"If you want realism," Klemets says, "cinema can deliver the illusion of realism better than any theatre production." Koldits objects to the very idea of "realism" as a genre representing anything other than another aesthetic response to life. "Realism," he says, "does not represent anything 'real.'"

Both directors look to Peeter Jalakas of Von Krahl theatre and Tiit Ojasoo of Theatre NO99 as representing the possibilities of a new direction in Estonian theatre. Jalakas is the instigator, owner, and manager of probably the most internationally connected theatre in Estonia. He is also one of the most shrewd theatre entrepreneurs in the Baltics, outflanking even Audronis Liūga in his ability to generate income for creative endeavors. Jalakas owns the fourteenth century building housing, in a renovated loft, his 150 seat black box theatre, but also the bar below and two adjacent restaurants. A sign in the bar reads, BUY A DRINK. SUPPORT THEATRE.

"It was a nice idea," he says. "But the truth is, the money we made downstairs (in the bar and restaurant) was lost upstairs (in the theatre)."

To solve his constant financial crises, he established one company to run the bar and restaurant and another non-profit that owns the theatre. That way he can finance risky projects from the income of the first company, yet because the theatre is a non-profit organization he receives a stable subsidy form the state, enjoys the use of his performing space free, and has his utilities paid. He also generates revenue from ticket sales and sponsors. And though he is relatively economically flush now, he cautions that too much money can create stagnation and a crippling sense of success.

"You need to be hungry," he says, suggesting that had he had enough money when he was first starting out he probably would not have survived. In the formative years of Von Krahl, the constant pressure of financial survival kept his work vital and alive. In Jalakas' opinion, once a theatre becomes "established" the people involved become lazy and smug, and they either expect the money to be there — which leads to complacency — or they panic if the budget is suddenly threatened — which leads to rashness and compromise. His other caveat concerning funding is that, when a theatre accepts money from the state it gives up control, so the less money Von Krahl receives from the state, the more freedom Jalakas retains for the kind of productions he wants to create.

Most of all, he says, he just wants to have fun. The motto of the bar is: PURE FUN. The motto of the theatre is: PURE ART.

"Given what we're doing, and what we want to do, we can't be concerned about audience or critics. The audience can do what it wants, and the critics" — he shrugs — "they have tried to put us in a box, labeling us experimental, alternative, epical, ethnic, carnival, social, but they can't decide, which is good for us because it means fortunately we are always changing, and that's what we want. Nobody knows what we might do."

Jalakas attributes his mercurial temperament less to his formal education than his experiences after graduation. He attended the Tallinn Pedagogical University and trained in the theatre department as a director, but after he traveled to Denmark Eugenio Barba at the Odin Theatre introduced him to the ideas of Grotowski — in fact, Jalakas credits Barba with introducing Grotowski to all of Scandinavia. Then in Germany he met Pina Bausch who exposed him to the theatrical possibilities of contemporary dance. This international, eclectic education illustrates Jalakas' hesitation to accept any notion of his theatre being necessarily "Estonian." He situates Von Krahl not within national borders but within an aesthetic community of theatres who share his vision.

"When you do theatre," he says, "of course it comes from your roots, but it must be understandable all around the world."

He concedes that Estonian theatre is traditionally text-based, and that the Estonian theatre system, for the most part, turns out better actors than directors. He explains this trend — a gross generalization but nearly unanimously acknowledged by people inside and outside professional theatre circles in Estonia — by describing a theatre culture rife with bureaucratic resistance to change and an entrenched allegiance to the German and Scandinavian state style of repertory theatre.

As artistic director of Rakvere Theatre[12] for two years, he speaks from experience. The problems — he left, he says, because he was forced to make too many compromises — are several. First, in a big structure, if you want to change its nature, if you want to build a system that "supports your vision," you must make institutional changes, and that means changing personnel from the ground up. Maybe now, he says, things are different because there are more opportunities for people to find work. But when he was at Rakvere people would be hurt financially if they were fired because it was impossible for them to find another job. So, the people employed by the theatre were more interested in a steady job than reforming the theatre system. Plus, according to Jalakas, the financial directors of large theatres read only the bottom line and shirk any responsibility for funding new ventures that might force them to find alternative sources of income outside the familiar formulas. Finally, the audience and their public mouthpiece — the collective voice of the critics — resist any change in the programs that might upset their usually reserved and traditional expectations.

The key difference between the normal state repertory theatre's approach to a production and that of Von Krahl, says Jalakas, is two-fold. First, the team at Von Krahl does not begin a performance as if it is a job they can leave at the office: the project becomes their lives; the actors must be totally immersed in the work. Second, the flexible approach Jalakas takes allows the team to approach the piece under creative consideration with no expectations. Part of the process is to have the performers forget everything they know or have come to expect previously about the work, engaging in a sort of Husserlean exercise in de-familiarization, developing ideas through improvisation and free association so that the role of the director is subsumed by what the ensemble extemporizes, inventing then re-inventing various dramatic contexts. Spontaneity, even during the formal performances, is expected and encouraged as part of the final product.

His approach, he hopes, moves theatre away from analysis toward presentation. He prefers to ask about a text: What can I do? Not: What is it? The actors and directors know the truth of their experience of the piece, but it is not their job to explain it to the critics and audience. He also keeps his distance from what he calls "social theatre" but questions what that term might mean. In his opinion, every work contains social relevance, but he prefers pieces that focus on aesthetic truths that no matter how "pure" the "art" nevertheless imply — obliquely but definitively — a social critique. Regarding the influx of pop culture, mass marketing and cheap commercialism that flooded the former satellite states after independence, Jalakas responds stoically: "Why be angry about rain?" He views popular culture as simply "another element of theatre." Yet even his aesthetic fatalism does not deter a streak of idealism in his philosophy. He expresses a surprisingly incongruous romantic notion that theatre can have a utilitarian, benevolent effect on society, a belief based in an odd trust in humanistic values.

"If our theatre does things that are good," he says, "this makes the world a better place."

This sense of lyrical beauty as a motivating force for goodness in the world is why he objects to much of the new work coming out of Ireland, Germany and England that seems designed to shock but offers nothing beyond shock itself. He cites Martin McDonagh's *Pillowman* as an example, readily admitting that much of McDonagh's other work is positive and engaging, but he dismisses *Pillowman* and similar works by English and German writers as nihilistic and sensational, works that leave audiences empty.

His objections to the raunchiness and violence in the work of McDonagh (and Sarah Kane, et al.) are hard to square with his own critique of nihilism, an in-your-face grunge-fest titled *Only Fakes Survive* (*Ainult võltsid jäävad ellu*) that chronicles (in its way) the rise and fall of the British marketing sensation The Sex Pistols. The piece, which purports to explore the question, What is punk? while challenging the premise and authenticity of the band, paradoxically tries to transform tastelessness and disgusting behavior into entertainment, a difficult trick that tries to use the punk paradigm against itself.

Loosely based on Julien Temple's film *The Filth and the Fury*, which critic J. Hoberman describes as "proudly cruddy," the play takes its title from an episode in the film when John Lydon (aka Johnny Rotten), "tearfully recalling the pathetic tale of Sid Vicious [...] tells Temple that 'only the fakes survive'" (Hoberman). The performance by Von Krahl, however, is more about the audience than the band, testing not only the viewer's aesthetics, sensibility and expectations about the nature of "art" or "theatre" but its patience too. A series of disgusting visuals interspersed with live performances of Sex Pistols' songs — members of the band collectively vomit in a bucket, wallow in colored liquid, simulate masturbation and coitus with a couch — the action is an assault on the senses, forcing the viewer to confront the same questions the Pistols forced into the face of a saccharized pop culture: Is this a talentless improvisation or a profound study of tastelessness? Must a critique become its subject? How much defilement can an audience endure before turning away, and does that act of rejection — that looking away — validate the action?

The cultural dilemma the performance (or treatise) provokes and the reactions from the audience it incites are, perhaps, more interesting in theory than praxis. The actual events on stage — the puerile play in the mucky sandbox of intentionally gross behavior — runs the risk of backfiring: as the viewer becomes inured to the repetitive vulgarity, the shock wears off quickly, replaced with a dull boredom, which in the end may explain the band's meteoric appeal and subsequent, equally hasty fall from critical and popular grace. With no talent beyond their Situationist/Conceptualist prefabrication to sustain them, they debunk their own mythological status with their pathetic need to be taken seriously. They have, in the words of another film critic, "long been obscured by their own legend" (Nelson). As Lydon says in the film, "When you feel powerless, you grab any power you can ... we managed to offend everybody" (qtd. in Nelson). Von Krahl's *Only Fakes Survive* attempts to challenge the demarcation between authentic theatre and intentionally putrid schlock, even if the result does more to blur the distinctions than to illuminate them.

The inspiration for the performance can be traced back to an event in Jalakas' youth that, as he tells it, begins to resemble a timely parable about the pitfalls of censorship and attempts at ideological purification. In 1979, when he was still a student, a Communist Party apparatchik who had heard The Sex Pistols wanted to discredit the punk movement as another indication of Western decadence, so he recorded several songs by the band and began to visit schools, playing the songs to the students. Jalakas jokes that maybe the man was a secret fan of the band, because, predictably, the man's plan backfired: after hearing the songs, the students were desperate for the music, and record sales soared. At that time, many records purchased by mail orders were confiscated, but the ones that got through became revered icons of freedom, cherished and copied onto tapes and distributed to the faithful like religious icons. No matter how stringently the officials tried to prevent Western influences — including punk — to "corrupt" the youth behind the Iron Curtain, their attempts proved futile. In fact, Jalakas suggests that the effect of social trends like punk may have been, at least in Estonia, more dramatic because of how rare the attempts at censorship made the recordings, guaranteeing them, by banning them, cult status. (This parable should serve as a lesson in the futility of censorship for Western countries — especially the United States — that, for religious, political or ideological reasons pursue their own programs limiting freedom of expression.)

Even given Anneli Saro's qualifications regarding the political impact of theatres during the Soviet era, Jalakas, like many artists in the former Soviet Bloc, laments the loss of whatever social influence, perceived or real, theatre enjoyed during the occupation. He too recalls people waiting a year for a ticket to see certain performances. And without exactly contradicting

Saro's point that much of the popularity of theatre during those times can be attributed to the fact that there was nothing else to do for recreation, Jalakas suggests that back then theatres offered a perspective that now is provided by newspapers and the church. But because during the Soviet era the press and the church were not functioning, all the good performances were political, coded with those famous "hidden messages." (For instance, *Hamlet* became an essay on oppression.) Jalakas still can only speculate as to why so many "coded" performances were allowed in Estonia that would have been banned elsewhere.

"Either the censors were too stupid to understand the subtext," he says, "or they just decided to let the people think what they want."

Jalakas is convinced that the theatre then was more honest, although there were, of course, ideological performances, demanded by the authorities, but, according to Jalakas, "only soldiers were sent to see them."

In his theory, during the transition the nature of theatre changed mainly because the newspapers and churches were restored to their normal place of influence within society. Ironically, this caused a problem for many directors who were considered "good" before the transition but could not adapt to a theatre that served no religious or political function, so they lost their touch and soon fell out of favor.

"They were politicians," Jalakas says. "But after liberation there was no message to hide."

The restoration of the press and the church as institutions of free expression also affected theatre attendance, for obvious reasons. And even though Estonia is now in a period of recovery, many directors still know only the Soviet system, so developing playwrights, actors and directors are, to their detriment (in Jalakas' view), still heavily influenced by the Soviet method, It will take, at least, he thinks, another generation to free Estonian theatre from the Soviet style system.

To qualify Jalakas' enthusiasm for experimentation, for "freeing the play from the text" and intentionally confounding audience expectations, Priit Pedajas, the Artistic Director of Estonian Drama Theatre and one of the old hands still working within the repertory system, states unequivocally that "there is not much new in Estonian theatre." He admits that the theatre is "looking for a new language"—especially young people with no experience of life under Soviet occupation, but Pedajas thinks the work of the so-called "new" directors is simply a rehash of the style employed by the old avant-garde movement "discovered by young directors who think it's new." Pedajas, who graduated from the Theatre Department of the

Conservatory of Tallinn in 1976, looks back to the late 1960s and early 1970s as a time when Estonian theatre experienced a radical renaissance. He notes how Soviet theatre critics were keen to visit Estonia (and other satellite states) because those cultural centers outside Russia were freer ideologically, therefore, according to Pedajas, more prone to experiment, creating a fresh, energetic theatre that made the Russian productions seem stale and listless by comparison. Though there were limits on themes and which playwrights could be produced, the Soviets considered theatre in Estonia to be a source for contemporary Western drama, a place where they could view quality productions of plays impossible to see, for instance, in Moscow. Even today, he says, the Russians are not exposed to much contemporary Western drama, not, as before, because of ideological sensitivity but because the Russian theatre companies cannot get good translators and the Western theatres that tour Russia perform mostly dated material.

Pedajas represents a disappearing breed of theatre practitioners in the Baltics, one still working who was also working during the Soviet period. And like the others, he recalls how the theatre was the only place to see honest critiques of the Communist Party, and he agrees with Jalakas and others who believe — incredibly — that the Soviets allowed the theatre to become this vehicle of resistance because the commissars just did not appreciate the power of the theatre. Pedajas, without being disingenuous, says flatly, "They didn't get it."

He also agrees that after the transition, life itself became more dynamic, so interest in the theatre declined. Yet he too senses a reawakening on the part of the public for quality entertainment, as if those who during the early years of independence were intoxicated by the possibilities of popular culture have recovered their sobriety, and now that they can again afford to splurge on entertainment, and because of the variety of performances available, they have returned to the theatre as a source of new ideas and provocative discourse.

For Pedajas, who traces his roots back to the late 1960s, when directors like Hermaküla and Tooming were the acknowledged forces shaping Estonian theatre, the role of the director is to interpret and provide a concrete frame for the action of a play, but he thinks directors should remain faithful to the text (unlike, for example, many of the more radical Lithuanian directors and young Estonians for whom the text is merely a suggestion). He thinks this faithfulness to the text comes from the Estonian tradition of text-based psychological realism derived from the German theatre and modified by the influences of Stanislavsky. Pedajas plays down the

Scandinavian influence, both historically and in the contemporary scene. But more significantly, he cites the waning Russian influence as the main reason for the changing direction of contemporary Estonian theatre (which may also explain the difference between Lithuanian and Estonian performances). He claims that not one of his current students in his acting class reads Russian. The students prefer British and American theatre, and given the choice between studying in Moscow and London, they invariably pick London.

One of the "young" voices agreeing with Pedajas that there is nothing "new" in Estonian theatre is Madis Kolk, editor-in-chief of the monthly arts journal *Theatre. Music. Cinema. (Teater. Muusika. Kino.)* Like Pedajas, he cites the work of Hermaküla and Tooming in the 1960s and early 1970s as having developed a physical theatre based more on Grotowski and Meyerhold than Stanislavsky, though the trend — like the driving social principles of so-called "68 Thought" itself — soon passed. But unlike the fate of so much avant-garde theatre, the work of Hermaküla and Tooming was not appropriated by the arbiters of popular mass-cultural tastes and recycled as mainstream style; it simply faded away. Audiences tired of experimentation and demanded a return to the message-based Aesopian story-line of a conventional theatre that they easily understood, that seemed relevant to their lives, providing entertainment they could respond to, that reflected their values in comforting aesthetics. Rähesoo explains:

> It [the work of Hermaküla and Tooming] found its expression in the freedom with which the play text was treated, in the aggressiveness and physicality of stage action, and in heavy reliance on symbols and metaphors. The aggressiveness [...] was a reflection of hysterical rage born out of a feeling of growing hopelessness. But for a wide section of the public, who otherwise might have shared that feeling, its theatrical form became a source of annoyance. Many theatre people, too, felt repulsed [70].

Just as in the time of Hermaküla and Tooming, the importance of the audience in determining the direction of theatre in Estonia cannot be overstated or underplayed. And the need both to cater to popular demands and to "educate" the audience into accepting new approaches reinforces the feeling throughout the Baltics that the market has too much influence on theatre, especially when it comes to nurturing new talent and experimenting with avant-garde approaches. As Pedajas makes clear, at the Estonian Drama Theatre, to stay viable financially, "we need two hits per season." To achieve this, compromises in aesthetic values must be made.

Kolk agrees that money is an issue — perhaps, in real terms, *the* issue — but the other problem, he says, is that because there is no official censorship anymore, the people are less inclined to view theatre with the same intrigue they did during the Soviet period. Critics looking for a scapegoat try to fix the blame on this factor or that trend to explain why theatre is not as popular as it was before independence, but to be fair, Kolk cautions not to use as markers of success similar demands as it did at the time of independence — social relevance, issue-orientation, political engagement — when, as noted, street life became more interesting than the vicarious life presented in the theatre. On the other hand, Kolk thinks that it is much too easy simply to conclude that people are no longer interested in issues or "high culture," preferring instead only the products of pop culture and mass-marketing, without examining more closely the complex psychological undercurrents determining the differences in taste and expectations between the social experience of people's lives during the Soviet period and life after independence.

What is needed, Kolk muses, is a theatre that offers a better quality of entertainment, the kind that uses elements of the media culture but recombines them in a fresh way that other media cannot. Even the experiments of Jalakas, for Kolk, do not necessarily represent a new direction in the theatre so much as a reworking of that 1960s "aggressiveness and physicality" with some technical elements unavailable in Tooming's time.

"In the end," he says, "the point is similar."

But Kolk does credit Jalakas with helping to liberate Estonian theatre from the tired aesthetics of psychological realism, although he is quick to qualify the notion that "mainstream" Estonian theatre represents true psychological drama in the original Stanislavsky mode. The basic principles are still Russian, he says, but he insists that it has become cliché among many critics to label mainstream Estonian drama as "psychological realism" when in fact it is often merely realism in the sense of a straight, well-made play, or pure entertainment, as it were, with no serious intentions (or pretenses). Part of this misunderstanding — or mislabeling — occurs because of the text-based traditions noted by Kolk and others as being at the historical core of Estonian theatre, which shifts the psychological basis for action in a performance — the key to Stanislavsky's method — to the story-telling in which action either illustrates a "situation" or advances the plot.

According to Kolk, critics are too easily excited by anything that deviates from the traditional dramatic style. For instance, stage anything that could be described as "physical" and the critics, in Pedajas' phrase, "shout it's new!" But for theatre to be considered truly new for Kolk requires more than tricks or games or mere "physicality." In Kolk's paradigm, Jalakas is too "radical," using technology and a multi-media approach to create what might, in the end, be considered more performance art than theatre. (Pedajas, for instance, calls Jalakas an "organizer," not disparagingly but as if he must be considered in a different context from "theatre.") Kolk complains that, given critical demand for something new, it is too easy to *appear* new without really creating anything innovative. (In Jaan Tätte's *The Highway Crossing*, for example, the characters make self-referential remarks about the fact that they are, after all, on stage, in a play, but the attempts to break the frame of the audience/actor relationship seems appended to the text and serves no organic or integral purpose in the structure or theme, so the effect is banal and sophomoric instead of post-modern or edgy.)

Kolk suggests that, with the acquisition of Mart Koldits as a director, Tallinn City Theatre, traditionally associated with the "old style" of psychological realism, is well-positioned to challenge the clichés plaguing mainstream theatre. Kolk cites Koldits' handling of *Tschapajev and Pustota* as a performance that, while maintaining what Kolk considers conventional theatre values still manages to transform those values into something authentically fresh. In Kolk's words, *Tschapajev and Pustota* "combines the Zen of Pelevin with traditional realism," creating a psychological theatre with post-modern overtones and indicating "a new direction in Estonian theatre."

Along with Koldits and Jalakas, two other directors Kolk considers to be working in authentically new directions are Tiit Ojasoo and Hendrik Toompere. Of the two, Kolk considers Toompere, perhaps, the more mature, in the sense that he has more experience, allowing his performances more consistency. Like fine wine, however, Ojasoo is still aging, and though Kolk thinks he has been overrated by critics desperate for anything they can tag as being "different," he is close to realizing his potential. Kolk cites Ojasoo's *Juliet* (*Julia*) along with Jalakas's *Estonian Ballads* (*Eesti Ballaadid*) as works that cut across the grain of mainstream theatre and yet have achieved immense popularity (although it is arguable, which is often the case with a Von Krahl production, if *Estonian Ballads* qualifies as "theatre" per se: the entire piece is a collection of traditional epic songs plus Butoh dance songs performed in a vast outdoor setting.)

But it is for Toompere that Kolk reserves his greatest appreciation. For Kolk, Toompere "brings together lots from the 1960s and 1970s" — stuff as diverse as the teachings of Carlos Castaneda and the theories of Grotowski — with a postmodern skepticism for fixed meanings and absolutes, creating a synthesis out of the seemingly contradictory characteristics of traditional psychological realism and the physical dynamism of a more metaphorical theatre. Kolk views Toompere's work as psychological drama filtered through Grotowski, so that it appears as both conventional and new, and therefore unique in contemporary Estonian theatre.

Like Kolk, Ojasoo considers the times of Hermaküla and Tooming as "the Golden Age" of Estonian drama, when, inspired by Grotowski and other new waves in Europe, those directors made a truly radical turn from the mainstream. But then, as now, Ojasoo notes, the audience quickly lost patience. They were less interested in aesthetic novelty than escapism, romanticism, or even activism — another form of escapism — all presented through more conventional venues. Ojasoo points out that the situation was the same in Moscow during the 1920s when Meyerhold introduced his experimental style to audiences steeped in strict Chekhovian theatre, and though he staged some memorable productions, the attendance fell off immediately and his reputation, at least with the general public, was seriously diminished.

In Ojasoo's opinion, whatever national identity that was once inherent in Estonian theatre disappeared after independence; as soon as the public no longer needed the allegorical component in public performances reflecting the political and social situation of the occupation, the theatre became generic, mired in the Soviet system but without the necessity or relevance as before. And it remains, Ojasoo says plainly, "boring for me." In his view, part of the problem is that the German-Russian model of the well-made play is not naturally Estonian. Like Koldits, he believes that the Estonian national character cannot be explained within the aesthetics of a bourgeois theatre represented by the German manor house tradition or the psychological fourth-wall theatre of Chekhov, but only by the illogic of pagan rituals — the theatre of Anne Türnpu, for instance, that emphasizes shamanistic dancing, intuitive rhythms and strange stories. Ojasoo gleefully describes Estonians as "greedy, jealous people" whose national character, for him, is best illustrated by *The Barn-Keeper* (*Rehepapp*), a novel by Andrus Kivirähk about a man who tries to enrich himself by exploiting dead souls.

Ojasoo considers *Juliet* his "most notorious" production. He takes the text from Shakespeare, but "only the lines the actors need to express themselves." He frames the performance as a production of *Romeo and Juliet*, not as a play within a play but as an exploration into the nature of the relationships between the actors and the characters they portray. His intention is to challenge the continuity separating stage life from real life, posing without necessarily answering the question: Which is the play and which is reality? The answer is not as obvious as it might seem.

Ojasoo centers the play on Mirtel, a young woman cast in the role of Juliet and the object of desire of every man she meets, especially her two "Romeos": Rasmus, with whom she is romantically involved, and Mait, who takes the role of Romeo in the production. The conflict inherent in the play intensifies when Rasmus becomes jealous of Mait's interest in Mirtel, not as Juliet of the play but as a young woman in "real" life. Ojasoo's intention is to explore how theatre conflates the actors' lives outside the play with the characters they play within it, and to question the traditional bright line of demarcation between "real" life and life presented on stage. By setting the production in a traditional "Italian box" stage at the Estonian Drama Theatre, Ojasoo plays on the audience's expectation of a traditional performance, a comfortable illusion shattered when the curtain opens: the audience, instead of seeing characters on a stage finds itself facing a huge projection screen playing a video shot by Rasmus of Mirtel practicing her lines in the bedroom of their apartment. The rehearsals that follow continue the disruption of expectations as the action alternates from video to cabaret (with a live band) to staged readings, auditions and period dances, with characters walking on and off the set, joining the band, mostly sticking to the Shakespearean script but decontextualizing it, appropriating the narrative from the original play and using it to signify situations in their "real" lives.

The men — the Capulets and Montagues — are dressed like Italian mobsters, and the only other woman in the play — Juliet's nurse — resembles a shrewd business woman more interested in pimping for Mait than rendering a classic tragedy. Mait's Romeo is a raw opportunist and sexual predator who sees his role in the play as a chance to sleep with Mirtel. The acting is often stylized and ironical, stripping the language of any melodramatic content. The actors consult their scripts, break into dance routines and nightclub acts, often trying to keep a straight face while delivering serious dialog, ridiculing the original action with mockery. The balcony scene is played on a step ladder. The stabbing deaths during the fight scene arise from jealousy and seem to be a mistake — a bit of action in rehearsals that got out of hand. The deaths — treated as real outside of the play — complicate Juliet's relationship with both her Romeos and her participation in the production, but earnest to a fault, she soon inevitably falls for the leading man and their bedroom scene is played with Juliet, in the afterglow of making love, doting on an obviously bored Romeo churlishly anxious to escape, their passion reduced to his giving her a parting, perfunctory kiss on the cheek.

Meanwhile, already unnerved about Mirtel's playing the role of another man's lover, and suspecting that Mirtel is in fact having an affair with Mait, Rasmus allows his insecurity to turn to anger and on a projected video-tape he rapes Mirtel. In an astonishing scene, the characters seen on the video suddenly burst through a blazing white light and enter the set as if they stepped live from the frame of the camera onto the stage. Distraught with guilt, Rasmus can only sit silently as Mirtel dresses and leaves him in their bedroom while she rejoins the action on stage. Again, the action of the play about Juliet and the "real life" situation of the actress Mirtel converge, providing Mirtel as much motive for drinking the

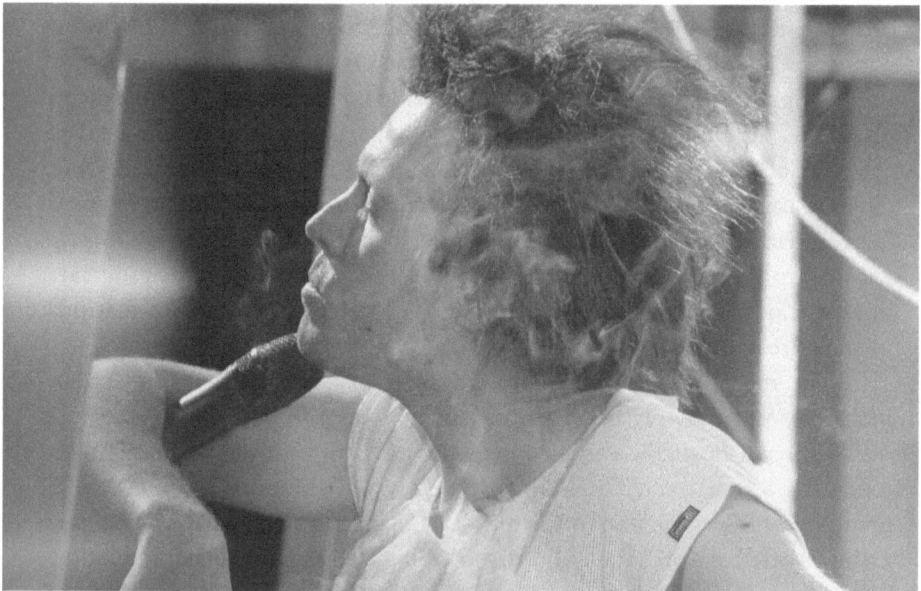

Mait Malmsten in Tiit Ojasoo's *Juliet* at the Estonian Drama Theatre. Ojasoo considers *Juliet* his "most notorious" production. Typecasting Malmsten, a well-known theatre star in Estonia, as "Romeo" creates an interesting layer of meanings where life inside and outside the play intersect. Ojasoo frames the performance as a production of *Romeo and Juliet*, not as a play within a play but as an exploration into the nature of the relationships between the actors and the characters they portray (photograph by Ene-Liis Semper).

poison as Juliet. For Rasmus, too, the demarcation between life and theatre is blurred when he must step "into character" to confront Mait and exact his revenge. When he asks Mait what he has to say about the situation, Mait stays in character, reciting lines from the play. But in a scene more reminiscent of *West Side Story* than the original *Romeo and Juliet*, Rasmus kills Mait before, fatally wounded himself, he falls dying into the arms of Mirtel. In a last dramatic rendering of the problematic issue at the core of the play, exploring the relationship between art and life, Mirtel walks away from the stage, towards her apartment, disappearing finally in the space between the two.

Whereas most attempts to make reality problematic usually devolve into juvenile exercises in post-modern excesses, Ojasoo relies on nuance, composing a self-referential model in which, to play Romeo, he cast Mait Malmsten, a star of Estonian theatre (fast approaching middle-age) already typecast as a "Romeo," a handsome "ladies' man." According to Ojasoo, Malmsten is no less vain in his off-stage life. So the casting, within the nature of the original play, created an interesting layer of meanings where life inside and outside the play intersected in a metaphor calling into question where the character begins and the actor stops, and vice-versa. In his actual life, Malmsten, an aging "Romeo," is cast to play Romeo the character from Shakespeare's drama, a role he is actually too old to play but tries anyway, hoping against all odds to render Shakespeare's character effectively. This structuring manages to conflate several clichés while considering the relationships in a fresh way that not only reinvigorates Shakespeare's play but also the audience's appreciation of the irony that, in itself, becomes a new, interesting reality created from basically hackneyed material.

Ojasoo mischievously asks, "When Romeo kisses Juliet, who is he kissing? Juliet? Or the young girl playing Juliet?" Indeed, the question reverberates throughout the performance. Who is *this* Romeo? An aging lecher having a go at a young girl, a serious actor searching for the psychological motivation for his character's action, some combination of truth and fiction that fuses into a complex synthesis conditional (and dependent on) the audience's understanding of the controlling irony?

Malmsten acknowledged this ontological dilemma during one rehearsal when he confessed to Ojasoo that there is "no one role of Romeo" he could play. That, says Ojasoo, is "the situation we started from," abstracting the roles into metaphors representing, not literally depicting, the relationships, distilling the essences, in a sense, to fit Ojasoo's ironic treatment of the play.

Another performance Ojasoo cites as an example of his direction in theatre is *Sometimes I Feel Life is Over and There is No Love* (*Vahel on tunne, et elu saab otsa ja armastust polnudki*). An actor is asked to read a poem, and then the "director" puts the actor through a series of physical exercises until the actor is "pushed beyond exhaustion" and literally collapses. Then he is asked to read the poem again, and this time the rendition is, in the director's eyes, closer to the truth he wants: a truly exhausted person on stage, not someone acting the part of an exhausted person. Another actor, instead of being physically "tortured" — Ojasoo's term — is dressed up like a clown before announcing to the audience that he will tell a series of jokes but with no plan — operating on purer improvisation — continuing until he runs out of ideas and becomes a senseless babbler, but the director has him keep going by asking the audience to help him, offering suggestions and making up material for him.

"Sometimes it works; sometimes it doesn't," says Ojasoo. But of course that is the point: neither exercise can be acted, only experienced, and each performance is different. The idea, similar to the conceit in *Juliet*, is to "touch the limits of what is playing and what is real. In *Sometimes I Feel* the actor is totally free to push the possibilities of improvisation, carrying on without a text. The director's job is to lead the actors to their limits, then beyond — in one case physically, in the other mentally — but the director can take the actors only so far or control them only so much, conceptualizing what he wants the actors to do, but after that the actors are on their own.

In another irony that seems too pat to be contrived, Ojasoo's Theatre NO99, a 200 seat black box financed by the State, shares a building with the Estonian Ministry of Defense. "We can't go on the roof," Ojasoo says, wryly, "because it's protected by cameras and wires and the Estonian CIA. About the name NO99, Ojasoo says, "It's just a number to start the countdown toward number one, which is our goal. Theatre can't last forever, so ..." He trails off, typically enigmatic.

Equally enigmatic is Hendrik Toompere's notion of "Zen theatre." The term (which Kolk uses also to refer to Koldits' work) implies nothing directly related to Zen Buddhism, but, Toompere says, refers instead to his interest in Zen paradoxes, "the idea that it is possible to construct scenes so they confront each other, collide and explode ... only then does the meaning become clear." The process implies a return to an organic appreciation of nature, "a de-ritualisation of everyday life" (Toompere, "First There was Nature"). He locates the crisis in Estonian culture "at the point of intersection between the mythological past and the mythological future." Mass consumerism may have replaced Soviet control of economic activity, but society is no less "threatened by the disappearance of individualism and the invasion of collectivism," as both reduce life to "everyday rituals and their concealed side." The process resembles a Hegelian dialectic, but the synthesis must occur emotionally, not rationally. Toompere's process also involves more than two ideas — the usual dyadic distinction in the Hegelian model — all conflicting and eventually discharging, but if the play is successful reassembling into new truths "beyond language" that must "just be understood."

Unlike a text-based playwright like Tätte, Toompere, echoing Koldits, is suspicious of words, stressing the impossibility of language to explain visual and emotional truths. But, he admits, relying on purely visual stimuli to communicate dramatic truths to an audience is risky because the technique, ambiguous by its nature, does not always work. Toompere claims a twenty-five percent success rate. He further quantifies his approach by speculating that his productions "should be sixty percent understandable through visual means." To underscore his faith in the visual aspects of theatre, Toompere lists, along with Kantor and Grotowski, the influence of Bosch, Bruegel and Dali, painters who inspired him to incorporate striking, complex images into his work.

Correlative to his emphasis on the visual at the expense of the oral, Toompere considers the text only an idea. "Narrative logic is not the most important element," he says, a precept that explains why, by his own confession, he has never staged Shakespeare. With more than a dose of tongue-in-cheek deference, he says, "Shakespeare is too good for me." What he means, in the context of his directing style, is that plays that are so well-composed and absolutely dependent on the words in the script render his approach unsuitable for doing justice to the piece. "Sometimes the text fights me," he says. "And if the text is stronger than I am, the play fails." Toompere prefers texts that do not dictate how the play should be directed — even further, as in the case of Shakespeare, he avoids plays in which the text is vital, indispensable for revealing the truth of the work. To overcome the artistic impositions inherent in a text-based play — written and designed for staging — Toompere chooses adaptations, of novels for instance, because the director is necessarily more free to interpret the material. "Nobody knows how to stage a novel," Toompere says, indicating that the sprawling text needs a visual rendering that, released from its genre, becomes an authentically new experience and shifts the relationship from writer-reader to writer-director-viewer, with the director positioned for an interdiction that allows a radical reshaping of the material.

Estonian theatre, in Toompere's opinion, is and has always been an actor's theatre. "Almost all the Estonian directors are actors," he says, an attribute he exploits from his own constant work as an actor that allows him "to see the play like a mirror." He admits that his sympathy — that is, his ability to identify firsthand with an actor's journey into a character — often works against his role as a director, interfering with the discipline he knows he needs to bring to a production to create the structure as he envisions it. Though he resists the tight blocking institutionalized by many professional directors — especially the Lithuanians — he acknowledges the conflict: "Maybe I'm too close to the actors and should be more assertive — less like an actor, more like a director." Still, his work as an actor combined with his director's "eye" allows him, as Kolk notes, to combine the psychological theatre of the Russians with the raw physicality of Tooming's approach to create a new synthesis — the result of his "paradoxical thinking" — that has become his signature style. Of the productions he considers successful — *Notos de Cochinas* by Rodrigo Garcia and *Festin* by Thomas Vinterberg and Mogens Rukov — Toompere cites Viktor Pelevin's *Hermit and Six-Toes* as a prime example of his style.

Pelevin's story relies on the absurdist notion of what might happen if a pair of "sentient" chickens developed not only will but also a talent for metaphysical systems and a desire for cosmological speculation, suggesting that the limited experience of chickens making sense of their lives is synonymous with man's attempts throughout history to understand the purpose of existence. The result is that *Hermit and Six-Toes* is both a comical story about two chickens stuck in a Soviet poultry combine and a philosophical discourse on love, truth, destiny and spirituality. As the two characters plot to scale the "Wall of the World," their reductive observations about life resemble the stratagems of transcendental philosophers, the implication being that humans who try to comprehend the origin and purpose of life, beyond mere survival, may as well be flailing around like a pair of chickens trapped in a poultry processing plant. When the chickens manage to escape the confines of the feeding pen, they end up on a conveyor belt delivering them to be butchered. But these two chickens, adhering, in their fashion, to the teachings of Socrates and Jesus, have been fasting to purify themselves. As Hermit points out in one of his sermons, "Your flesh is sinful, because of it the gods strike you down." They have also been exercising their wings, hoping to fly — even though neither is quite sure what "to fly" means. In a final hilarious twist, Hermit and Six-Toes resist being slaughtered at the last moment by the gods — workers in the processing factory — by flying through a broken glass window to freedom.

The story, an obvious satire of communist ideology, is also an ironic critique on the futility of mystical philosophers to provide useful insight into the ultimate mystery of life. The two chickens, reluctant prophets exhorting their "flock" to exercise and fast to resist being slaughtered, are in the end thrown back on their own desire and resourcefulness to take control of their individual destinies. (The processors delay killing them because they are too scrawny, and the strength in their wings allows them to fly to freedom.) Though Pelevin maintains a Malthusian bottom line — humans are no different from chickens being fattened at the trough, uneasily awaiting their day of slaughter — he manages to elevate the struggle by Hermit and Six-Toes merely to survive into an epical human event.

Transferring the action of *Hermit and Six-Toes* to the stage suggests several problems for Toompere, not the least of which is that the actors play chickens (plus an equally inquisitive rat) — all with a penchant for philosophical disquisitions. Also, Pelevin's text, heavy on conversation, lacks engaging dramatic action. In response, Toompere reduces the story to its essence and sets the action within a minimalist world of interlaced bars and staggered platforms on which the actors swing and strut, molting and preening and clucking their discourse. The challenge, and therefore the appeal of the play for Toompere, is for the actors to present faithfully the unique perspective Pelevin develops through his characters, respecting their limitations as creatures whose philosophical queries pose questions beyond their experience while making them human enough to engage an audience's empathy. The characters are not allegories; they do not represent: they exhibit the characteristics of chickens, albeit with the anthropomorphisms Pelevin assigns them. Their humanity is expressed in their frailty, in their vulnerability, but also in their cunning — in the manner of Tom Sawyer or Brer Rabbit — and their absolute desire for freedom.

The play is typical of projects favored by Toompere. It is, first, adapted from a text that was not originally a dramatic piece, allowing Toompere a clean slate on which to visualize the story. Second, the play fits the Lutheran tradition of a text-based sermon extolling the virtues of discipline, hard work and brotherly love. Finally, because of the static nature of the material, the actors must provide the central dramatic action by their physical rendering of the psychological state of the characters that are, after all, anthropomorphized chickens. The action remains faithful to Pelevin's text.

The characters, in their dirty white feathers, are a study in high contrast: Hermit is condescending, proud and stoical, while Six-Toes is tenuous, nervous and needy. They scurry around the stage, twitching and syncopated, Hermit philosophizing and Six-Toes agonizing about their situation, until Hermit establishes authority by foretelling the exact moment when darkness will fall, like a Pre-Socratic predicting an eclipse. In the ensuing darkness, they discuss the nature of fear. When the lights come up, the characters are roosting in the scaffolding. Six-Toes, weak-willed and fearful, spouts the standard Soviet narrative of their situation — the "official formula" — couched in ideological clichés that, when challenged by Hermit, he can only explain in circular arguments. "In the center of the world," Six-Toes recites, "is the two-tiered feeder. [...] The place of an individual is determined by his social worth and services. [...] Outside the Socium is the Great Waste, bordered by the World-Wall" — the Iron Curtain. Hermit, more purposeful and courageous, sees the world in concrete terms, identifying their environment as, in the language of the gods, the V.I. Lenin Poultry Factory, a huge closed space from which they must escape if they want to realize their potential in freedom. When Hermit explains that their life began in "white spheres," Six-Toes faints. Revived, he begins to recall his birth, nesting and brooding, and inspires a comical chicken-or-the-egg debate that, in this case, is decidedly ontological.

They devise a plan to "infuriate" the other members of the Socium so they will expel them over the Wall of the World, and amidst a flurry of feathers they make their escape out of the Socium onto a conveyor belt in a corridor leading to Shop Number One, the site of what they know will be the "Decisive Stage" in their quest for meaning. Again in darkness, they wander a path through the factory, trying to avoid the ubiquitous rats. The rat they finally encounter — One-Eye — turns out to be Hermit's friend. She is called One-Eye because her "third eye" is open. She too is a mystic, an enlightened fellow-traveler. However, her world is subterranean, and her journey into freedom will lead her into the sewers of the factory. As Hermit explains when he declines to follow her, "Down is not our way."

Amid the screams of the slaughter house and a snowstorm of plucked feathers, Hermit describes the gory details of life after death: "Our bodies are dissected and fried in huge pans. Sometimes we are baked whole in iron chambers [...] boiled in monstrous pots [...] frozen in blocks of ice." Hermit, however, has a plan, and exhorts Six-Toes to begin exercising his wings to prepare to fly to freedom. During their workouts, they listen to the voices of the gods, at one point interrupting their regimen to sing in supplication, but frantically continuing their practice, flapping among the chains and bars of the scaffolding. Their predicament becomes dire when Six-Toes is tagged with a blue ribbon — presumably because of his six toes. Hermit interprets this as a sign of the gods recognizing Six-Toes as a prophet, so he devises a sermon, imploring the other chickens to "overcome sin" by fasting, claiming that their feeding habits, which fatten them, are the root of their transgressions and the reason for their suffering at the hands of the gods. But the gods are not placated. The voices disparage the scrawny chickens — assuming the feeder must be broken — and they dismiss Hermit's prayer as so much "squawking." Grabbed by a butcher, Six-Toes pecks him in the eye and escapes. In a mystical moment of decisiveness, the chickens — transformed from theoretical beings to ones of action — overcome their limitations and fly to the top of the scaffolding where they perch in silhouette, framed by a russet glow from the window.

Toompere is convinced that Estonian theatre can be "internationalized" by relying less on text-based scripts and creating more visually dynamic performances because, he says, "images speak a universal language." Even so, he understands that part of the importance of theatre lies in its ability to keep the language alive, especially the stories crafted from the national speech that are essential in maintaining the unique Estonian culture alive. It is this chauvinism that, according to Toompere, provokes audiences to resist physical, metaphorical and/or purely visual theatre. Because of this resistance on the part of the audiences to abandon, in a sense, their cultural roots as they perceive them being preserved in the language of the theatre, Toompere concedes that compromises must be made or the audiences will quit supporting theatre. "If they don't understand," he says flatly, "they won't come." In a 2005 interview in *Estonian Art*, Toompere explains that he understands the hesitation of the Estonian audience to embrace more avant-garde works, while recognizing the dilemma as more than a mere an aesthetic phenomena for artistic directors and the writers, actors and directors they support:

> ... a touch of documentary has become a necessity, because everything is illusory and nothing can be trusted. Newspapers, television, chat rooms [...] it is all one big illusion [...] People no longer want to see quite so much artistic imagery in theatre but prefer, rather, authentic reality [...] the spectators must believe in what they see on stage, and therefore whatever takes place there has to have at least some resemblance of real life [qtd. in Epner].

To educate an audience — that is, to create an ideological and aesthetic base that accepts and even expects experimental work — could put the very existence of theatre at risk.

But Toompere is optimistic. Convinced that people are fed up with the artificial realities of newspapers and advertisements, he believes theatre offers something real in a world where society seems more and more unreal. To this end, he advocates "environmental theatre" — that is, staging plays outside the normal confines of a theatre, setting *Festin*, for example, in an old German manor house because the characters in the play were wealthy and accustomed to that world, or staging *Rosencrantz and Guildenstern Are Dead* in Padise Monastery because it suits the time and theme of the play (as Klemets did by staging McGuinness' *Someone Who'll Watch Over Me* in Kõismäe Tower). Toompere insists that to fill the "emptiness of reality" in Baudrillard's post-modern nightmare of media fabrication, people are hungry for a realism only theatre can provide.

"Environmental theatre works closer to cinema," he says (echoing Klemets), "but in theatre the audience sees real people, up close, in an actual space, not a set. Everything is real — even the illusion of real is real."

Working in a totally different direction from her contemporaries (validating, perhaps, Toompere's observation that people need "a touch of documentary" in their lives), yet no less concerned with the relationship between what is "truth" and what is "real," Merle Karusoo investigates life theatrically through a process critics refer to as "documentary theatre." Indeed, Madis Kolk questions if her method can be categorically considered theatre. "She is on a mission," he says, suggesting that her approach resembles more art therapy or an encounter group than true dramatic presentation. There are no scenes, sometimes no "action," only people talking, sometimes actors, other times actors not acting but talking about themselves. Rähesoo suggests that the modern prototype for this kind of play began with Madis Kõiv, and his self-described "'memory plays' based on his personal reminiscences (*Returning to Father—Tagasitulek isa juurde*)" ("The Estonia Drama Revisited" 28), which even Kõiv, anticipating Kolk's qualification above, described as "'untheatrical'" (qtd. in Rähesoo, "The Estonia Drama Revisited" 28).[13] But critics like Paulus describe Karusoo as being "in a class of her own."

Steeped in the tradition of Soviet documentary films, Karusoo says her goal is to "gather life stories together" using memories. She describes both her purpose and her method as a process of recovery, in the sense of regaining and healing. She explains that the first mass deportation in 1944 created a psychological condition in Estonia, through Soviet repression, she calls "memory blocks." By forbidding people to discuss the Estonian Republic, the situation from 1918–1940, and punishing anyone who dared tell their children about the former independent state, the Soviets in effect tried to erase the collective memory of Estonian culture. By the time of the second mass deportation in 1949, the ability to enjoy any group identity was further restricted when harsh repressive measures were again imposed — for instance, not allowing more than three people to congregate in public at any given time and enforcing rules of silence on anyone associated with the deportations.

But in the 1980s, during the period of Gorbachev's *perestroika* and *glasnost*, people did begin to talk, and as this gradual recounting (and acknowledgement) of the atrocities began to percolate through the public, Karusoo says she discovered the phenomenon of "memory blocks." She recalls teaching acting in 1982, when people had just begun to feel free enough to openly discuss the Estonian political and social situation. She encouraged her students to open up about their concerns, their personal problems, to voice criticism of the Soviet system that they knew was depriving them of the opportunities for free expression and career choices others their age enjoyed on the other side of the Iron Curtain. As these young people explored — and vocalized — their various issues, they suddenly began talking about parents who had been arrested and grandparents who had been deported. One student's monolog detailed a visit she made to the Berlin Wall — a topic deemed taboo by the authorities, or the *Glavlit*, the organization responsible for controlling the content of publications and performances but which also had the power to restrict the topics of private meetings and even casual conversations.

When she composed these students' stories into a stage presentation, the censors told her to take out the offending material — about the arrests, the deportations, the impressions the student shared about her trip to the Wall. Karusoo says she faced a decision: to perform the piece with the material left in and risk punishment or remove it and compromise her values and the truth of the students' experiences. She discussed her dilemma with friends and colleagues from the University of Tartu and decided to perform the work in 1982 only six times to a select, obviously sympathetic audiences.

"Only six hundred people saw it," she says.

But that work, *When Space is Over-Crowded* (*Kui ruumid on täis*), was a landmark performance for Karusoo because it represented the first time that she could remember when a group of people were openly talking about themselves, criticizing the situation, honestly confronting life under Soviet control and, in defiance of the *Glavlit*, sharing their ideas with others in a public space.

In another attempt, with *Children's Lives* (*Laste riskiretk*) — originally titled *Children's Trip of Risks*, implying a neologism from the word "crusade" ("ristiretk") — Karusoo used the same technique, this time taping over thirty hours of material to create two performances — one that was allowed by the *Glavlit* and one that was banned. Again, her compatriots in Tartu considered the tapes dangerous, but they convinced her to go ahead with the production. In 1987 she staged *Report* (*Aruanne*), which chronicled the lives of elderly people — many victims of the infamous "memory blocks" — and she noticed that with this work her method of recovery was successful in both senses: not only were stories of the times graphically recalled, but once the memories became stories, more and more people from the audiences — old people invited to the performance — began to tell their stories, creating a cathartic, therapeutic purging of repressed memories.

A freak event provoked her next project, technically more of a true documentary than her previous work. During the difficult years of transition just after independence, a former classmate was senselessly murdered by a gang of strangers. As she watched the court proceedings she asked herself, as if the answer would explain or help her cope with the absurdity of what had happened, "Who are murderers in Estonia?" Trained as a sociologist, she used her skills to research and interview forty murderers in prisons around Estonia and found only one Estonian among them. (The gang that killed her friend was composed of a Belarusian, an Estonian-Russian and a Russian girl.) Ironically, these "outsiders" were runaways from Russian poverty, raised in Estonian orphanages and, in a sense, victims of society themselves. Titled only in English as *Save Our Souls*, the performance played in Estonian and Russian, using actors from mixed families so they could express the truth and tragedy of the inequities of the mismatched cultural realities.

As for her method, Karusoo claims that her impatience with the trappings of conventional theatre is based on her faith in verisimilitude. "My problem," she says, "is that the words people use are more important than so-called acting and playing." To resolve this need to present her subject but not necessarily to perform it, when she does use a more traditional dramatic method, instead of the actual people whose stories she is recasting, she has the actors assume the role of the person telling the story. Some work contains more theatre elements than others, and she admits that she prefers to use only words, but she also understands that audiences like theatre, so she tries to incorporate dramaturgical aspects into her work as long as these "effects" do not interfere or obfuscate her strong sense of truth.

4

Latvia: Focus on Process — Actors' Theatre

Guna Zeltiņa, from the Institute of Literature, Folklore and Art at the Latvian Academy of Sciences, traces Latvian theatre to "the days of the pagan ritual" (37), suggesting that "theatre has been one of the most permanent passions of the characteristically reserved, Northern-tempered Latvian people" (37). Rähesoo agrees, noting that "[f]olkloristically the Finno-Ugric inheritance connects the Estonians to the shamanistic world of the hunters and fishers of northern Eurasia [and] Latvians and Lithuanians [...] with the agricultural beliefs and customs of the regions lying to the south" (*Estonian Theatre* 14).

But though its roots are firmly planted in the pagan world of North European tribalism, Latvia shares its modern cultural heritage with the Teutonic and Hanseatic traditions of Estonia. Valda Čakare, a critic and Professor of Theatre and Drama at the Latvian Academy of Culture, flatly rejects the notion that Latvian theatre stems from pagan rituals: "Latvian theatre did not develop out of its folklore. On the contrary, it was strongly influenced by Germany, from acting style to theatre architecture" (82). For Čakare, the independence movement of 1918 created a paradox that remains influential today: "The national liberation was simultaneously a rejection of German supremacy and an adaptation of their cultural institutions" (82). Lithuania, itself a former imperial country, fiercely resisted assimilation, but after its strategic alliance with Poland its cultural roots ran deep into the Catholic tradition, while in Protestant Latvia and Estonia "the German element became predominant" (Rähesoo 14). Rähesoo points out that Riga was a hub for the Livonians as early as the twelfth century, and later in the modern period developed into a financial and cultural nexus for the entire Baltic German community. He writes:

> Speaking of Baltic German theatre one must also mention Riga as the biggest city and cultural centre of the region. Until 1917 it was also the administrative centre of a district (Livonia) comprising northern Latvia and southern Estonia. It had a sizeable Estonia community, and people from southern Estonia (including Tartu) often had more business in Riga than in Tallinn. Undoubtedly many of them also visited its thriving German theatre [22].

Most critics mark the establishment of the Riga Latvian Theatre (Rīgas Latviešu teātris) in 1868 as the beginning of professional theatre in Latvia. A project envisioned by a group of Latvian intellectuals, private employers and merchants gathered under the rubric of the Riga Latvian Society, this early theatre, although heavily influenced by the German styles of the times, established regular performances in Riga, initiating the trend towards a national Latvian theatre. The Riga Russian Drama Theatre (Rīgas Krievu drāmas teātris), the oldest professional theatre still operating in Latvia, and the oldest Russian Drama theatre outside of the Russian Federation, opened in 1883. Under the guidance of K.N. Nezlobin and K.A. Marazhanov, the Riga Russian Drama Theatre established a "director's theatre" faithful to the principles of realism. During the 1890s, the first of the mature and original Latvian playwrights began to emerge, most notably Elza Rozenberga, known by her pen-name, Aspazija, and Rūdolfs Blaumanis, whose play *Tailor Days in Silmachi* (*Skroderdienas Silmačos*) is considered by some to be the most loved play in Latvian theater history. Following this "renaissance," the New Riga Theatre (Jaunais Rīgas teātris) was founded in 1908 to stage the symbolic verse dramas of Janis Rainis, one of Latvia's most important poets.

The Latvian National Theatre (Latvijas Nacionālais teātris) was established after Latvia declared its independence in 1918. And although the German influence on Latvian theatre continued as emphatically as it had in Estonia, the Russian influence, especially the predominant style of psychological realism, soon dominated the training of actors and directors. By 1920, however, The Art Theatre (Dailes teātris), under the management of director-actor Eduards Smiļģis, introduced a physical and metaphorical style of theatre, stressing music, lighting and movement over psychological intensity, more in the tradition of Meyerhold and Alexander Tairov. When Latvia was annexed by the Soviet Union in 1941, ideological pressure from the Communist Party stifled much of the creativity of the resurgent theatre; however, the Soviet occupation in 1940, then again after World War II, secured the dominance of Russian dramatic literature and theatre methodology, especially Stanislavsky's approach. In 1945, all Latvian theatre companies officially became state theatres, operating with significant government subsidies involving large resident acting companies.

As in the other Baltic states, the 1960s in Latvia were a period of experimentation with various styles, including new approaches to psychological realism in the work of Alfrēds Jaunušans and Oļģerts Kroders, Brechtian expressionism in Ādolfs Šapiro, and the introduction of a modern verse theatre by Pēteris Pētersons. In 1970s The Art Theatre, under the direction of Arnolds Liniņš, revived the experimental style of Smiļģis, the founder of The Art Theatre. Other playwrights that achieved national status as innovators include Gunārs Priede, Pauls Putniņš and Harijs Gulbis, and Māra Ķimele while in the 1980s a new generation of directors — Valdis Lūriņš, Kārlis Auškāps and Valentīns Maculēvičs — began to revitalize and modernize classic Latvian and contemporary plays. These directors — especially Šapiro at the revamped Latvian Youth Theatre (Latvijas Jaunatnes teātris) and Arkady Kacs at the Riga Russian Drama Theatre — emphasized a more poetic-metaphorical theatre. Inspired by the pioneering work of the older generation, a new group of dynamic younger directors like Alvis Hermanis, Viesturs Kairišs, Dž. Dž. Džilindžers, and Regnārs Vaivars began experimenting with a more visual, physical theatre — incorporating into their productions post-modern strategies and mixed-media performances — while others, like Kroders, Ķimele and Felikss Deičs revived the tradition of staging realistic psychological and philosophical dramas. The 1980s also produced female playwrights like Māra Zālīte and Lelde Stumbre, who brought feminist perspectives to the Latvian stage.

By the 1990s, as elsewhere in the former satellite countries, Latvia faced two interrelated problems. First, the collapse of the state subsidy system for funding theatre arts created economic hardships for even the most established troupes. By 2003 only eight professional theatres were subsidized by the government, five of which were in Riga. Zeltiņa complains how "spiraling inflation [...] forced [theatres] to engage in a desperate battle for survival in their search for private sponsorship" (37), causing "a complete rejection of ideology" (37). This loss of social relevance combined with the correlative reduction in state funding created an aesthetic deficit. "In most cases, artistry and experimentation were superseded by commercially-safe ventures" (39). Most theatres, if they did not simply shut down, were so compromised by their pandering to mass cultural tastes — reduced to staging "'forbidden fruit': plays by Western and Latvian émigré authors" (37) — that the once engaged theatre of social activism that until 1991 had "played an important intellectual and spiritual role in Latvian society" (37) abandoned its mission, as it were, failing not only "to reflect the current tensions in the society" (37) but also stifling artistic creativity, cultivating an environment so sterilized that "Latvia's own playwrights withered" (37).

Many critics hope for a revival of traditions in a new theatre language, citing both Gaļina Poliščuka and Hermanis as the primary reformers — Poliščuka for her revisionist treatment of classic plays recast using contemporary techniques and language, Hermanis for his sensitive turn to the human individual as a proper subject for theatre. These critics prefer Poliščuka's ability to present dated material in fresh ways to the dated techniques associated with Stanislavskian realism and Hermanis' focus on psychology to the abandonment of all pretense to realism by the likes of Džilindžers. Ieva Zole encapsulates the feeling of many progressive critics when she admires directors who "return to the human being [...] to the study of man as an individuality" (qtd. in Grīnbauma) and disparages those who seem more interested in sheer theatricality:

> Thus the theatre in Latvia moves on taking a step backwards to take on board human meaning. Therefore discarding different marginal phenomena that are staged for the box-office purposes only to sink into oblivion after seeing them, the serious theatre of Latvia is looking in one direction, speaks about the same things although through the use of different forms, manner of representation, means of expression [qtd. in Grīnbauma].

She cites the work at New Riga under the management of Hermanis as evidence that Latvian theatre can be accepted — understood and appreciated — in foreign countries without sacrificing its national identity. New Riga, she writes, "has brought the name of Latvia into the world and proved that it can be done also by an art form closely linked to this country" (qtd. in Grīnbauma).

Riga

From inside the city center, including the medieval section, Riga appears as a small but thriving metropolis. The streets, tastefully lined with posh shops, inviting restaurants and quaint cafes, are bustling, orderly and clean. Embassy Row and the Art Nouveau sections are polished and fashionable. The parks are manicured. The Old Town is heaving with tourists. The Bentleys, Beamers and Benzes do not look as out of place on the smart streets of Riga as they do in Vilnius or Tallinn. The beggars are less visible — except for the occasional teenagers dressed in Diesel ski jackets and Calvin Klein jeans trying to pass themselves off as eleven year old Russian orphans panhandling the pedestrian zones, or the odd handicapped derelict loitering by the central shopping mart jingling change in a can and mumbling prayers.

The prosperity is historical. Founded in 1201, Riga has always been an important international commercial hub. In the fourteenth and fifteenth centuries, it was the most developed center of the Hansa Union, ideally situated on the cross-roads between Eastern and Western Europe as well as between Russia and Scandinavia. Now, Riga is not only the largest city in the Baltic States but also the most important center of industry, finance and transport in the Baltic region. In addition to its commercial success, the city's architecture is well preserved and impressive, ranging from the compactness of the medieval fortified town with its irregular form and urban density, to the wide nineteenth century boulevards that resemble the Ring Strasse in Vienna, including an ensemble of Art Nouveau buildings famous throughout Europe.

Outside the city center, however, excluding the odd pockets of novelty in the suburbs (some featuring a unique collection of old wooden houses), the indicators of the economic split between those in the higher income brackets and the others struggling for a decent salary (or subsisting on meager pensions and inadequate incomes) is painfully evident.

While Latvia hosts important theatres outside the capital — including the "big three" of Daugavpils Theatre (Daugavpils teātris), Liepāja Theatre (Liepājas teātris) and Valmiera Drama Theatre (Valmieras Drāmas teātris) — the core players work in Riga.[14] Of the major theatres in the city, the most traditional — i.e., the one catering to the largest bloc of theatre-going audiences seeking popular entertainment and Latvian classics — is the National. The stately building housing the theatre sits alongside the sweeping Basteja boulevard on the edge of the city canal (pilsētas kanāls), adjacent to the Old Town. The interior is not as spacious as it would seem, given the appearance of the facility from the outside, but the main performance area, with its loges and contoured balcony ensconced in its recently renovated baroque interior — an impressive example of an old style German design — still manages to seat 780. Another smaller basement space called Actors Hall, seats 100, and an even more intimate space, the New Hall, is used for experimental work and staged readings.

The building originally housed the Second Riga City Theatre (Otrais Rīgas pilsētas teātris); in 1918 it became the National. (Independence for Latvia was announced from its main stage.) During the Soviet occupation in 1940, its name was changed to simply the Drama Theatre (Drāmas teātris) to indicate its annexation. But in 1988, reflecting Gorbachev's initiatives, its name was reinstated as the National. It bills itself as a "traditional repertory theatre, preferred mainly by audiences adhering to stable values, usually — the elder generation" ("Latvian National"), and it prides itself for the "cultivation of constant, positive ethical ideals." Known for "staging Latvian classics" such as *Tailor Days in Silmachi* as well as plays by established modern Latvian playwrights, the National considers itself an actors' theatre, allowing the company precedence over the work of its directors.[15] The National rarely stages foreign plays or contemporary work by young Latvian playwrights. In fact, except for anomalous productions like Vaivars' adaptation of *A Clockwork Orange*, the National resists deviating from its traditional program, staging avant-garde and experimental pieces on both its main stage and its smaller spaces only when hosting festivals and showcases like Homo Novus and Spēlmaņu Nakts.[16] This adherence to traditional "safe" theatre combined with its tentative willingness to indulge more aesthetically risky work creates an odd, somewhat conflicted approach to its stated "mission," an antithetical doubling evident, for instance, when it presents a decidedly middle-brow musical like *The Sphinx* (*Sfinksa*), then provides the space to stage a more experimental dance piece like *One More Night and One More Morning* (*Vēl viens vakars vēl viens rīts*). Though both the audience and the actors at the National resist change, as the stable audience ages and is replaced by a younger generation with a more progressive sensibility, adaptation is inevitable.

Evidence of the National's awareness of this evolution from stodgy predictable classics to more edgy experimental performances is indicated by its inclusion in its repertoire of Gaļina Poliščuka's treatment of Rainis' play *Blow, Wind!* (*Pūt, vējiņi!*), a classic reworked through a feminist perspective and staged in a contemporary fashion that marks a radical departure from the National's usual, more conservative style.

The action of the play is based on an old marriage ritual in which men cross the Daugava (the largest river in Latvia) to choose suitable wives from a local village. (The title is borrowed from a song sung by young men

Rēzija Kalniņa in Gaļina Poļiščuka's treatment of Rainis' play *Blow, Wind!* at the Latvian National Theatre, Riga. Poļiščuka's approach illustrates a strong tendency in contemporary Latvian theatre to rethink the staging of classic plays, thus preserving Latvian heritage while using modern acting methods to reinvigorate the dated material. This consideration represents a determined attempt to connect the country's past with its present, employing contemporary sensitivities while maintaining the eternal elements of traditional tragedy. In this way Poļiščuka remains faithful to the historical aspect of the piece while presenting the material as a current predicament. She manages to accomplish the nifty (and difficult) trick of transforming traditional folk customs into a modern context, using contemporary stage language, without ruining the uniqueness of the original play (photograph by Ojārs Jansons).

bragging about their virility.) In this telling, a boatman named Uldis and a male companion arrive at the farmhouse of a wealthy landowner who lives with his daughters Zane and Anda, along with another girl Baiba, an orphan who lives with the family. A year before Uldis had been involved with Zane, and both she and her mother now expect Uldis to marry her. Instead, Uldis is intrigued with Baiba, who vehemently resists his advances and proposals. Because getting a husband is not only one of the few methods to achieve prosperity available to the village girls but is also more often than not a question of survival, the two sisters engage in a savage competition for Uldis, but he continues to pursue Baiba. At first, Uldis wants her only because she rejects him, but later he begins to appreciate her idealism. In the end, Baiba realizes that Uldis' love for her is genuine and agrees to go with him, but seeing that her happiness results from the misfortune of others, she drowns herself in the river.

The performance space is a bare black floor bordered with a wooden frame like a sandbox and flanked by bleacher seating on either side. Arrayed around the frame are various farm implements — traditional tools and baskets along with costumes on wooden scarecrow-like manikins. The effect creates a scene from a museum, where historical artifacts are on display. The actors and musicians enter from the audience in normal street clothes, like students visiting an exhibition, but soon each one pauses before a display and begins to undress, stripping out of their contemporary clothes and donning the costumes of the play, allowing the audience to witness the transformation of the actors into their characters and the creation of theatre time and place, as if carving out a magic space of verisimilitude while acknowledging the limitations of realism. The process also strips away the romantic notions usually associated with Rainis' play and highlights the brutal naturalism that distinguishes Poliščuka's production from more traditional renditions.

Poliščuka's approach illustrates a strong tendency in contemporary Latvian theatre to rethink the staging of classic plays, thus preserving Latvian heritage while using modern acting methods to reinvigorate the dated material. This consideration represents a determined attempt to connect the country's past with its present, employing contemporary sensitivities while maintaining the eternal elements of traditional tragedy. Curiously, this rendering of *Blow, Wind!* provides a sharp contrast to her earlier work, where she seemed to succumb to the pervasive trend of trying to "contemporize" classics by, for instance, casting Macbeth as a fascist motorcycle gangster, Romeo as an earnest California mall rat, or using multi-media extravaganzas to resituate the time and setting of the original conditions of the dramatic situations. In this piece Poliščuka eschews anachronistic elements and uses no special effects (except for professional lighting): the ambient noises and the music are created live by the actors, the songs and instruments the same today as a hundred years ago. In this way Poliščuka remains faithful to the historical aspect of the piece while presenting the material as a current predicament. She manages to accomplish the nifty (and difficult) trick of transforming traditional folk customs into a modern context, using contemporary stage language, without ruining the uniqueness of the original play.

For Poliščuka, the social issues evident in the play are both universal and particular to Latvia's present situation. The sisters Zane and Anda represent superficial values, using their looks and sex to try to win the favors of men, the same way, suggests Beata Baranovska, Poliščuka's producer, many women from former Soviet bloc countries are "selling" themselves to Westerners, specifically those coming to the Baltics to procure wives. Baiba, in contrast, is authentic; she lives in harmony with nature and resists the temptation to compromise her values for the sake of easy success. Baiba's death in the end is actually restorative, allowing her to preserve the intensity of her joy and integrity, leaving the others alienated from both nature and human dignity.

Not all of the National's forays into reworking classics through modern staging techniques and contemporary acting methods are so radical or successful. *The Sphinx* (*Sfinksa*), for instance, written by established contemporary playwright Māra Zālīte and the composer Jānis Lūsēns and co-directed by Regnārs Vaivars, one of the new generation, and Edmunds Freibergs, the more seasoned Artistic Director of the National, is based on the life Eližens Finks, an astrologer and socialite. Before disappearing into a Soviet gulag, Finks famously predicted that Latvia would regain its independence. The piece mixes film-noir, jazz dance, live rock music, circus stunts, cabaret and magic realism to convey the decadence of the years between World War I and World War II. The plot documents the encroaching impact of Italian and German fascism in Latvia, the equally devastating annexation by the Soviets, and the collapse of the moral, social and spiritual values of the culture.

The performance is predictably sentimental and schmaltzy: a typical old-fashioned musical with flashes of inspired choreography and dramatic effects (attributed by some critics to Vaivars). The overall effect is unapologetically kitsch — designed for mass appeal, reflecting, after all, the National's relationship with its audience. Still, the text represents Zālīte's long-running interest in connecting popular entertainment to poetic themes that explore Latvian national identity.

One of her major projects in this quest stems from a medieval myth set in pagan Latvia during its conquest by German Crusaders that recounts the exploits of Lāčplēsis the Bear Slayer who defends Latvia from assorted invaders.[17] The legend was reworked in the nineteenth century into an epic by the Romantic writer Andejes Pumpurs, and in the early twentieth century was developed into a verse play, *Fire and Night* (*Uguns un Nakts*) by Rainis. Continuing this tradition, and to stimulate and respond to the mounting resistance to the Soviet occupation and the new nationalist movement ignited in Latvia by Gorbachev's *perestroika*, in 1988 Zālīte wrote *Lāčplēsis*, based on the myth of the Bear Slayer. Ten years later she returned to the theme of Latvian nationalism, penning *Kaupēns, My Dear* (*Kaupēns, mans mīļais*), in part based on the legend of Kaupēns, a famous thief and murderer from the 1920s whose name has been immortalized by a popular love song from which the play takes its title. Kaupēns is opposed by his antagonist, the Poet, a gentle man of contemplation, but who in the end loses even his lover to the murderer, punctuating the irrationality of human nature and the sexual attraction of violence. When the play was performed at the 2001 Contemporary Drama Festival, the program noted: "The central theme of the play is the complex, multi-faceted love/hate relationship of Kaupēns with a society [...] which during wartime teaches a man to kill but in peacetime condemns it [and in which] the mass media profit from reporting crime, and through that reporting often breed more crime by people like Kaupēns who thrive on perverse notoriety" (*Skate 2001* 41).

Zālīte's version explores how the outlaw and the poet express two sides of the Latvian national character: the extroverted man of action who does not hesitate to do whatever is necessary for survival, combined with the sensitive, introverted thinker representing the naturally reserved Latvian personality. In this context, *The Sphinx* represents a continuation of Zālīte's exploration of what she identifies as an essential duality defining the collective Latvian psyche, while also investigating Latvian identity within the destabilizing context of globalization, connecting Latvia's history with current events.

Zālīte is as much at home on the small stage as she is working in the epic style on the National's main stage. Her two-person play *All Humans Are Cats* (*Visi cilvēki ir kaķi*; originally titled *Zemos Nodoklis*) demonstrates how her minimalist style can also express universal tragic elements. Staged in the tiny loft-style space above the main performance hall at the Russian Drama Theatre by Felikss Deičs, one of the directors working with Šapiro at the former, highly regarded Youth Theatre, the play indicates the influence of Beckett but achieves an intimacy and passion that sets Zālīte's work off as patently original, analyzing the lives of people who share an unpleasant past and who are now marginalized by society. *All Humans Are Cats* offers a sly comment on contemporary life in the "new" Latvia while emphasizing the timeless values that elevate her play out of mere topicality into a universal tragedy.

The sparse set, barely able to contain its few props — a chest of drawers, a bed on wheels, an end table with a telephone, a small television, piles of books, a tree set into a "garden" niche in the back, a wall plastered with newspapers and photographs of cats — nearly spills into the bleacher seating running the length of the stage. A rope strung horizontally from one end of the room to the other is used as an effective tool for Zente, an old woman who occupies the bed, to pull herself along. Her ex-husband Herman allows her to live in the apartment as long as she continues to pay rent (and a commission when he goes shopping for her, mainly to buy cat food and litter). He converses with her about how much money she owes him, his plans to move away as soon as his emigrant brother returns from Cleveland, and daily updates about a Spanish soap opera. The couple, it seems, can express their harsh love for each other only through bickering, jousting over money and expenses, and arguing about the moral status of the characters involved in the hopelessly convoluted plots of their daytime soap — as if old age has reduced their desire to pettiness.

For his part, Herman lives with the illusion that his brother from Cleveland will show up any day and deliver him from poverty, but the reality of his brother is intrinsically suspect. For Zente, her comforting illusions are invested in her make-believe cat. Her reasoning is simple: "Cats are better than people. They don't start wars or privatization." Her obsession, however, has become so acute that she sends Herman out to buy cat food — a special brand with trout — that she eats herself, insisting the food — like the litter that is never used — is for her ubiquitous but invisible cat.

Herman demands that Zente "get rid" of the cat or he will throw her out. He offers to take the cat's place in her affection, as he had in their younger days when she used to call him "Mittens." She retorts that unlike Herman, her cat does not drink or smoke; plus, her cat has a passport. Herman insists that his brother's arrival is imminent and so Zente must leave to make space for him. Seduced by commercialism, he brags that he and his brother will "shop till we drop."

Soon, however, the illusions that have sustained them in their loneliness and alienation begin to unravel, as does the tapestry of deceit they have used to disguise their pasts from each other. Zente reveals to Herman that she knows he murdered her former lover, a Czech KGB agent. But unknown to Herman she brought the body back from the woods where Herman had hanged the man "like a cat" and buried it under the lilac bush. Her reasoning is that now, if Herman sells the house, the new owners will find the body and will arrest him for his crime. She tells him that she stayed in the house not for him but out of love for her KGB lover.

His revenge is not to tell her about the soaps anymore, though his immediate worry is that his property is about to be confiscated because he is in arrears for property taxes, and both of them now face eviction. When she asks if Herman can at least save his television, he confesses that, in fact, it has never worked and his reports to her have all been cribbed from the TV guide. When she asks him why he has spent so many years talking to her about the soap opera, he says that since his family was tortured and lost in the deportations to Siberia, except for his brother, who he still insists lives in Cleveland, the soap opera provided him with a sense of family, one he could talk to her about. She in turn confesses that her television has been working the whole time, and she no longer needs his reports. In the end, even the eviction notice turns out to have been a mistake, but they discover the error too late. Herman poisons himself, and in a gruesome parody of *Romeo and Juliet*, Zente kills herself too. Only the soaps continue, until the lilac bush falls out of its gate in the wall, spilling onto the stage in a final image of the inability of even theatre to sustain the illusion of life.

The play resonates with meaning for Latvian audiences. On a contemporary social level, the play exposes the distressing plight of the elderly, whose pension programs are constantly at risk in the free market system, whose family properties are threatened by gentrification, and whose abandonment by members of their extended families as they seek employment abroad have left them lonely and isolated in an unfamiliar world that offers little sympathy for the old, the destitute, or the infirm.

The play also dredges up issues many Latvians would prefer to ignore or forget. Herman complains that his family disappeared in a Soviet gulag. Zente confesses that she granted sexual favors to her superiors at the Central Committee to advance her career; though never more than a secretary, she enjoyed caviar and other elaborate perks while her peers had to settle for much more modest fare. Not as pervasive today as during the Soviet-era of corruption and elitist hypocrisy, means of advancement for women in contemporary Latvia are still exploitative in the professional world. The crass commercialism that comes with privatization, the constant need for money and the ideology of measuring value by cost, not quality, causes Herman to calculate the worth of his actions — what others may discount as acts of compassion — in terms of an economic bottom line. He constantly nickels-and-dimes Zente until finally he is driven to suicide, partly (or especially) because of the government's threat to evict him and confiscate property that has been in his family for generations. Also, his faith in his brother is based more on his brother's wealth than any genuine filial affection. All bonds are reduced to economic exploitation, in Herman's case the desire for a bigger apartment and a shopping spree, as if his brother were a modern Robin Hood dispensing money, not justice, compassion or traditional family values.

Theatrically, the play appears to adhere to the tenets of naturalism, but it also creates a kaleidoscopic world of illusions that not only comments on the nature of the theatre but also on the tendency in contemporary society to forsake the actual world for a virtual reality with no real consequences that can be switched on and off like a television (neatly illustrating Baudrillard's theory of how society seeks "ecstasy" by willfully engaging the displacement of reality). The real world is replaced by wishful thinking, the displacement of an actual life with that of an onanistic, imaginary surrogate existence conditioned by avoidance, denial, and, finally, pure desire, whether nostalgic or utopic, nonetheless impossible. The danger in this masturbatory withdrawal from the real — as indicated by Zente's playing with her puppet cat — is reminiscent of Paul in Lawrence's "The Rocking Horse Winner." In this sense, *All Humans Are Cats* displaces metatheatrical assumptions that belie its naturalistic structure, and by its design illustrates the fragile construction of a Latvian society confronting its identity, both as a precious illusion and a hard reality.

While the Main Hall at the National provides all the space and mechanics to accommodate full-scale spectacles like *The Sphinx*, its New Hall at the rear of the complex has begun to be used for works-in-progress, readings and smaller, more experimental black box productions by new writers and directors such as Anta Priedīte, a young recent graduate from the Department of Choreography at the Academy of Culture and the 2003 winner of the Spēlmaņu Nakts' award for outstanding debut. When she was nominated for Best Choreographer at the 2004 Spēlmaņu Nakts, Zeltiņa noted how "her choreography broadens the micro dramaturgy of the performance by revealing the relations among the characters not only with the help of words and dialogues, but also through dance and movement — especially the deepest, hidden layers of the relationships" (qtd in Grīnbauma).

Her performance piece *One More Night and One More Morning*, based on a series of "internet diaries" by the Russian writer Dmitrijis Gorčevs, plays like a student showcase, heavy on metaphorical interpretations, physical theatre, dance routines, improvisation and game playing, narrated by frequent voice-overs and characters directly addressing the audience. Two empty bathtubs dominate the minimalist set, with a red ladder between them and miscellaneous objects — sports coats, silver serving trays, a door hanging horizontally from the fly. The feel is industrial chic, the bright metal ceiling, bare white walls and stark black floor hardly separate from the chairs-on-bleachers seating.

The lights come up on four actors, two men and two women. One of the women reads a letter garbled by the recorded voice-over narrative while the others pantomime various activities — dancing, playing ball, other childhood games — creating a dramatic contrast between the static noise of the reader and the silent action of the other players and implying the impending youthful confusion of being thrown into life, realized in the next scene by a clever birthing image as three of the actors huddle in the womb-like tubs while the fourth, the other woman, stands halfway up the ladder, seemingly capturing the exaggerated breathing of the others in an ever expanding balloon. She caresses the balloon as it swells, like a woman admiring her belly late in pregnancy, until the balloon bursts with a loud bang and the others tumble from the tubs into the world of the play and the action proper begins.

The title illustrates their emergence into the normal activities of life, suggesting, first, a night of insouciant revelry followed by the morning hangover of regret and recrimination, and, second, the day of a life full of activity followed by the inevitable, motionless silence of death. The actors play through a series of events tracing their progress from childhood to young adulthood to maturity, graduating from pillow fights to clubbing, drunken shenanigans to sexual awakening. As each stage of their education devolves into chaos and recklessness, they are interrupted by an adult father figure (incongruously dressed in a formal white suit, cutting a figure uncannily resembling Ricardo Montalban in his role as Mr. Roarke on

Fantasy Island) who does not necessarily organize or channel the children but acts more like a counter-force, never imposing order but always offering choices, encouraging the children to enjoy their youthful exuberance — at one point even suggesting that they might be happier living a shallow "television" life. But even as he stresses that the choices the children make are what will create their characters, his presence restores order and perspective, guides the children through more complex and sophisticated interpersonal engagements, cajoles, criticizes, corrects and celebrates each stage of their maturation process, coaching them through the rituals of school, work, dating, marriage, parenthood and the foibles of adulthood — affairs, disillusionment, physical debilitation, ending in the stasis of death.

The play as performed suffers from some novice miscues — gratuitous soliloquies, overwrought and often inane comedy, amateur dance routines — mainly due to a lack of confidence on the part of Priedīte, as if she is still trying to find her footing, as it were. But some moments demonstrate talent that will surely be channeled into more original and challenging performances. A series of sex tableaux, for instance, constructed by the cast in the dark then illuminated by match-light, create a successful chiaroscuro effect interesting even outside the context of the play. (Priedīte admits she rehashed the scenes from a student project in which the assignment was to create five-minute pieces, so those bits were, as she puts it, "already tested," explaining why they were among the most successful elements in the production.)

More interesting is Priedīte's attempt to transcend the local aspects of the play by having the actors detail their particular Latvian experiences in a way that elevates the exercise to represent the universal pathos of children growing through their innocence, maturing, accepting responsibility, realizing the brevity and fragility of life. In this way, Priedīte illustrates the concern, common with the new generation, of using circumstances of their particular nationality only to frame more general, collective emotions, thereby releasing the theme from its local context to appeal to a wider audience. The pillow fights, the adolescent excessive drinking, the experiments with sexuality, the parental confusion and concern embody common experiences of generational conflicts inherent in any culture. Priedīte is unconcerned with overarching historical parallels; there is no political subtext, no social statements beyond the immediate issue of "growing up." This lack of political framing may seem trite, but the story is meant to be engaging on a strictly personal level without any pretensions to existential themes or heavy philosophical baggage.

This intentional lack of historical perspective marks a distinctive shift in thematic structuring from only a few years earlier, when theatre, to regain its pre-independence stature, felt compelled to address the "new" situation. The result is that for many young artists the theatre is no longer a vehicle for political expression or a tool for social amelioration; it is a personal mode of expression in which technique gives form and substance to an otherwise unremarkable story.

Priedīte readily admits that she created the piece in response to what she sees as a decadence permeating contemporary Latvian theatre — especially evident in performances "where actors are mainly talking, with no action." She prefers a "physical narrative" that renders oral expression moot, allowing the play to be understood outside its verbal context. Her initial impulse was to use two Russian actors speaking Russian mixed with two Latvian actors speaking Latvian, but in the end she had to settle for only one Russian performer — a female dancer who speaks Russian throughout the piece. This polyglot approach reinforces the idea that the action can transcend linguistic and cultural differences and communicate with audiences on a more visceral, alogical level of experience.

Priedīte claims to have happened upon the "diaries" while surfing the internet, and was immediately drawn to the central paradox of Gorčevs' style: the intimacy and the universality of his narrative depicting the everyday lives of ordinary people (a theme suddenly popular in contemporary Baltic theatre, embraced by Karusoo in Estonia, for instance, and Hermanis in Latvia). The approach closely resembles a pseudo-documentary that attempts to achieve a greater semblance to reality than a "straight" drama. Priedīte, however, uses the docudrama format only as a foundation for her metaphorical interpretation of the characters' relationships. She explains the pace of the performance — moody and meditative in spots, then accelerating through time like fast-forwarding a video — as reflecting the contemporary media-driven sense of time, flashing through history in a seamless stream of images, often juxtaposing indiscriminate events without context or any attempt to fix significance to an event beyond the immediate sensation of the moment (Baudrillard's "ecstasy"). Yet she hesitates to editorialize, she says, insisting she takes no moral stance toward the situation; she merely presents the material, leaving ethical judgments to others. By appropriating and exploiting the form of new media as a frame, however, she acknowledges "the way things are" and accepts her complicity, offering both an appreciation of and a critical comment on the nature of commercial art — of advertising reflecting *and* creating our current reality — in which life is reduced to "quickly changing images." Still, she maintains her moral neutrality: "Maybe the modern world is too fast, but maybe people like it that way."

Regarding some of the seemingly arbitrary aspects of the set, the scenographer, Liga Lazdina, a third year student at the Art Academy of Latvia at the time of the premiere, explains the problems in terms of the limitations of the performance space. Whereas the bathtubs proved essential, the horizontal door, originally supposed to serve as a child's slide through the "door" of experience, could not be utilized as intended because the stage was too small. That the set is malleable, however, and easy to transport, is an advantage for touring the piece, and that the play worked anyway, without the slide sequence, testifies to the flexibility of the production, another perceived advantage, keeping the production fresh. "Actors who are continually forced to improvise," says Priedīte, "are usually at their best performance level."

Because of the balkanization of the theatre community — between the repertories's determination to stick to the classics and the need to offer more experimental work to younger audiences — many critics hesitate to draw any generalizations about the direction of Latvian theatre today or to recognize any over-arching themes or movements that might suggest definitive trends. Ieva Zole, Assistant Managing Director of the National, a theatre critic and the author of *Pēteris Pētersons*, the authoritative book on one of the most influential directors in the history of Latvian theatre, neatly summarizes the contemporary situation: basically every theatre in the country — the National, the Art, the New Riga, etc. — caters to the expectations of its stable audience and hires directors that fit the aesthetic ideology of the respective audiences. But because audience expectations drive the venues, Zole admits that the repertoires will change only when the audience changes. For now, audiences — for the most part — demand entertainment. Zole attributes this to a deficiency in the education system that stresses business and vocational/technical programs over humanities. And while acknowledging that audiences will certainly change, she fears that their sensibility will coarsen further, devolving into a need for ever more commercial, popular, comfortable forms of entertainment. She questions whether, in the near future, what now is considered conservative classical theatre — Chekhov or Turgenev, for instance — will be understood by future audiences. Her pessimism may seem extreme, but on the evidence of the situation, her attitude may prove prescient. The problem, in her view, is two-fold: If the audience is lost, the theatres will lose income and decline, but by pandering solely to the tastes of the popular demands of the audience, the theatre risks its artistic integrity.

As for the dearth of original plays being staged in Latvia by Latvian playwrights, Zole suggests that until the indigenous playwrights embrace more physical, metaphorical processes they will remain provincial. She notes that many Latvian playwrights consider contemporary Latvian theatre "too cosmopolitan" and lament the fact that the plays receiving the most attention within professional circles do not address strictly Latvian themes. This split in sensibility — with the writers concerned with local issues and directors more interested in formal experiments — fuels a simmering controversy. Most of the dynamic directors tend to import foreign plays for the chance to stage challenging material, while the popular audiences will support a Latvian playwright even if his or her work is what Zole calls "second-rate." This clash between popular chauvinism and eclectic elitism has led to the odd situation of mediocre plays being staged in halls for huge audiences and important contemporary imports being relegated to small halls.

Zole speculates that the general Latvian theatre-going public is concerned with other issues — a decent working wage, inflation, health insurance, family security — and so when they go to theatres they want to be distracted, entertained: they do not necessarily appreciate the nuance of aesthetics, meta-theatrical theories or the intricacies of contemporary postmodern experiments. According to Zole, Latvians are still heavily influenced by Soviet socialist realism, so they are skeptical of formal, theoretical theatre. Also, the majority of the audiences are more interested in the personalities of the actors, often following favorite actors from one performance to another regardless of the "director's vision" or the aesthetics of the production. The problem for repertory theatres (especially of the old school, like the National) is to choose plays that satisfy both the audience and the directors while adhering to the general cultural ideology of the repertory venue. But this actor-based approach also presents a problem for the ensemble-based theatres (like the New Riga, which purports to have created a more flexible, independent style of repertory) because the critics — echoing the attitude of the general public — complain that the actors' personalities are lost in the collective approach, proving that theatre in Latvia, much like in Estonia, remains an actors' theatre, subordinating the writer and director to the status of accessory to a "star" system that continues to resist more metaphorical, non-realistic treatments.

Zole traces two schools of contemporary theatre back through a specific lineage to the beginnings of the twentieth century. On one hand are the psychological realists, starting with Alfrēds Amtmanis-Briedītis at the National Theatre, then continuing through the work of Ķimele and Šapiro; on the other, the metaphorical, non-realistic school associated with the Art Theatre begins with Smiļģis and Pētersons and continues through Hermanis, Kairišs and Vaivars. That the psychological school — in Zole's paradigm — ends with Šapiro, who hit his prime in the 70s and 80s, and the metaphorical school includes three young directors — Hermanis, for instance, was born in 1965 — is evidence that the traditional approach so popular with the general audience is losing favor with progressive critics like Zole (though she is, admittedly, professionally associated with, the National, the most traditional of the repertories).

Valda Čakare concurs with Zole that the audience drives the venue in Latvian theatre. She attributes this hesitancy to experiment on the part of established repertories to the influence of German theatrical trends combined with Russian realism that still pervades popular Latvian culture. Čakare suggests that Latvian theatre shares with the Estonian model a "decayed German classicism" in its acting tradition and is distinct from the Lithuanian tradition of directors and actors whose education and cultural influences are so intimately associated with Russian theatre. She also agrees that the Lutheran influence is as strong in Latvia as it is in Estonia and contributes to the text-based approach preferred in Latvian theatres, opposed by the visual, more metaphorical drama in Lithuania produced in the Catholic tradition of ritual and spectacle. She qualifies the idea that Latvian theatre can be categorized as an "actors' theatre," however, suggesting that, while it is true that until recently there was no school in which to train directors, many actors nevertheless established their own strong directing style by sheer necessity. She cites Smiļģis as the first Latvian director working on a European level and credits him with introducing Stanislavsky to Latvia — even though, oddly enough, Smiļģis began his career as an expressionist in the style of Tairov. It was only after the Soviet occupation, when the authorities "suggested" that he work in the State approved style of social realism, that he made a conscientious shift to Stanislavsky's style. Today, he is still associated with the experimental theories of the avant-garde, and his influence on the Art Theatre separates it from, for instance, the National (though there are signs that even the Art Theatre is becoming more commercial due to its need to maintain an income in an age of depleting state support). Smiļģis' contribution to the present situation is unusual because though he is credited with the experimental work in the early days of the Art Theatre, his influence on the general public remains grounded in Stanislavskian realism, so he is ironically credited with contributing to the resistance on the part of contemporary Latvian audiences to postmodern trends.

Čakare recalls how during the 1990s theatres were marginalized and confused, having lost their focus, meaning and purpose. To recover their relevancy, each of the prominent theatres tried to compete with the sudden influx of popular culture by seeking a particular niche: the National staging Latvian historical and contemporary plays, the Art Theatre producing contemporary commercial imports and homegrown experimental extravaganzas, the Valmiera continuing the tradition of psychological realism, and so on. This has been the case ever since.

But for the most interesting and original work in contemporary Latvia, Čakare cites New Riga Theatre under the guidance of Alvis Hermanis as the true heir to Smiļģis' progressive traditions. While the other major theatres, in Čakare's view, are still trying to strike a viable balance between satisfying their audience's expectations, trying to maintain a profitable bottom line and keeping their directors involved in new, interesting material (but not, of course, to the extent that they alienate their precious paying audience), Hermanis at New Riga is one of the few practicing directors to challenge both the critics and the audience with his own often radical aesthetics. For her, Hermanis represents one of the few new theatre artists who successfully "deviates from the script," experimenting in the context of a Latvian tradition that tends to favor straight, mainstream literary plays. In his *Latvian Stories* (*Latviešu stāsti*), for instance, Hermanis presents a panorama of stories simply told by a series of characters created from interviews conducted by actors with ordinary people and then transformed into dramatic monologs presented in six separate performances.

After graduating from the Conservatory, Hermanis honed his style at New Riga, working alongside Juris Rijnieks, the progressive artistic director bent on transforming the theatre, weaning it from its repertory structure toward a project-oriented house, inviting directors and actors from other theatres both from inside and outside Latvia to stage specific works. Čakare remembers how Rijnieks at first created "a remarkable dialectic between [his] ironic vision of new Latvian problematics and his universalist theater of poetic images" (92). But unable to refuse jobs to people who had more enthusiasm than talent, according to Čakare, Rijnieks reverted to the repertory model and reduced the theatre, in Čakare's words, to "a trash box."

Hermanis took over as artistic director in 1997 and immediately imposed his own radical vision of trying to sell formal experimentation and stylized performances in a thoroughly anti-realistic fashion — selling "art" as a high-concept commodity. One of the first of the experimental directors invited by Hermanis to help revitalize New Riga was Baņuta Rubesa. Born to Latvian refugees in Toronto, Rubesa moved to Latvia in 1998. In 1999, Hermanis asked her to stage a performance, telling her she could do "anything." (Rubesa recalls that the New Riga at that time was floundering, so Hermanis had nothing to lose.) Hoping to shock the theatre out if its malaise from years of stale Stanislavsky-style realism, she chose Schnitzler's *La Ronde*, a fairly scandalous play when produced with fidelity to the original version, but Rubesa decided to deconstruct the text, not only shifting the time and location to reflect the contemporary sex scene in Riga but also to stage the series of vignettes that make up the narrative throughout the New Riga complex — in cloak rooms, bathrooms, the lobby, anterooms — and incorporating improvisations, audience participation, video, elements of poor theatre — running throughout the building simultaneously, using an "ushers guide system" to lead the audience from set to set: eleven scenes, eleven minutes each.

At first, Rubesa says, Hermanis was incredulous, but because he had, after all, agreed that she could do "anything," he had no choice but to accede and backed the production unconditionally. The critics, predictably, were scandalized, but for the most part the audiences were intrigued and in Rubesa's admittedly less than objective opinion it was this production that re-invigorated public (and professional) interest in New Riga. As for the critics, Rubesa has grown accustomed to her status as perennial "outsider" — no matter that Latvian is her first language or that she resides permanently in Riga with dual citizenship. She complains that the Latvian critics intuitively object to performances that run counter to their expectations.

"The critics in Riga are some third species," she says. "They do not reflect the popular opinions or the attitude of professional theatre practitioners."

Typically, what sparks the ire of the critics, or at least explains their hesitation to accept experimental work, is their lack of experience with alternative approaches like those of Hermanis and his productions at New Riga that often challenge the nature of theatre itself. Many of the theatre professionals, especially the older ones, were educated in Russia where they were exposed to various and unconventional performances alongside the preferred Stanislavskian model, so they are more flexible and informed when evaluating new approaches. The general public, too, though for the most part conventional in their tastes and conservative in their expectations, are hungry for new ideas — especially the younger generation — so they are also more curious and forgiving when confronted with alternative-style productions. The critics, however, lacking a pluralistic education, remain rigidly fixed in their preferences, as if the trends in contemporary Latvian theatre were an aesthetic turf war waged against foreign elements that might somehow taint the pure spirit of traditional production values. As Rubesa acidly remarks, "If a production does not feature a beautiful set and brilliant costumes, the critics will not take it seriously."

More important than the audiences' appreciation or the critics' rejection of her staging of *La Ronde* was Hermanis' reaction. According to Rubesa, her new approach inspired him to investigate the experimental possibilities in his own work. He had by the time of her performance managed the difficult task of dismantling the repertory system at New Riga — the "Achilles' heel," says Rubesa, "of Latvian theatre" — transforming the stale, flagging theatre into a productive, project-based troupe composed of professionals of his own choosing, maintaining his state sponsorship while completely revamping the management. (His claim that if he can do it, others can too, irritates proponents of the independent theatre movement who interpret his success as more the result of luck, timing, circumstances and a major charm offensive rather than raw talent.)

Rubesa's next performance was equally controversial. Her staging of Carol Churchill's *Top Girls* provoked a much needed dialog, she says, addressing the current issue of financial equity within the current social climate she describes as a dog-eat-dog, capitalist system: a decidedly Malthusian ethos based on survival of the fittest. Perversely, the locals read the ostensibly feminist play not as a feminist tract but as simply a portrait of women dealing with the world as it is, patriarchal, certainly, but complex in ways that transcend categories. The critics, she says, again "didn't get it" and mainly wrote about the "pretty actresses."

The critics and the older generation of audience members that rejected this approach found the attempts by Rubesa and Hermanis to reform the theatre into a more dynamic vehicle cold and empty and lacking any sense of humanity. But because the younger generation — especially university students and new directors — responded positively to the fresh approach, Hermanis was encouraged to continue evolving. (Of course, many of those who appreciated Hermanis' experiments had been trained in the aesthetics of theory and viewed the plays from a more formal perspective.)

By the end of the 90s Hermanis changed again, retaining his stylized design and action but combining it with an acute investigation into human psychology, creating a hybrid of formalism and everyday realism that satisfied the critics and teenagers alike, though the general public remained skeptical.

Undaunted, Hermanis continued to pursue meta-theatrical issues concerning the possibilities and limitations of theatre, its relationship with "real" life, and the ambiguities and variants of "theatre language." With productions like *The Inspector General* (*Revidents*), *Long Life* (*Garā dzīve*), and especially *Ice* (*Ledus*), based on the story by the Russian novelist Vladimir Sorokin, Hermanis secured his reputation as an outstanding European director (confirmed by a profile of him in the Baltic Air in-flight magazine). Part 1 of the play, subtitled *Collective Reading with the Help of*

Alvis Hermanis's *Ice. A Collective Reading of the Book with the Help of Imagination in Riga*, based on the story by the Russian novelist Vladimir Sorokin. Hermanis deliberately challenges the framing aspect of the performance space to close the gap between the actors as real people and their roles as performers by collapsing the distance between the audience as viewers and their participation in the theatrical experience (photograph by Gints Mālderis).

the Imagination, was staged in Frankfurt with members of the Schauspielfrankfurt ensemble, Part 2 at Gladbeck's Maschinenhalle Zweckel (an old factory space that included installations using live exhibits), and Part 3 at New Riga theatre.

That the story deals with the idea of a utopia creates an immediate overall controlling connotation: theatre itself is an impossible idealization of expression — a simulated experience that cannot be realized ever as being "true" in any literal sense. But to challenge the framing aspect of the performance space and to close the gap between the actors as real people and their roles as performers, and to reduce the distance between the audience as viewer and their participation in the theatrical experience, Hermanis has his actors during the performance simply face the audience and read from Sorokin's novel. They distribute three collections of photographs: one, a collection of staged shots showing the performers posing "in character," another of pornographic fantasies, and a third of real historical figures. For Hermanis, these three assemblages represent the current collocation of theatrical motifs in vogue in Latvia: everyday social concerns (which he revisits in *Latvian Stories*), titillating voyeurism (decadent attempts at prurient entertainment), and traditional depictions of historical theatre (akin to the mainstream venues offered by the National). According to Čakare, Hermanis self-consciously dismisses all of these approaches as he attempts an original mode of theatrical experience that will be free of any past associations and will constitute a fresh, truly new approach.

Just as Sorokin's novel deals with people trying to recognize each other in a search for identity — beating on people's hearts with an ice hammer to determine

Alvis Hermanis (photograph by Gints Mālderis).

kinship and authenticity — a painfully violent ritual — Hermanis portrays theatre the same way, beating the hearts of the spectators to achieve a sympathetic understanding of the human situation. But the hammers in the fictionalized depiction on stage are not real hammers, only empty bottles. So theatre for Hermanis is like these hammers, never real, always merely representative, a notion that seems sophomorically obvious, except in the hands of a director like Hermanis the issue is cast in a phenomenological context, so that the very idea of existence, knowledge and how experience is rendered is brought into question. According to Čakare, *Ice* was cathartic for Hermanis: having dispensed with the detritus of his former productions — trashing visible objects and confetti from his own contributions to theatre — Hermanis offers a sort of resolution at the end of *Ice*. The actors skate around the stage, periodically stopping to sharpen their blades. As the lights go down the skates glint, flashing, until in blackout the only lights are these pinpoints striking off the blades — tiny sparks of light — of truth — that sometimes theatre can produce.

Vilis Daudziņž (*top*) and Guna Zariņa (*following page*) in Hermanis' *Latvian Stories* at the New Riga Theatre. Dispensing with the modes of theatrical presentations and opting instead for a straight delivery, an adumbration with hardly any fictional structuring, this is theatre reduced to voice and delivery, expressed with sensitivity, exposition without dramatic effects (photographs by Gints Mālderis).

Hermanis' interest in what Čakare calls "stylized realism" fed his concern for social issues, and from that confluence of forms he produced an acknowledged *tour de force*, *Long Life*, followed by his equally celebrated *Latvian Stories*—two sides, essentially, of the same thematic coin. *Long Life* depicts the stories of five elderly people living in communal apartment complex in Riga. The set is constructed as a cut-away so the actions of all the players can be presented simultaneously. But true to his counter-intuitive style, Hermanis casts young actors — each around thirty years old — to play the elderly without make-up. There is no text; instead of dialog, the actors use paralinguistic forms of expression, punctuated only by traditional Latvian songs popular with the older generation, to express the comically desperate struggle for territory and dignity that marks the days of the elderly in the play. Using beautifully graded lighting and remarkably focused actors, Hermanis creates a delicate, revealing piece of social realism.

Čakare suggests that the key to the success of this performance lies in how Hermanis presents the characters without romanticizing them or making them seem overly pathetic or tragic but balancing their pathos with humor to keep the realistic portraits honest. Zole notes that, as the play is a companion to *By Gorky* (*Tālāk*), a piece inspired in part by Gorky's *The Lower Depths* and portraying the lives of young people in a reality television show, both plays resonate with contemporary *and* universal meaning: "Today's people are of both kinds, the old ones without a future and the young ones with one" (qtd. in Grīnbauma). Critic Ingrida Vilkarse appreciates how the physicality of the actors drives the action "peacefully and deliberately as a stream of consciousness and ascribes each happening with almost existential relevance" (qtd. in Grīnbauma).

Latvian Stories continues Hermanis' investigation into both a more realistic style and the dramatic potential expressed in ordinary lives, although Zole sees in the performances a chance for Hermanis to remain true to his theatre while identifying his style as strictly Latvian: "to seek and find what is intrinsic to being Latvian is more important than its ultimate discoveries" (Zole). Presented as a product of his *coup d'etat* at New Riga, the play is arguable more theoretically provocative than dramatically engaging, and therein, as it were, lies the rub. The New Riga complex itself, its non-descript façade facing a cross-street in the city center, has an "in your face" feel that begins in the main lobby where stenciled graffiti announces an attitude graphically depicted on the egg yolk yellow walls, the foyer exuding the charm of a dilapidated one star hotel circa early 1960s. "Fuck Art" reads one inscription, in English. Another, in Latvian, translates to "Poetry is Terrorism" ("Poētiskais terorisms"). Another, again in English, reads "Life Not Lifestyle," and yet another in Latvian roughly translates to "Protest for the Beauty of Soul!" ("Streikojiet par Dvēsēles skaistumu!").

A performance of one of the monologues, staged in one of several performance spaces surrounding an impressive courtyard — this time in an upstairs loft-style black box — indicates Hermanis' interest in "pure" acting. By stripping away the normal theatrical framing devices, he exposes the medium for what it is, an actor becoming another person indulging an audience in an act of empathetic identification. The impulse driving this approach seems to suggest that all the props and scenery and elements of dramatization directors use to enhance the presentation in "typical" theatrical productions tend, instead, to falsify rather than clarify the action. In this instance, the set consists only of a bare stage and a backdrop collage of photographs depicting apartments in various stages of lived-in disarray. The actor simply sits on a stool between the audience and the photo-collage, telling the story of the character he has assumed.

The method of *Latvian Stories* is similar to the Estonian writer Merle Karusoo's Documentary Theatre, composed of collections of stories collated from interviews, often recited verbatim, the director dispensing with the modes of theatrical presentations and opting instead for a straight delivery, an adumbration with hardly any fictional structuring. This is theatre reduced to voice and delivery, expressed with sensitivity, exposition without dramatic effects. The comparison to Karusoo recalls the Estonian critic Madis Kolk's question: "Is it theatre?" That issue, of course, intrinsically problematic no matter how it is framed, is impossible to settle. A traditionalist could argue that without dramatic structure — i.e., an applied technique of metaphorical, naturalistic or mimetic strategies of representation beyond mere recitation — the monologues, delivered, granted, with sensitivity and immediacy, might just as well be performed as a book reading. In this sense, *Latvian Stories* represents an end of "theatre," where any story told with precision (in this case) or without (a rambling cell phone call, for instance) passes for drama. The approach implies nihilism within the genre: theatre reduced to the art of storytelling, stripped of verisimilitude or, indeed, of any enhancement by visual means. The argument from genre insists that the beauty and appeal of art, per se, is form. Life, after all, is contingent, art arranged. And it is in that arrangement, the structural semblance of reality — not in its naïve presentation, which by its ordinariness is boring — that the craft of the artist imposes design on the chaos of experience. Only a dilettante would complain that theatre somehow sacrifices its value by its artifice; in reality, theatre as a genre posits quite the opposite: beauty is form, art the skill of shaping experience. Hermanis' collection might be engaging, but the stories are not his, not the actors,' and in the end not the "real" story of the clerk, the bus driver, or the unemployed student who inspired the original piece. But this seems to be his point: to challenge representation at all levels. As critic Silvija Radzobe observes, writing about his diptych *By Gorky* and *Long Life,* "Hermanis is experimenting with the perception mechanisms of the audience" (qtd. in Grīnbauma). The writers for the Latvian Theatre Workers Association brochure of Latvian Theatre 2003 insist the key to Hermanis' style as "simplicity." They describe his *The Story of Kaspar Hauser* (*Stāsts par Kasparu Hauzeru*) as "a German Romantic phantasmagoria" and equate the performance with a fairy tale, noting that the "language of a fairy tale is never complicated" (Raudseps).

Hermanis' talent is certainly mercurial; he is uncomfortable settling into one style or another. Sympathetic critics (and there are many convinced that he is one of the most creative directors in Latvia) situate *Latvian Stories* in a continuum of his artistic development. His plays, characterized by his self-conscious attempts to rethink traditional styles and aesthetics, resemble dramatic pastiches, combinations of images from different periods of history collated to challenge the nature of theatrical experience. But for all his theorizing and innovative staging, Hermanis' productions are typically actor-friendly. An actor himself (nominated for Best Actor of the Year in Latvia at the 2004 Spēlmaņu Nakts for Jean's role in *Miss Julie* [*Jūlijas jaunkundze*] directed by Māra Ķimele), he focuses on personality-dominated work; even his "stylized realism" is grounded in respect for the actor's skill at bringing a character to life. His reputation, however, has been established as a director. He has won a slew of awards, including Best Debut as Director and the Play of the Year in 1993, the prestigious Young Directors Project Award for *The Inspector General* at the Saltsburg Theatre Festival (2003), and yearly awards in 2000–2004 for both Best Director and Performance of the Year in Latvia. His work with New Riga Theater has been performed in festivals in Russia, Poland, Lithuania, Estonia, Slovakia, Czech Republic, Finland, Germany, Austria, USA, Canada, France, Belgium, Switzerland, Hungary, Netherlands, Italia, Serbia and Montenegro.

Aside from the recent acclaim afforded him by the general community of European theatre aficionados and critics, appreciation locally also remains solid. Indra Roga, for instance, one of the most respected young actresses in Latvia, recently noted for directing *Nora* (*Leļļus nams*) based on Ibsen's *A Doll's House,* names Hermanis as the best of the new breed. In her view, Hermanis is "always looking for a new understanding of theatre" and she suggests, somewhat incongruously — given the structure of *Latvian Stories*— that his actors never dominate his productions. For her, Hermanis' productions are centered on his vision of making New Riga a "director's theatre."

Roga admits to being unsure as to whether she prefers acting or directing. When she is "in process," she says, she would rather be acting, responsible only for herself. (Professionally, she qualifies her remark, stressing that a good actor is responsible for everyone involved in the play.) But directing, she says, allows her "to make a new world, a new reality." That "new reality" entails freeing herself from traditional readings of a play, reinterpreting not only the shape of the play but also the central theme. But even with her tinkering, she is well aware that many young directors still consider her approach structurally conservative, based in that Latvian treasure: stylized realism.

As if to verify this judgment by her peers, she professes in her production of *Nora* fidelity to Ibsen's vision, although most critics after viewing the play agree that Roga basically redefined Nora as a more sexually charged woman and weakened the ending by mitigating the consequences of her final decision to leave the family. Still, Roga insists her interpretation is in line with Ibsen's. In theory, she says, directors should not impose their concepts too quickly on the text; they should instead "open" the play, even if that implies working at the periphery of consensus. Weak material, she says, *requires* directors to take liberty with the scripts. But when it comes to masters — in this case Ibsen — she defers to the text. "If a director thinks he is better than the work," she says, "he or she might be blind to new possibilities." She also trusts directors trained as actors more than directors who approach theatre from a literary or theoretical background. "The director must know the actor's skill," she says. Relying on her own training as an actor, she makes no apologies for insisting on Stanislavsky's approach. She expects her actors to conduct background research, etudes, improvisation, to merge, she says, "self and character into their magical roles"; she allows for "a few spots" to be open for spontaneity in the performance but tightly blocks the choreography.

It was her director's curiosity, combined with an actors' passion for a strong character, that caused her to reconsider Ibsen's well-worn classic, and her production does offer a new angle on Nora and her relationship with her husband. In Roga's staging, Torvald is much less of a manipulator, Nora more sinister. When she first approached the character, Roga says she understood her "as a child, not a normal woman." But in Roga's

(*Above and top right*) Indra Roga directing herself in her adaptation of Ibsen's *A Doll's House* at the Latvian National Theatre, Riga. A good example of stylized realism, her production offers a new angle on Nora and her relationship with her husband, Torvald. In Roga's staging, Torvald is much less of a manipulator, Nora more sinister (photographs by Ieva Kauliņa).

production, Nora never gets beyond that childish impetus to amuse herself, and in the end joins the children in ring-around-a-rosy. In a telling reversal, Roga accuses Nora of playing with her husband, not the other way around. Even her flirtation with Dr. Rank is more sexually calculated than naïve, especially in the scene where Nora shows off her Christmas stockings; in Roga's rendering, the stockings are real: Nora slips them on in a brazen and provocative performance. Not until Torvald, having discovered Nora's scheme, becomes violent and physically abusive does he seem unsympathetic and cruel — a flaw, perhaps, in the directing, as Torvald's change seems particularly abrupt, and given the tenor of the preceding action, out of character. Equally incongruous is the beautiful tableau Roga strikes — as actor and director — in which Nora, instead of angrily rejecting her role as the mother and wife in Torvald's doll's house, hinting at suicide and abandoning everything she has lived for, joins in her children's game. In Roga's view, Nora is not an innocent destroyed when her childish whims are suddenly played out in the brutal adult world where mistakes can have deadly consequences; rather, she seems in the end of Roga's play not to understand the consequences of her actions any more than at the beginning and merely regresses into another childish fantasy.

Her ambivalence toward Torvald and her reassessment of (and difficulty with) Nora might be seen as a sign of the problems inherent in directing herself, though Roga admits that she frequently invites Michail Gruzdov to coach her. "It's not unusual," she says, "in the Russian tradition for an actor to continue being trained ten years after graduation." (Gruzdov, the Artistic Director of Art Theatre, happens also to be her husband.) Čakare suspects a willful misreading, suggesting that Roga intentionally tries to finesse Nora's leaving — especially considering the implications of Nora's abandoning her children. What Ibsen might think of what some critics consider a radical departure from his shocking and devastating dénouement is speculative but not beside the point: Roga's treatment, despite her professed allegiance to Ibsen's script, calls into question whether she can remain faithful to a text in which she has invested so much of herself.

Many young actors and directors do not have the advantages Roga enjoyed: training at the Latvian Academy of Culture, then studying in Russia and marrying her professor (who happens to run the largest theatre house in the country). One Artistic Director determined to discover new and not necessarily traditionally schooled talent, recruiting both from within and without the established actors' educational system, is Anna Eižvertiņa, founder of The Stage Theatre (teātris Skatuve). Founded in 1991, The Stage is a product of the changing situation during the 80s and 90s that was so detrimental to the established theatres — even fatal for some, like Šapiro's Youth Theatre — but which proved conducive to the establishment of a vibrant network of independent theatres defiantly determined to counter the direction of the large repertories that until then had defined mainstream Latvian theatre.

A graduate of the Russian Theatre Academy in Moscow (GITIS), Eižvertiņa returned to Latvia to work at Liepāja, but after five performances she returned to Moscow hoping to marry her fiancé. When her engagement did not work out, she finished her master's degree and decided to return to Latvia, but at that time in the professional theatre world, because positions were tenured, she could not reclaim her former directing job, so she had to settle for an assignment in the Ministry of Culture where she worked for seven years, concentrating on new Latvian dramaturgy in the Department of Theatre.

When a directing job opened at Daugavpils, she took it (where, incidentally, she taught Indra Roga). Her new professional role allowed her the chance to study directing in Moscow (where she met Nekrošius), a move she says she made more out of necessity than choice because at that time the best directors were not teaching and Latvian academies concentrated strictly on training actors. Not planning on staying too long at the Daugavpils, she nevertheless worked there for six years, from 1988–1994 — a time she describes as perhaps the most exciting and disappointing eight years in contemporary theatre, beginning with the hopeful period of the "new awakening," where the spirit of activism and the push for independence energized the theatre, and ending with the decline of relevance and stagnation, when theatre was relegated to being just another entertainment venue, its former status displaced by politics, despondency, and the influence of crass Western popular culture.

Out of this malaise, indeed because of it, a group of directors decided to try to reinvigorate the theatre outside of the enervated and by then decadent repertory system by creating a truly independent theatre that would allow the directors total control over their projects. (After all, she says, every director wants his or her own theatre to create an ensemble sympathetic to the director's vision.) The first independent theatre in Riga, The Pocket (teātris Kabata) had been in existence since 1987, hosting a permanent troupe of actors and directors. After 1996 the directors decided to bring together various theatre personnel for project-specific productions, but the Pocket's dedication to progressive theatre declined after the 90s and has since been reduced to musical hall productions and performances for children just to stay alive in its present location within the city center.

To counter this slide into a "music hall" aesthetic and to continue to provide a venue for serious theatre, Eižvertiņa organized a group of film and theatre artists around a space she found — a former cinema house in a dilapidated area outside the city center which they began to renovate into a working theatre dedicated to producing Latvian plays, calling it The Little Riga Theatre (Rīgas mazais teātris). The theatre quickly went dormant because of in-fighting between the playwrights and their general dissatisfaction with the location of the space in a seedy, socially depressed area, a former Soviet workers' sector outside the city center. Eižvertiņa, however, viewed the location as one of the theatre's finest aspects. She mocks the dissidents' objections to the locale by citing the refrain from Chekhov's *Three Sisters*: "To Moscow! To Moscow!" Eižvertiņa, contrary to her colleagues, was firmly against the "centralization of art" and so resisted the seduction of being in the city center, too close to the traditional repertory companies representing the "establishment," as if the geography of the city itself were a metaphor for her independence, her location away from the center reinforcing her status as "outsider."

Having taken control of the building — in essence, by default —

Eižvertiņa tried to organize a stable troupe of actors mainly consisting of former students within the theatre structure she now called The Stage — based on the unique design of the space, featuring a floor sloped toward a raised thrust stage in a black box studio. But this idealistic plan collapsed in the harsh economic reality of the 90s, when she could no longer sustain the role of "creative mother," especially when many of her troupe became more interested in creating families than art, and so she was forced finally to abandon the idea of an idealized ensemble and opted instead for a project-based approach.

Her theatre developed in three distinct directions. The first she describes as "performance as project," in which she chooses actors to perform premieres of world and Latvian drama in new translations, stressing that she only stages plays that have otherwise never been produced in Latvia. The second direction highlights her role as an educator, allowing her students an opportunity to practice their craft in front of an audience as part of their training process. (She mentored many of the top personalities in the professional theatre community, sponsoring the first performances by Regnārs Vaivars, Dž. Dž. Džilindžers and Zane Kreicberga.) The third direction involves her work with the immediate neighborhood outside the doors of The Stage, not the most salubrious part of Riga — the community is rife with disadvantaged youths prone to violence and criminality. Responding to this social malady, Eižvertiņa began offering private acting classes for at-risk children aged 14–18 who participated in activities at the theatre. She also donated private acting classes, focusing on the basics — speech, movement, dance and acting techniques — to students who hoped to pursue careers in theatre but also to underprivileged students from the local area who would otherwise not be exposed to acting in their ordinary schools. She admits that not many of her students succeed as professionals but insists that her classes develop personality, responsibility and character. Just as importantly, her students gain a sensibility that will produce an educated theatre audience schooled in the appreciation of contemporary theatre, and so Eižvertiņa feels she is directly contributing to the viability of theatre by creating an informed audience, an essential ingredient for maintaining a healthy art environment.

Whereas independence sparked an interest in developing small theatres as alternatives to the dispiriting state run systems, the transition was traumatic for the major repertories, both economically and artistically. No better example of this paradox — of sudden political freedom leading to an equally precipitous demise — can be cited than the story of the Latvian

Youth Theatre (Latvijas jaunatnes teātris), which Čakare describes as "the most dramatic event of that period [and] a heavy loss for Latvian culture" (87). The "official" line places the responsibility of the failure of the theatre on minions at the Ministry of Culture for not appreciating the work of Ādolfs Šapiro, the illustrious director responsible for transforming what began as a Soviet state-dictated acting program for children into a serious — some say the most important — theatre organization in Latvia. Čakare, for instance, claims the ministry "accused Šapiro of not employing all the actors in the company, for stoppages, for choosing 'incorrect' repertoire" (88). Others claimed it was prejudice — Šapiro was a Ukrainian Jew — that drove him into self-exile, causing one prominent theatre impresario to immigrate to Israel in protest, but this account is discredited by most objective critics who recognize that Jews in Latvia are well-assimilated and evidence of institutionalized discrimination is anecdotal at best.

The truth, according to Zeltiņa, is, as usual, more complex and inextricably tied not to the macro-management of the Ministry of Culture or any form of state sponsored anti-Semitism but to Šapiro's own stubbornness, conceit and artistic temperament.

Šapiro assumed control over the Youth Theatre in 1962. By the 1980s his theatre was recognized as one of the most innovative and dynamic companies in the country, hosting two professional troupes, one for the Russian language productions and one for Latvian shows. By this time Šapiro had earned a reputation outside of the country, and was traveling frequently. Traveling outside of the Soviet bloc during this period was restricted, but Šapiro was allowed to tour widely with a select group of actors (composed mainly of his favorites and students) — producing his versions of Brecht's work, for instance, all over Europe. But it was not necessarily Šapiro's ability to travel throughout Europe that caused the fatal friction within his company; it was, more seriously, his flagrant favoritism that eventually created resentment among the actors left behind: the actors who were not part of his touring group remained idle as long as Šapiro was away, their theatre dark. Zeltiņa recalls how Šapiro's extended absences became a national scandal. (In 1987 an article appeared in the national press titled, "One Year in the Youth Theatre without Šapiro.") Because Šapiro actually forbade members of the theatre not selected by him to travel professionally outside the country, both critics and players in his own company began to accuse him of running the theatre as if it were his personal fiefdom and referring to the idle actors derisively as Šapiro's slaves.

After independence, circumstances in the professional theatre began to change quickly. Meritocracy slowly began to replace cronyism — at least, sinecures were no longer guaranteed, theatre companies had to apply for funding, and actors and directors were suddenly competing for employment, hired on annual contracts subject to renewal. Šapiro considered the new system an affront to his status and resisted the changes. But Zeltiņa cites a dispute in 1990 concerning the site of the Russian component of the Youth Theatre as the decisive event marking the end of Šapiro's career in Latvia. The Latvian troupe was housed in what later became the New Riga Theatre, located in the heart of the city center, with the Russian troupe in a former Baptist Church building. When the church appealed to have its building returned, Šapiro objected, but the Ministry overruled him and moved the Russian troupe to a location outside the city center. Although Šapiro tried to salvage the Russian contingent, he could not overcome the problems already inherent in a difficult situation — some out of his control but many caused by his own lack of leadership and discretion: first, while the Latvian troupe was coherent and highly successful, the Russian troupe suffered from defections, with many actors leaving to work in more prestigious theatres in Russia, for instance, but also because in Riga the Russian population is segregated — in Riga more than in the provincial areas — and, second, because there was a backlash after independence for the animosity left over from the occupation.[18] (To put the occupation in perspective, Čakare writes, "not only was the invasion of culturally less developed Soviet troops seen as a powerful loss of freedom, but as a deep humiliation" [81].)

The real problem was Šapiro himself, traveling abroad with his favorites while leaving those out of favor idle at home, promoting himself at the expense of his colleagues, refusing to abide by the new meritocracy, and failing to realize that, after all, his Russian troupe was not as talented as he pretended, mainly because the members preferred to work in their native country. The last straw, according to popular lore, occurred when Šapiro insisted on casting his second wife, Irina Fjodorova, as Juliet opposite a Romeo who was only twenty. The actor playing Romeo objected and left the performance. The rest, as they say, is history. The anecdote most cited by critics who now, more comfortable in the cushion of historical distance, can recall the affair with bitter humor, runs, "Every Meyerhold has his own Zinaida Raikh." So Šapiro had his Irina.

After thirty years at the forefront of Latvian theatre, Šapiro announced that Latvia was too small for his talents, and he left the country. Drifting from one theatre to another, Šapiro faded into mediocrity. His Latvian troupe, partially disbanded, reformed as the New Riga, while most of the actors from the Russian troupe sought work in Russian or joined the Russian Drama Theatre in Riga.

Šapiro's legacy lives on in the new work of Hermanis and Džilindžers, but most critics agree that, even given the examples of strong directors like Šapiro and Smiļģis and their contemporary heirs, Latvian theatre remains essentially actor-based, with many Latvian directors having trained first as actors. One young practitioner, however, representing a new generation who disagrees that a good director must first be trained as an actor, is Mārtiņs Eihe. His production of *The Blue* (*Zilā*), written by Gunārs Priede, a significant Soviet-era playwright whose work was often banned, illustrates his interest in moving away from a traditional actor-based performance toward what he calls "magic realism." Although trained as an actor, Eihe says his acting experience is merely a "bonus" when it comes to directing, so he can tell, for instance, when an actor is cheating. In a tongue-in-cheek moment of self-deprecation, he recalls a former teacher telling him, "All bad actors are going to be directors."

Nominated for Best Debut at the 2005 Spēlmaņu Nakts, and performed in one of the three main spaces at New Riga — this one a black box with a raised stage and "dining room chair" seating — *The Blue* crosses minimalism with mixed-media to jazz-up and contemporize what is basically straightforward Grotowskian "poor theatre." The tiny stage is bare, but from the front of the stage out, over and through the audience, a network of chrome rails with what appear to be subway straps attached support a half-dozen video monitors, intended to produce the effect of the audience traveling on a mass transit bus, while on the screens a single image of a cow floats against a dull blue and white background.

Suddenly the monitors flash a red alert warning, the lights go down, and a loud siren blasts. A man in a wheelchair rolls onto the set; three other actors sit offstage facing the rear curtain. The story unfolds as each actor takes the stage to interact both with each other and with the audience directly, working within a realistic frame and yet breaking the frame by what amounts to confessions directed outside the "time" of the play.

The story deals with the events leading up to a tragic automobile wreck and the aftermath, told in what amounts to flashback dialog delivered in a series of visits during a day in the life of the survivor, the temperamental, spoiled son of a wealthy family, and his mother. The son, Juris, while driving drunk, killed his father, his grandmother and another woman in a head-on collision that also left the passengers in the other car with debilitating injuries. His mother, Rasma, has sold everything and moved from Riga to a house by the Black Sea in Georgia hoping to facilitate her son's recovery.

On the day of the present action, a former acquaintance, Linda, turns up with a male co-worker, Vidvuds, ostensibly on a business trip, but both harbor ulterior motives, Linda hoping Juris will give her money to support a son she has never acknowledged, Vidvuds expecting to cultivate a lover to take his mind off his own family problems.

Juris, strapped into his wheelchair, solipsistic and obsessed with guilt and despair, seems like an agent of expiation, a prompt for expurgation, as the others, while confronting him must ultimately confront themselves. Even his mother, who has been living the role of martyr, collides with a past that proves as slippery, duplicitous and, finally, as fictional as Juris' present sense of reality. For Rasma, her self-righteousness stems from her belief that Linda slept with her husband, causing her to leave him, destabilizing the family and contributing to Juris' bouts of alcoholism. Linda explodes this myth when she explains that Juris brought her to the house but left her alone. Entranced with the wealth of his parents, Linda had bathed in the comforts of the house, enjoying luxuries that were absent in her life of poverty. She merely fell asleep in the master bedroom and never saw Rasma's husband.

All of the family's tragedies — the parents' divorce, the death of the grandmother, the injuries to others, both real and imagined — result from action initiated by Juris, a self-centered slacker who had friends only because he had money and a car. As a defense mechanism, Juris has become fixated on the semi-mythical Latvian "blue" cow that is immune to diseases. According to Juris' version of events leading up to the wreck, all four occupants of the car, just minutes before the crash, saw one of these cows and had stopped to marvel at it. Juris recounts how at that moment he saw the car — a black Volga — through the eyes of the blue cow: "four objects driving fast — no one wants them." In the end, Juris steps out of his wheelchair and plunges off a precipice to his death.

What at first appears to be a gratuitous use of the bars and video monitors through the course of the play becomes symbolically significant, the bars an image of Juris' confinement in the wheel chair, the monitors on which the white lines of a highway scroll by in super slow motion indicating his conscience fixed on the accident and the blue cow that he has come to pray for like some idealized *deus ex machina* that will deliver him from his physical and psychological suffering. Eihe suggests that the extended set of bars and monitors should also create in the audience a sense of collectively traveling the same highway, emulating Juris' journey toward self-recognition, a simple attempt to create a subjective verisimilitude that also explains the staging, combining realistic interaction among the characters interspersed with their attempts to rationalize their motives by plea bargaining with the audience. Significantly, Juris is the only character who does not address the audience, reinforcing the idea that the entire "vision" of the play is constructed through his perspective as the audience experiences not so much a play as the working of Juris' mind.

Traditionally, the themes coursing through Priede's script deal with moral corruption engendered by envy, an indictment of the economic inequities endemic in the cronyocracy that passed for communism under the corrupt Soviet regime. These themes — the recklessness of spoiled youth, class envy, the desire for love and the impossibility of innocence — are universal, and the action of the text, in this sense, transcends the particulars of the Latvian social context. But Eihe is less interested in themes than presentation, so that the staging itself becomes an editorial on current values. The quick scenes, the actors reciting summaries of their situations, the brevity of the play itself— running a short hour at most — represent for Eihe the reality for a young audience demanding immediate, abbreviated shots of information, their attention span conditioned by news flashes, high speed video games, MTV collages, e-mail correspondence and fifteen second advertising spots. Even the use of the video monitors, providing a visual portal into Juris' mind and signifying his fixation, was as much a practical component for Eihe as a metaphorical one. He explains, "The young audiences today expect video," as if they might trust the play and be more inclined to accept its theatrical truth as long as it included some aspect of electronic media.

Eihe admits that relying on visual stimuli can be tricky and counterproductive, especially if the monitors distract the audience from what is happening on stage. For instance, Eihe first tried looping a series of car crashes on the screen feed, but the audience became more interested in the video than the action of the play, so he settled for the more surrealistic slow motion track of the highway lines sliding diagonally across the monitors.

Eihe also confesses that he first conceived of the production as a radio play, another indication of his privileging electronic tools of communication over staged drama — a tendency realized in practice by his working away from sustained dramatic scenes, opting instead for explication, exposition and quick dramatic vignettes. His ideal, he says, would be to create a piece for one actor and one spectator, offering this example as homage to Hermanis, referring to the technique he used in *Latvian Stories*. Eihe is convinced that working without props or other actors for support, an actor achieves a purity of intention missing in more elaborate productions; alone with only his skills, he must conjure up "more intensity from his soul."

Part of his need to pressure his actors into what he calls "psychological tests" (which resembles the experiments by the Estonian director Tiit Ojasoo in pieces like *Sometimes I feel Life is Over*) can be traced to his disdain, shared almost universally by every young director, for the repertory system at the major theatre companies, in his case at Liepāja. His complaints, echoed by other dissatisfied directors, include the length of time set aside for rehearsals — mainly because actors come to the play at hand without having read the script, so a lot of time is wasted — weeks, he says — reading the text before getting the actors on the boards; low salaries, forcing actors to work other jobs outside the repertory, not that moonlighting is the problem, but because these jobs often involve actors playing to the audience in amateur productions their performance in the repertory can become contaminated, the practice of pandering leeching into their professional work; the fact that jobs are tenured — once hired into the repertory, actors are not expected to compete for their jobs, often for the rest of their careers, with some positions being handed down from one generation to the next — so that the talent in the repertory can be compromised with no recourse, whether the actors become hams, alcoholics, dilettantes; and finally that the plays — three or four a year — are not always very challenging, so many directors become bored. Eihe, like most of the new generation, prefers project-based theatres, but freelancing is difficult given the scarcity of opportunities and the uncertainty of earning a steady, sustainable income.

Eihe concurs with other critics that suggest the general tendency in Latvian theatre is more closely aligned with Estonia than with Lithuania, citing the text-based theatre (for example, *The Blue*) that dominates the popular programs, and he agrees that this phenomenon results from the historical affiliation of Lithuania with the more visual aspects of Catholic rituals and Latvia's allegiance to the sermonizing traditions associated with the less ceremonious Lutheran tradition. To change Latvian theatre from "talking" texts to more visual dramatic productions, he suggests combining the two approaches, striking the kind of balance he notes in

Hermanis' *Ice*, where the dialog, though minimized, is elevated to poetry (or sometimes merely read from the text) and because the visual component drives the story the dialog becomes not a complementary element but, ideally, just an accessory.

The main problem he says he faces as a young director entering the professional theatre world now, during a time of dynamic, shifting aesthetics, is not to be overly influenced by the work of other directors recognized as "new." Eihe cites Nekrošius, with whom he studied, paraphrasing T. S. Eliot: "The best director is the one who steals from others."[19] One of the best of these "thieves" is Dž. Dž. Džilindžers[20] who once described himself, referring to his impression of the Latvian critics' response to his work, as "a stomach ache or a malignant tumour that has to be cut out" ("Synopsis of the Stage" 213). Rubesa describes him as a nihilist. "He has a Russian world-view," she says. "He believes there is no truth, no values." This evaluation, which in fairness is meant by Rubesa as a compliment, not a criticism, is qualified by Džilindžers: "Why is there postmodern, ironic attitude towards truth? Because all the truths — religious, moral, generally human have been degraded [...] postmodernism irony discloses relativity of truth" (214).

On stage this ironic distance creates a cool formalism that Rubesa is quick to contrast with Hermanis' "warmth and sincerity." Džilindžers' actors are told "not to play the character but the idea." She cites his production of Camus' *Caligula* (*Kaligula*) as an example of a new level, a high mark of professionalism in Latvian theatre, praise carefully couched in a purely aesthetic context — a tacit acknowledgment of Džilindžers' postmodern prowess that precludes any sentimental, naturalistic or romantic notion of theatre as a medium for humanism.

Ironically (which in Džilindžers' case is a given), he praises Caligula as exactly that: a humanist. But this category, like Rubesa's description of nihilism, must be understood in a strictly Nietzschean sense. Nietzsche called for a revaluation of values because in his view the credibility of morality in theory and practice has been corrupted by the very "moralists" whose own prejudices supplant any transcendental notion of justice (arguing also that language itself, as a limited system of signifiers, renders transcendence impossible). Abstractions must be understood for what they are: illusions reified to serve political, religious or humanist agendas. "The struggle against *purpose* in art is always a struggle against the *moralizing* tendency in art, against the subordination of art to morality" (Nietzsche, *Twilight* 81).

Džilindžers' *Caligula*. Art Theatre, Riga. An extravaganza of Total Theatre, part Broadway musical, part West End farce. By staging unabashed theatrical celebration of anti-theatre, absurdity and vaudeville, borrowing liberally from Artaud and Preminger, Brecht and Tarantino, Džilindžers manages to remain faithful to Camus' philosophical intent (photograph by Jānis Deinats/"Fotocentrs").

For Džilindžers, Caligula "uses his power to fight against the essence of what it means to be human because people are not living truth, so they are unhappy" — or, in Caligula's famous maxim: "Men die; and they are not happy" (Camus, *Caligula* 8). Džilindžers believes that Caligula's ends are noble, but his methods — his "tools" — are not successful because Caligula, after all, is all too human, a product of "the old truths" that he realizes are worthless. Caligula's violence is caused by his inability to escape his humanity. If this sounds familiar, it is because during productions Džilindžers tends to avoid the script at hand and immerse himself instead in a variety of texts — including an eclectic array of philosophical works and American pulp fiction — and he quotes Dostoyevsky as easily as he does David Lynch. He insists, somewhat disingenuously, that his purpose in staging *Caligula* is not to explore the nature of freedom or rebellion; the play is simply an excuse to present a dramatic spectacle about which the audience may draw its own conclusions, ethical or aesthetical. Džilindžers' disclaimer mirrors both Camus' observation that *Caligula* is "an actor's and director's play" (Camus, Foreword v) and Nietzsche's enigmatic quip that "existence and the world seem justified only as an aesthetic phenomenon" (Nietzsche, *Basic Writings* 141). Džilindžers' approach follows Camus' stated purpose: "For the dramatist the passion for the impossible is just as valid a subject for study as avarice or adultery" (vi).

The production is an over-the-top example of Total Theatre, part Broadway musical, part West End farce, a theatrical celebration of anti-theatre, mixing absurdity with vaudeville, anachronistic elements with historical accuracy, borrowing liberally from Artaud and Preminger, Brecht and Tarantino, while remaining faithful to Camus' themes and overall structure. The tone is set from the opening scene when Caligula drives a minivan recklessly down the steps of a tremendous Roman arch, its bass amp thumping rap. More graphic scenes follow, including a game of Russian roulette and using humans as bowling pins. Random executions litter the stage, and at one point Caligula rapes a patrician's wife while another is forced to eat the flesh of his roasted son. But Džilindžers never succumbs to melodrama or naturalistic gore. His sadistic humor so stylized that he never pretends his performance is anything but an artificial theatrical indulgence.

In one of the funniest scenes — and the nastiest, given Latvia's Romantic nationalism embodied in the spirit of unity felt during the late 1980s, just before independence — Caligula orchestrates a variety show in which the patricians are forced to perform song and dance routines (a grotesque parody of the version by Camus where Caligula forces the poets to improvise poems on the subject of death). After several ridiculous attempts at disco and hip-hop, an earnest young man solemnly strums a guitar and sings one of the most beloved songs of these precious "years of enlightenment." Just as the dewy-eyed audience begins to applaud lightly, respectfully, some quietly singing along, filled with chauvinistic pride and nostalgia, Caligula, sitting among the audience, suddenly stands and deliberately shoots the singer dead. The shock in the auditorium is palpable, and Džilindžers exploits it ruthlessly, freezing the scene in silence for several minutes, provoking the now uncomfortable audience into applauding this time as if that would kick-start the action and move the play away from this obviously unsettling episode. But Džilindžers holds the scene even longer, testing the audience's patience and indulgence, until he achieves the desired effect: turning the audience's romantic nostalgia back on itself, an aggressive, unapologetic assault on the sentimental pap infecting the popular culture. Only then does he allow the action to proceed.

It is facile and reductive, and for Džilindžers irrelevant, to seek in his desire to stage *Caligula* recent historical parallels — reading the play as a morality tale about Soviet totalitarianism, for instance, or viewing Caligula as an image of a monomaniacal American neo-con. In the end, however, in a scene ripped straight from the headlines, Caligula assumes the role of a suicide bomber in a final act of terrorism against the state, the senators, and himself.

While Džilindžers might agree with Camus' sentiments, particularly that Caligula's "error lies in negating what binds him to mankind [... as one] cannot be free at the expense of others" (Camus vi), Džilindžers' target is not philosophical: it is Latvian culture (and the global culture generally, he would argue, resisting any identification as a nationalist playwright). His concern is not man's condition: it is performance values. The bottom line for Džilindžers is simply to entertain himself. If as a side-effect he can invigorate Latvian culture, so much the better. But he is as pessimistic as Ieva Zole about the future of Latvian theatre. Whereas Zole complains about the education of the audience as a prerequisite for advancing the culture within the theatre community, Džilindžers' complaint is leveled against the young directors who, in his view, are too timid. They graduate with fresh ideas, he says, but almost to a person quickly fall into a predictable pattern, tinkering with possibilities but settling for what audiences and critics expect, especially those involved in repertory theatres, although Džilindžers makes no distinction between the established repertory troupes and the so-called independent theatres.

"Even Skatuve," he says, "is essentially a repertory system."

Regarding his contemporaries, he admires some of the work by Gaļina Poliščuka, especially her staging of *Romeo and Juliet*, and he says he appreciates Koršunovas, mainly for his style, not necessarily his individual performances. "Every show is the same," Džilindžers says of the Latvian director, "as if he is making the identical show over and over again." He expresses a qualified respect for the work of Regnārs Vaivars, saying he showed early signs of talent, "but the critics killed him," forcing Vaivars to leave theatre for a commercial advertising job. Four years later, Vaivars returned to theatre, this time embracing psychological realism. "The critics this time gave him a prize," Džilindžers says, wry but dismissive. "And killed him a second time." Eihe's *The Blue* earns a shrug, indicating Džilindžers' boredom with language-based dramatic realism. Of Roga's *Nora*, he agrees with Čakare that the title character as played by the director is a perversion of Ibsen's intent and cynically sums up the problem: "Feminism."

As for the directors at the forefront of Latvian theatre, Džilindžers is not shy about citing himself and his friend Alvis Hermanis as the only two working at the margins that demarcate anything that could be described as truly "new." Though he acknowledges they are using different approaches, for him their purpose is the same: to challenge the status quo, what he describes as the tired, dull, text-based psychological realism that he considers the bane of contemporary Latvian theatre. On the differences in their styles, Džilindžers explains that Hermanis "calculates" before the performance exactly how he wants the piece to work and brings his calculations to rehearsals, shaping the play to conform to the ideas he has worked out ahead of time. For Džilindžers, his understanding of how the play will be shaped begins in rehearsals. He prefers to approach the process with only a loose idea of what will happen, attentive to what he calls "the accidental factor," allowing spontaneity to serve the play as much as any preconceived notions about what should happen.

For Džilindžers, psychological realism is "finished — there's nothing new." He admits that he incorporates some elements of realism in his work, but only "small episodes" that are effective only because he re-contextualizes those moments, contrasting them with other forms. Studied realism no longer works because in his view the audience is impatient. The spectator today, he says, is accustomed to immediate access to innumerable sources of information (the same point Eihe makes). This impatience keeps the audience "a step ahead" of the delivery mechanism, as it were, of information within the context of realism. To appeal to a new audience, new forms — not necessarily inferior or less legitimate — must be employed to reflect the reality of an age of integrated information systems. This failure to synthesize the visual elements with an accelerated dialog — to acknowledge that, like Estonian theatre, and in contrast to the Lithuanians, Latvian theatre still relies on "too much talking" — will, he says, eventually kill off contemporary audiences.

"Written words," he says, "hinder the imagination."

Džilindžers' disdain for psycho-realism — "I hate it," he says bluntly — and what he derisively refers to as Latvia's "actor's theatre — is seriously evident in his production of *Penelope and Dick*. He reduces Maugham's comical but subtle psychological study of marital infidelity and the willful deceit of the couples involved — a staple element of stereotypical British discretion, decorum and the art of keeping up appearances — to an absurdist farce that has little to do with British behavior and everything to do with Džilindžers' own love affair with the quirky, Warholian, image-saturated landscape that passes for normalcy in the new fangled, consumer-driven contemporary Latvian society.

Whereas Maugham shellacs the veneer of social manners by which the Edwardians masked their perversities and maintained their peculiar façade of normalcy, Džilindžers works from a prime-time soap ethos in which vixens vie for incompetent males, sex is never an end in itself but always merely another option in an arsenal of manipulative tools, and personal obsessions — fitness, pornography, alcohol, religion — become interchangeable cultural commodities, nothing more than convenient lifestyles, as ephemeral as the guts of a lava lamp.

What at first seems irreverent — Džilindžers ridiculing a pop-art culture he obviously adores — belies a more serious critique. Džilindžers, typically, prefers to hedge his moral intentions: eager to claim the mantle of a po-mo alchemist turning trash into gold, he is less willing to acknowledge

Dž. Dž. Džilindžers' version of *Penelope and Dick* at the Art Theatre, Riga, illustrates his disdain for psycho-realism and what he derisively refers to as Latvia's "actor's theatre." Džilindžers reduces Maugham's subtle psychological study of marital infidelity and the willful deceit of the couples involved to an absurdist farce celebrating Džilindžers' love affair with the quirky, Warholian, image-saturated landscape that passes for normalcy in the new-fangled, consumer-driven contemporary Latvian society (photograph by Jānis Deinats/"Fotocentrs").

his role as ethicist. His irony more closely resembles that of an old school reformer like Kierkegaard than the easy cynicism of Joe Orton. Any moralizing in the play, he says, occurs "by accident." Yet he identifies his "mission" as a "fight against untruths." He argues that if people are "living old truths, they become lies." He says that in his version, unlike Maugham's original, he has Dick kill Penelope because to let the couple continue living as they have would affirm the established values that are actually, in the context of the play, decadent and useless. "Truth," he says," is a new thing that happens to you in a different context." Penelope's murder destroys the "old truths" and forces the survivors to rethink their values. In an existential coda, the *raison d'être* of his own career, he adds, "You have to recreate truth to survive life."

Džilindžers and Hermanis work at opposite ends of a stylistic continuum, philosophically and practically, but they are responding to what appears in contemporary Latvia to be a theatre of exhaustion, and each director in his own way confronts the same issues: re-energizing an enervated theatre, exploring the aesthetic edges of performance art, and increasing the audience for Latvian theatres.

That Džilindžers and Hermanis are constantly seeking new creative

Rēzija Kalniņa in Džilindžers' version of *Penelope and Dick* at The Art Theatre, Riga (photograph by Jānis Deinats/"Fotocentrs").

avenues for their dramatic productions is evident in the variety of strategies they incorporate into their new material. Džilindžers displays a range of influences, pulling ideas from a variety of sources such as contemporary media, situation comedy and epic theatre that demonstrates a postmodern love of pastiche, of new ways to use old material, exploiting the empty rhetoric of hype and dissonance for dramatic effect. His are anti-aesthetic performances, subversive in the sense that Džilindžers' work represents the reality of social mutation, comical nightmares that are simultaneously a product and a critique of multinational capitalism. Of course, Džilindžers moves seamlessly from the kitsch and camp of *Penelope and Dick* to the sentimental tragedy *Melancholic Waltz* (*Melanholiskais valsis*), a certifiably weepy musical, which merely illustrates another facet of his postmodern sensibility: a polished eclecticism.

Hermanis shares Džilindžers' sophistication, as well as his uneasiness with a settled definition of theatre. His distrust of genre and unity, in an Aristotelian sense, forces him into meta-theatrical commentary even as he tries to refine the form. This aestheticism leads him to despoil his previous work, divesting it of any significance beyond a reservoir for exploitation, recombining old material that then informs, comments on, and eventually subverts his next project. A purist, Hermanis defines the essence of theater as "storytelling and physical presence" ("In the Strange Club"). Contrary to Džilindžers' media saturated productions, Hermanis believes that soon "theatre will be the only form of art escaping electronic transformation," and at that point theatre will be returned to its amoral, aesthetic essence: "I never looked at theatre as a tool for improving the world. I think that theatre needs to be a pure art-form."

The last issue is perhaps the trickiest: maintaining Latvian identity in a work while making it accessible and desirable for a foreign audience. Hermanis thinks theatre "will always be local and should be rooted in a local context." Lauris Gundars, director, playwright, and one of the principals at the independent Theatre TT (Teātris tt), does not hesitate to identify "this LANGUAGE problem" ("Theatre as Art") as the most difficult factor to overcome in theatre. Gundars points out that the British and Americans can tour English-speaking countries with huge markets and audiences, but Latvian artists, Gundars complains, "can't go to Helsinki to act [...] Even to Lithuania! And this is a very specific thing for a small country." Films seem to have overcome the problem of globalization because they are so easily disseminated, plus they can be dubbed or subtitled into various languages. Theatre is more difficult to travel for obvious reasons, including expenses for actors, arranging for spaces, constructing sets, etc. But it is language — even more than using localized situations — that presents the most severe drawback for exporting dramatic works from one country to another. Hermanis believes "there is something un-natural about theatre going abroad" ("In the Strange Club"). As for the language issue, he is philosophical: "more important than the language you are speaking is whether you have something to say. Then language doesn't matter." Gundars is even blunter. "I think it is almost impossible to write down something 'global,'" he says, claiming that theatre by its nature is not necessarily an exportable commodity, as a play is "made in a special place and it is very big problem to make it in another place" ("Theatre as Art"). He cites his own *Touching the White Bear* (*Pieskaries baltajam lācim!*) as an example of a play that deals with a strictly Latvian theme — the mass deportation of by the Soviets of Latvians to Siberia — that could appeal to a wider audience outside of Latvia, but "only because of the performance." In an attempt to have his play speak a common language, as it were, Gundars developed it poetically, allowing the images and situations in the performance to "address the public aesthetically, politically [...]. The play follows the editing principle, [in which] the images move around in time and space directed by relativity in the rules of the play" (Kļaviņa 16).

Gundars expresses a mixture of surprise and contempt at the Art Theatre's decision to stage Martin McDonagh's *Pillowman* (*Spilvencilvēks*) "because this play is totally not Latvian. The British kind of writing and the Latvian theatre ... We are VERY different" ("Theatre as Art"). He compares his reaction to the reception of Koršunovas' production of *Shopping and Fucking* when it came to Latvia. "After the first act, only one-third of the audience stayed. The British are thinking in a different way." Although Gundars resists the importation of plays, he is not averse to the principle of viewing works from other countries or the need to have Latvian plays performed abroad. His skepticism about the cultural translation is syntagmatic, not ideological: "The topic for all of us is the same — the mysterious human. For me, personally, it is important to see my plays staged outside Latvia, mainly because it promotes the essential role of drama in our domestic theater" (qtd. in Kļaviņa 14–15).

Gundars frames the problem of maintaining a strong alternative theatre in terms of the expenses involved, especially concerning space: "it is almost impossible to make alternative theatre [...] in Riga [...] because it is impossible to FIND a place where to play even for a hundred people" ("Theatre as Art"). He also notes that most of the theatre-going public in

Riga associate "theatre" with a building, "and if there is a theatre company without a building, one that is working in different locations, it is a very hard job to inform people about the performances and sell tickets." Gundars names the New Riga under the guidance of Hermanis as the ideal synthesis because it is "state owned, but at the same time it's alternative."

Another promising movement attracting many of the top writers and directors is what Hermanis (and others throughout the Baltics) defines as "ecological" theatre. "Theatre needs real physical contact between artists and spectators. This makes the position of theatre very special" ("In the Strange Club"). This ecological positioning — that is, staging works in site-specific locations outside traditional theatre spaces, like Varnas setting *Wasted Land* in the abandoned Pravda building in Vilnius, or Klemets performing *Someone Who'll Watch Over Me* inside Köismäe Tower in Tallinn — opens a specialized discourse that Una Chaudhuri identifies as "platiality" denoting "the signifying power and political potential of specific places" (5). Situating a play ecologically also acts to liberate the audience from its expectations the same way exile for Chaudhuri can be emancipating: it posits the performance as an event rather than a viewing, transferring the action from a closed, tightly controlled environment into a more organic, spontaneous setting, allowing the location to infuse the play with meaning missing from the sterile, artificial confines of a theatre stage.

One example of this trend in Latvian theatre is Baņuta Rubesa's *Escape from Troy* (*Glābšanās no Trojas*). Based on versions of the fall of Troy by Euripides and Seneca, combined with elements of Toronto-based writer Ingrida Viksna's novel, *We Have to Wade into the Sea*, which recounts the plight of refugees fleeing the Soviet army's advance on Riga as the German's were retreating at the end of World War II, the play finds historical parallels between the tragedy of ancient Troy and the more recent horrors of World War II. Performed on the coast near Liepāja near the actual spot where Latvians hid in the woods waiting to board boats to take them to Sweden, the play is a spectacle of environmental theatre, a depiction of a tragic period in Latvia's past framed as an historic epic event.

The action begins with a chorus of young people, dressed in contemporary casual beach attire, relaxing at a picnic on a pebbly beach by the sea. Their complacency is interrupted by the dramatic arrival of Hecuba on crutches, accompanied by Cassandra, Andromache and her son Astyanax. Hecuba announces that Troy is burning, and that the only chance to escape the marauding Greeks is to board the boats and go to sea. Aeneas, an insurgent with the Trojan underground, explains that only people on a

A good example of "environmental theatre," Baņuta Rubesa's *Escape from Troy* parallels the tragedy of ancient Troy and the plight of refugees fleeing the Soviet army's advance on Riga as the Germans were retreating at the end of World War II. Performed on the coast near Liepāja near the actual spot where Latvians hid in the woods waiting to board boats to take them to Sweden, the play is a spectacle depicting a tragic period in Latvia's past framed as an historic epic event (courtesy New Theatre Institute of Latvia).

special list — the privileged, the politicians, artists and scientists — will be allowed onto the boats. The women struggle to accept their fate — Cassandra, Andromache and Hecuba assigned as chattel to Agamemnon, Achilles and Odysseus respectively. As they lament their fate, the first boats appear, but Aeneas threatens to shoot anyone not authorized to board, and the boats stay off the beach. By the time Helen arrives, the others are desperate, but she has only contempt for them, believing she will be returned to her husband Menelaus and convinced he will forgive her for being wrongly abducted and forced into marrying Paris. A Greek patrol kills Aeneas, then arrests Astyanax, accusing him of writing an SOS message in a bottle, and executes him too. Finally, the last boat arrives to deliver the women to Greece as slaves, but Cassandra predicts that Troy will rise again.

The similarity between the fall of Troy and the plight of Latvian refugees fleeing the devastation wrought by two murderous occupation forces is distinct. But the historical parallels provide only the excuse for Rubesa to explore the possibilities of staging the play on location. Some particulars of the production — for instance, the numerous anachronistic elements — do reinforce the historical connections, but it is the location that gives the performance its power. Her choice of material, complemented by the historically accurate setting — transposing the tragic events of the Greek siege of Troy to the shores of Latvia and integrating the text with the environment — not only brings immediacy to events thirty centuries apart but also lends an aura of authenticity to the material and underscores the desperation of any refugees fleeing war, ancient or modern.

Again, according to Rubesa, critical response was muted. "The critics dismissed the event," she says. "They couldn't be bothered to make the trip."

Rubesa explains the attitude of the critics not in terms of laziness or reflexive prejudice against her as an outsider but as a codified determination on the part of the general population in Latvia to avoid discussing painful or uncomfortable historical subjects.

"Everything from the 1930s to the 90s is off-limits," says Rubesa, especially the mass deportations, the occupation years, the repression, the censorship, and the general political realities of the second half of the twentieth century. *Touching the White Bear* is the one notable exception, but even that play makes the point rhetorically: "There are less and less people for whom the words Siberia, deportation, camp mean part of their lives. [...] Why do we have to be quiet then? [...] Are we able to give answers when we are heroes or cowards [...] if we avoid the inevitable past? (Kļaviņa 15).

In Rubesa's view, the difficulty the Latvians face in trying to maintain a progressive theatre movement is both inherent and practical. First, by its nature the country produces a small pool of talent, and echoing the concerns of Zole, Rubesa agrees that in a society pressuring young people into careers that earn them a sustainable living wage, few choose to study humanities. They focus instead on information technology or opt out of higher education altogether for the immediate if meager incomes available in the growing service sector based on the ever increasing rates of tourist traffic. Others immigrate to more economically developed countries in the EU, often sacrificing their professional training for less skilled labor simply to earn comparatively better salaries. On the practical side, except in the rare ensemble approach, no component within the theatre community's creative process stresses or supports the development of new playwrights; specifically, there is no module to nurture, encourage, test and rework new, potentially decent scripts that need the kind of creative workshop treatment so prevalent (and arguably productive) in Western organizations, professionally or as part of the university creative writing programs.

Gundars concurs. "Fifteen years ago," he says, "I was the only writer and the youngest one, because the people who worked during the Soviet times stopped writing totally. [...] Because earlier it was a different reality, it was either propaganda or anti-propaganda." Now, he says, "theatres don't trust our new playwrights. Old playwrights are not writing" ("Theatre as Art"). He has initiated a special course focusing explicitly on new playwriting — exactly the "creative catalyst" Rubesa predicts will revitalize Latvian theatre.

Other evidence of a flagging theatre can be seen in how many "imports" are now included in most seasonal programs, especially the work of Irish and British playwrights. For instance, the critical appreciation for McDonagh's *Pillowman* (Gundars' complaint a notable exception), lies not in its images of the totalitarian police antics reminiscent of the Soviet bloc security apparatus; instead, the appeal is based in cultural, historical and economic realities Latvians perceive to share with Ireland. But most surprising, given the talent of the Latvian theatre professionals, is that The Art Theatre's performance of *Pillowman* was directed by Jan-Willem van den Bosch, a Dutchman living in England, and the set was designed by David Fielding, also of England.

For Latvian theatre to continue evolving in a progressive direction, most young professionals agree that restructuring the repertory system is a priority. It is the kind of reform from which almost all other reforms — funding, aesthetics, audience appreciation — will follow. Although sputtering attempts have been made to maintain a healthy "alternative" theatre circuit, besides Theatre TT and The Stage, very few rogue troupes can manage to sustain themselves.

Notes

1. Although the Lithuanian director Jonas Vaitkus from the Lithuanian National Drama Theatre concurs with Saro on this issue, Priit Pedajas, the Artistic Director of Estonian Drama Theatre, disputes the idea, and concurs with Latvian critic Valda Čakare's more benign view that there was simply no opportunities to study directing in the Baltics because the universities had no programs for training directors.

2. Zane Kreicberga, Director of the New Theatre Institute of Latvia, lodged the same complaint that many theatre directors made in Lithuania, that in Latvia the quality of the playwriting is stale compared to the dynamic styles of the new directors. Yet the writers still question why their scripts are not produced. In one anecdote, she relates how Dž Dž Džilindžers agreed to direct *The Nice Feeling of Cleanness* (*Labā tīrības sajūta*), what Kreicberga termed an "old-fashioned" play by Pauls Putniņš (see pp. 243–251, and also note 20). Džilindžers took the rather straightforward realistic play and completely abandoned the intention of the playwright, stylizing the action and actually turning the play into a parody of realism. Outraged at first, Putniņš changed his tune when he realized how much the audience enjoyed the performance. As Kreicberga noted wryly, and accurately, nicely summing up the discrepancy in the level of talent and sensibility between the new directors and the practicing playwrights, "Džilindžers saved the play."

3. Many critics disparage Lebeliūnas' approach. Markevičiūtė labels his style "typical actor's staging to show people's feelings," illustrating the prevailing sensibility of the Lithuanian audience generally as well as critics who favor a "director's theatre" over an "actor's theatre."

4. Sajūdis, which means "Movement" in Lithuanian, was a forceful political council composed of Communist Party members and nonparty members to organize the Lithuanian Reconstruction Movement and to lend support to Gorbachev's policies, but it also promoted Lithuanian national issues, including the restoration of the Lithuanian language, secret details of the Nazi-Soviet Nonaggression Pact, revelations about the atrocities committed during the Stalinist years, and environmental protection.

5. See Ramunė Markevičiūtė's essay "The Energy of Transit: Theatre in Non-traditional Spaces" in *Kulturos barai*. Rpt. in *Eurozine* 2005. Trans. Aušra Simanavičiūtė. <http://www.eurozine.com/articles/2005-10-19-marcinkeviciute-en.html>.

6. According to Skendelienė, "The older generation of directors is the alumni of the Russian Theatre schools (except J. Miltinis, who studied in Paris in 1932–1936). It wasn't until 1990 that the first artistic directing school was established in the Music Academy, Vilnius."

7. The question of nationality was a tricky one in Estonia in the nineteenth century. The author of *Kalevipoeg*, Kreutzwald, had Estonian parents but he studied and lived in German-speaking environment. The same applies more or less to Koidula whose mother

was German. All educated or wealthy people became Germans by their social class.

8. In Tätte's production of the play, the man appears with a fish-like face and open mouth, suggesting the golden/magic fish.

9. Vrgoč, writing about the identical phenomenon in Croatia, explains this turn away from politics to more formal considerations in detail in his article "Croatian Theatre at the Close of the Nineties: From Political Queries to Aesthetic Challenges."

10. See note 7 above. Many young Estonians like Koldits defiantly speak of the nineteenth century Estonian Germans as if it they were entirely separate from the indigenous Estonians, while the reality of their relationship is more complex and the differences between the "pure" Estonian and "German" are often indistinguishable, or at least so interconnected as to erase clear demarcations between them.

11. Freelance director Larry Zappia from Croatia, speaking at the Q Theatre in Helsinki, Finland, during the November 2003 Baltic Circle conference, concurred with Laasik about the negative effects of small countries trying to achieve status as transnational theatres. He notes that "transcultural bonds are hard to form" and labels the kind of theatre that denies its own cultural roots "airport theatre" or "theatre of no-belonging." He attributes this phenomenon to the fact that "minorities have this feeling of being threatened, that they are going to assimilate and vanish."

12. For Jalakas, the Rakvere Theatre represented the epitome of bureaucratic ineptitude, and he considered its problems to be endemic and institutional. Rähesoo describes Rakvere as the one theatre in Estonia where "working conditions are the hardest" (170).

13. Külli Paulus, who concedes that Kõiv's "material is hard, or even impossible, to adapt for the stage, quotes Priit Pedajas as saying that "staging Kõiv's plays is well nigh impossible."

14. The eponymous Daugavpils resides in the second city to Riga. The Liepāja, also named after its host city, is the oldest professional repertory theatre in Latvia. The Valmiera, again named for its city of residence, experiments in psychological realism in its two small halls while producing melodramas, comedies and performances for children on its main stage.

15. Ieva Zole, Assistant Managing Director at the National, disputes this self-characterization, insisting that the directors have more autonomy than the theatre itself would like to admit.

16. Homos Novus ("new man") is an international festival of contemporary theatre organized by the New Theatre Institute of Latvia. Spēlmaņu Nakts ("night of the actors") is an annual showcase of Latvian plays selected by prominent theatre critics followed by an awards ceremony culminating on November 23 to commemorate the birthday of the famous Latvian theatre director Eduards Smiļģis.

17. The myth of Lāčplēsis is similar to the Estonian epic *Kalevipoeg*. The creation of literary epics in both Latvia and Estonia coincided with the romantic national consciousness in the 19th century.

18. Zeltiņa recalls Russian shopkeepers after independence telling her daughter to quit speaking the "dog language" of Latvian and to speak the "language of Lenin."

19. "Immature poets imitate; mature poets steal…" from "Philip Massinger" (158).

20. Real name: Raimonds Rupeiks. Džilindžers takes his stage name from the 1968 film *Dillinger Is Dead* by the Italian director Marco Ferreri. Džilindžers claims that after he viewed the film, "the images" haunted him until he decided to appropriate the name, but he insists that the colorful sobriquet has nothing to do with his perceived "outlaw" status.

Works Cited

Atėnai, Šiaurės. Program from "Madagascar." The State Small Theatre of Vilnius. <http://www.vmt.lt/en/pages/view/?id=50&PHPSESSID=2338efa47f009e75ac971fb2540be726>.
Avotins, Viktors. "Dances in a field of real competition." *Neatkariga rita avize* Nov. 29, 2000 Riga, Latvia <http://www.vip.lv/jti/Publikacijas/avot_en.htm>.
Bajorinienė, Elona. "Theatre in Twilight." Trans. Aušra Cizikienė. *Krasnogruda* no. 8 (1998). <http://www.pogranicze.sejny.pl/archiwum/krasnogruda/pismo /8/eural/bajori.htm>.
Balevičiūtė, Ramunė. *Kultūros barai*. <www.sirenos.lt>.
Baltic Theatre Policy Review III. Riga, Latvia. <http://www.vip.lv/jti/EN_new/projects/policy.htm>.
Baudrillard, Jean. *The Ecstasy of Communication*. Trans. Bernard and Caroline Schutze. Ed. Sylvère Lotringer. New York: Semiotext(e), 1988. 12.
Buglewicz, James. "Czech Cinema: An Interview with Michal Bragant, Czech National Film Archives." *Slavic and East European Performance* vol. 20 no. 3 (Fall 2000): 35–42.
Čakare, Valda. "The Ecoglogy of Theatre in Post-Soviet Latvia." *Eastern European Theatre After the Iron Curtain*. Ed. Kalina Stefauova. London: Routledge, 1998. 81–97.
Camus, Albert. *Caligula*. In *Caligula and Three Other Plays*. Trans. Stuart Gilbert. New York: Vintage, 1960. 1–74.
_____. Foreword. *Caligula and Three Other Plays*. Trans. Stuart Gilbert. New York: Vintage, 1960. v–x.
Carlson, Marvin. "Report from Estonia." *Slavic and East European Performance* vol. 19, no. 1 (Spring 1999): 62–65.
Chaudhuri, Una. *Staging Space: The Geography of Modern Drama*. Ann Arbor: U of Michigan Press, 1995.
Eliot, T.S. "From Philip Massinger." *Selected Prose of T.S. Eliot*. Ed. Frank Kermode. New York: Harcourt Brace, 1975.
Epner, Eero. "More of 'Me.'" *Estonian Art*. The Estonian Institute, Jan. 2005. <http://www.einst.ee/Ea/1_05/epner.html>.
Gardner, Lyn. "Attempts on Her Life." *Guardian*, 31 July 2004 <http://www.guardian.co.uk/print/0,3858,4983005-108884,00.html>
Górski, Wieslaw. "Memoirs of the Warsaw Uprising." *Slavic and East European Performance* vol. 20. no. 1 (Spring 2000): 45–47.
Grīnbauma, Krista, ed. Spēlmaņu Nakts program Teara balva 2003/2004. Trans. Dana Fiļipišina and Viktors Freibergs. Riga: Ulma, 2004.

Grinvalds, Dainis, and Ingmars Caklais, et al. *Skate 2001.* Trans. Katarina Hartgers and Margita Gailīte. Latvian Contemporary Drama Festival. Riga: Latvian Theatre Union, 2001.
Gundars, Lauris. "Theatre as Art in the Era of Globalization." Baltic Circle 2005. <http://www.q-teatteri.fi/baltic_circle/dramagora/HOMONOVUS/tas.php>.
Hermanis, Alvis. "In the Strange Club of Theatre Freaks." Baltic Circle 2003. <http://www.q-teatteri.fi/baltic_circle/2003/newsletter/mon241103/strange.html>.
Hoberman, J. "Work in Progress." *The Village Voice March* 29-April 4, 2000. <http://www.villagevoice.com/film/0013,hoberman,13613,20.html>.
Kessing, Katja. "Interview with Oskaras Koršunovas: 'the spectator is not to deliver its reason at clothes.'" Trans. Jūratė Pieslytė. Goethe-Institute Vilnius. <http://translate.google.com/translate?hl=en&sl=de&u=http://www.goethe.de/prs/int/de16175.htm&prev=/search%3Fq%3Dkessing%2Binterview%2Bkorsunovas%26hl%3Den%26lr%3D>.
Kivirähk, Andrus. *The Estonian Funeral.* Trans. Triin Sinissaar. Unpublished photocopy. 2002.
Kļaviņa, Ilze, ed. *Skate 2003.* Trans. Ieva Ērnštreite. Latvian Contemporary Drama Festival. Riga: Preses Nams, 2003.
Kruus, Priit. "Future Classics: How Should Freedom Be Used." *Estonian Literary Magazine* no. 20 (Spring 2005). <http://www.einst.ee/literary/spring 2005/index.html>.
"Latvian National Theatre." *Homo Novus Program,* 2002.
Liniņš, Eduards. "Baltic Theatre Policy Review." *Homo Novus 1999.* The New Theatre Institute of Latvia, 2000. 36–40.
Marcinkevičiūtė, Ramunė. "About Us." *OKT main.* Trans. Artur Zapalowski. <http://www.okt.lt/main.php3?menu_id=5&lang=e&parent=5&sid=&spauda=>.
Nelson, Sean. "Only Fakes Survive. The Sex Pistols' Story Told from a New Perspective: the Band's." *The Portland Mercury* April 27-May 3, 2000. <http://www.thestranger.com/seattle/Content?oid=3809>.
Nietzsche, Friedrich. *The Basic Writings of Nietzsche.* Ed. and trans. Walter Kaufmann. New York: The Modern Library, 1968.
_____. *Twilight of the Idols and The Anti-Christ.* Trans. John Hollingdale. New York: Penguin, 1985.
"Nomadism and Airport Theatre." *The Baltic Circle Festival Newsletter.* Nov. 24, 2003. <http://www.q-teatteri.fi/baltic_circle/newsletter/mon241103/nomadism.html>.
Paulus, Külli. "Estonian Dramaturgy—a Moment on Stage." *Estonian Literary Magazine* no. 6 (Spring 1998). <http://www.einst.ee/literary/spring98/06drama.htm>.
Pelevin, Victor. *4 by Pelevin.* Trans. Andrew Bromfield. New York: New Directions, 1994.
Rähesoo, Jaak. "The Estonia Drama Revisited." *Slavic and East European Performance* vol.18 no.1 (Spring 1998): 23–29.
_____. *Estonian Theatre* (Tallinn: Estonia Theatre Union, 1999), 13.
Raudseps, Pauls, trans. *Latvian Theatre 2003.* The Latvian Theatre Workers Association.
Rudzīte, Ilze. "Preventive Medicine for the Latvian Theatre Policy." <http://www.vip.lv/jti/Publikacijas/pote_en.htm>.
Šabasevičinė, Daiva. "Jonas Vaitkus—teatro gyvasties ieskotojas." Trans. by Aivaras Mockus. Teatras vol. 19 nos. 1–2 (2005): 79.
Salomonsson, Annika. culturebase.net <http://www.culturebase.net/artist.php?689>.
Skendelienė, Rūta. "Lithuanian Theatre in the Last Ten Years: Directing, Acting, and New Forms of Expression." *Trans: Internet-Zeitschrift fur Kulturwissenschaftern* no. 9 May 2001. <http://inst.at/trans/9Nr/skendelien9.htm>.
Staniškytė, Jurgita. "New Representations: The Languages of Contemporary Lithuanian Theatre." *Lituanus: Lithuanian Quarterly Journal of Arts and Sciences* 48.3 Ed. Violeta Kelertas (Fall 2002). <http://www.lituanus.org/2002/02_3_03.htm>.
"Synopsis of Stage Directors' Discussion 'The Basic Values Cannot Be Denied.'" *Post Mod-*

ernisms: teātri un drāmā. Ed. Silvija Radzobe. Trans. Viktors Fribergs. Riga: Jumava, 2004.
Tätte, Jaan. "Happy Everyday!" *Naidendid. (Plays)*. Trans. Triin Sinissaar. Tallinn: Tallinn City Theatre, 2002.
———. "The Highway Crossing, or A Tale of a Golden Fish." *Naidendid. (Plays)*. Trans. Krista Kaer. Tallinn: Tallinn City Theatre, 2002.
Tjarve, Baiba. "Passing on Knowledge." *East West Theatre*. Paris: Theorem, 2005.
———. "Performing Arts Policy in Baltic Countries." <http://www.vip.lv/jti/EN_new/publications/performing_arts.htm>.
Toompere, Hendrik. "First There was Nature, Then There Came Culture, and Then Rituals." *Estonian Culture*, Feb. 2003. <http://www.einst.ee/culture/II_MMIII/toompere.html>.
Vasinauskaitė, Rasa. "From Metaverbal to Metascenic Conception." *OKT main*. Trans. Antanas Danielius. <http://www.okt.lt/main.php3?menu_id=5&lang=e&parent=5&sid=&spauda=>.
Vrgoč, Dubravka. "Croatian Theatre at the Close of the Nineties: From Political Queries to Aesthetic Challenges." *Slavic and East European Performance* vol. 20 no. 1 (Spring 2000): 52–60.
Zeltiņa, Guna. "Latvian Theatre in the 90s: Trends, Repertoire, Personalities." *Slavic and East European Performance* vol.17 no.1 (Spring 1997): 37–48.
Zole, Ieva. "Performance Night Musings or Seeking (Understanding) One's Own." Trans. Dana Filipisina and Dace Smits. Teātra balva Spēlmaņu nakts 2004/2005. Riga: ULMA, 2005.

Index

Adamkus, Valdas 34, 156
Aesop (and Aesopian language) 14, 22–23, 29, 50, 64, 85, 137
Albee, Edward 24, 27
Aleksaitis, Valdis 36
All Humans Are Cats 165–168
Allik, Jaak 17
Amtamanis-Briedītis, Alfrēds 174
Andersen, Hans Christian 57
Animal Farm 127–129
Antonioni, Michelangelo 36
Aristotle (Aristotelian) 204
Art Fort (Vilnius) 52–54, 67
Art Theatre (Riga) 7, 157–158, 172–175, 188, 198, 202–203
Artaud, Antonin 31, 49, 55, 198–198
"Atgaiva" 32
Atkočiūnas, Rolandas 35
Attempts on Her Life 74–79, 87–88, 101
Auškāps, Kārlis 158
Avotins, Viktor 16
L'Avventura 36

Bajorinienė, Elona 21, 44–46, 66
Bakus, Egidijus 53, 56
Balevičiūtė, Ramunė 47, 61, 87, 90, 92
Baranovska, Beata 164
Barba, Eugenio 133
Barker, Howard 63
The Barn-Keeper 142
barn theatre 34
Baudrillard, Jean 13, 36, 39–40, 73–74, 168, 171
Bausch, Pina 133
Beckett, Samuel 24, 63, 96, 166
Belarus 8
Benedict XVI 123
Bergman, Ingmar 41, 119, 120

Bičkutė, Valda 90
Blair, Anthony Charles Lynton (Tony) 20
Blaise 48
Blaumanis, Rūdolfs 157
Blok, Alexander 49
Blow Up 36
Blow, Wind! 161–164
The Blue 193–196, 200
Bolsheviks 1
Bosch, Hieronymus 127, 147
Boyakov, Edward 17
Bragant, Michal 15
Brecht, Bertolt (and Brechtian) 32, 66, 96, 158, 198–199
The Bridge 96
Brook, Peter 41, 60, 62
Bruegel, Pieter 147
Budrys, Povilas 47
Buglewicz, James 15
Bukšnaitytė, Alma 19–20
Bulgaria 16
Bush, George Walker 14
By Gorky 182, 184

Čakare, Valda 174–175, 179–182, 188, 191–192, 200, 211
Caligula 197–200
Calvin, John (and Calvinism) 108–109
Camus, Albert 197–200
Capitalism 20, 31, 33, 39, 78, 122, 204
Carlson, Marvin 11–12
Castaneda, Carlos 142
Catholicism 7, 11, 23, 74, 80, 84, 108, 123–124, 156, 174, 196
Černiauskaitė, Laura Sintija 73
Charlie! 35, 107
Chaudhuri, Una 206

Index

Chekhov, Anton Pavlovich (and Chekhovian) 36, 54, 63, 65, 96, 122, 130, 142, 172, 189
Chekhov, Michael 32, 41, 49
Chernobyl 21
Chetchnyans 31
Children's Lives 154
Children's Trip of Risks see *Children's Lives*
Churchill, Carol 177
Clinton, William Jefferson 20
A Clockwork Orange 161
Close City 52–59, 67, 70, 73, 81, 105
Cobain, Kurt 80
The Cousin of Saaremaa 93
Crime and Punishment 64
Crimp, Martin 74, 87
The Cripple of Innishmaan 131
Croatia 15, 212
Czech Republic 8, 16, 94, 184

Dali, Salvador 147
Daudziņž, Vilis 180
Daugavpils Theatre 160, 188–189, 212
Dauguvietis, Borisas 41
Daunoraviciutė, Ingrida 71–73, 80
Deičs, Felikss 158, 166
de Man, Paul 60
Demons 87
Denmark 8, 28, 54
de Pontcharra, Natacha 87
de Tairov, Alexander 157, 174
Dillinger Is Dead 212
A Doll's House 184–185
Dorst, Tankred 47, 88
Dostoyevsky, Feodor Mikhailovich 63, 65, 69, 87, 96, 198
Džilindžers, Dž. Dž. (Raimonds Rupeiks) 158–159, 190, 193, 197–204, 211–212

East Prussia 6
Eco, Umberto 85
Eihe, Mārtiņs 193–198, 201
Eižvertiņa, Anna 188
Eliot, T(homas) S(terns) 197
environmental theatre 46, 93, 152, 206–207
Escape from Troy 206–208
Estonia 6–7, 11–12, 1–18, 23–26, 28, 54, 93–155, 156, 173–174, 184, 201, 211–212
Estonian Ballads 141
Estonian Drama Theatre 7, 115, 131, 139, 143–144, 211
The Estonian Funeral 109
Estonian Theatre 6
Euripides 206
European Union 1, 3, 5, 7, 21, 28, 52, 54, 56, 67, 72, 73, 86, 92, 107, 124, 209

Fantasy Island 169
A Farewell to Arms 49
Fellini, Federico 36, 90
Ferreri, Marco 212
Festin 148
Fielding, David 209
Filipovič, Inga 88–89
The Filth and the Fury 135
Finks, Eližens 164
Finland 6, 8, 18, 23, 108, 120–121, 184, 212
Fire and Night 165
Fjodorova, Irina 192
Flaubert, Gustave 65
Flying Theatre 41
The Fourth Chair 36–40
Freibergs, Edmunds 164
Freud, Sigmund 49, 120

Garcia, Rodrigo 148
Gardner, Lyn 74
Gargantua and Pantagruel 50
Germany (and German) 11–13, 27, 93–94, 108, 114–115, 121, 124, 130–131, 133, 142, 156–157, 160, 174, 184, 206–207, 211–212
Gerould, Daniel 5
Ghosts 120
Ginger and Fred 36
Giniotis, Aidas 79–80
Gintautaitė, Airida 53, 56
glasnost 11, 81, 153
Glavlit 153–154
Glinskis, Juozas 31–32
Glinskis, Konstantinas 41
Gorbachev, Mikhail Sergeevich 31, 81, 153, 161, 165
Gorčevs, Dmitrijis 169, 171
Gorky, Maxim (Aleksey Maximovich Pyeshkov) 182
Górski, Wieslaw 15
Graužinis, Cezaris 74–78, 80, 87–88, 101
Grishkovets, Yevgeniy 59
Growtowski, Jerzy 49, 60, 74–75, 119, 126, 128, 132–133, 142, 147, 193
Grušas, Juozas 31, 43
Gruzdov, Michail 188
Guerra, Tonino 36
Gulbis, Harijs 158
Gundars, Lauris 28, 73, 204–206, 209

Hamlet 137
Hanseatic 28, 156
Happy Everyday! 96, 101, 104–107
Havel, Vaclav 2
Hedda Gabler 44–47

Hegel, Georg Wilhelm Friedrich (and Hegelian) 60, 147
Heidegger, Martin 60
Hellwig, Hilda 120–122
Hemingway, Ernest 49
Herkus Mantas 43
Hermaküla, Evald 94–95, 138–139, 142
Hermanis, Alvis 28, 59, 158–159, 171, 174–185, 193, 196–197, 201, 203–206
Hermit and Six-Toes 148–151
The Highway Crossing 101–104, 122, 141
Hitler, Adolf 115
Hoberman, J. 135
Husserl (and Husserlean), Edmund 134

Ibsen, Henrik 23, 44, 119, 120, 184–186, 188, 200
Ice 178–181, 197
The Inspector General 178, 184
Intercult 16, 59
Ionesco, Eugene 49
Ivanovas, Sergejus 88–89
Ivaškevičius, Marius 22, 28, 52–59, 67, 70, 73, 81, 90–91, 105, 107, 109

Jalakas, Peeter 23, 132–137, 140–141, 212
Jampolskis, Marius 46
Jänes, Pille 116–119, 122, 126
Jankevičius, Agnius 63, 87–88
Jansonas, Egmontas Georgas 63–66, 70, 72, 92
Jarry, Alfred 85
Jarzyna, Grezegorz 59
Jaunušans, Alfrēds 158
John Paul II (Pope) 123
Juliet 141–146
Jurašas, Jonas 41

Kacs, Arkady 158
Kafka, Franz 126
Kairišs, Viesturs 158, 174
Kalev's Son 93, 131, 211–212
Kalevipoeg see *Kalev's Son*
Kalniņa, Rēzija 162, 203
Kane, Sarah 71, 135
Kant, Immanuel 58
Kantor, Tadeusz 55, 119, 147
Karusoo, Merle 23, 26, 152–155, 171, 183
Kaunas (Lithuania) 5–6, 20, 22, 33–51, 52
Kaunas Little Theatre 19, 34–41
Kaunas State Academic Theatre 41–44
Kaunas Youth Chamber Theatre 46–51
Kaupēns 165
Kaupēns, My Dear 165
Kažemēkas, Gintautas 39
Kažemekienes, Inga 39
Khrushchev, Nikita Sergeyevich 43, 63, 94

Kierkegaard, Søren 203
Ķimele, Māra 29, 158, 174, 184
Kivirähk, Andrus 23, 109–113, 142
Klaić, Dragan 18
Klemets, Eva 23, 29, 96, 98, 100–101, 128–132, 152, 206
Koidula, Lydia 93
Kõiv, Madis 152, 212
Koldits, Mart 23, 115, 106, 118, 126–132, 141–142, 147, 212
Kolk, Madis 139–142, 152, 183
Kõre, Hele 98–99
Koršunovas, Oskaras 17, 22, 44, 69–70, 80–87
Kreicberga, Zane 7, 190, 211
Krėvė-Mickevičius, Vincas 43
Kroders, Oļģerts 158
Kuhlmann, Annelis 28
Kuodytė, Viktorija 46–47

Laanesaar, Monika 125
Laasik, Andres 95, 123–126, 212
Lāčplēsis the Bear Slayer 165, 212
La Mama Theatre 40
Lamp, Ann 104
Landsbergis, Algirdas 43
Latvia 7–8, 11–12, 16–18, 23, 25–29, 54, 73, 108, 123, 156–210, 156, 211
Latvian National Theatre 157, 160, 162, 164, 168, 172–175, 179, 185
Latvian Stories 175, 182–185, 196
Lawrence, D(avid) H(erbert) 168
Lazdina, Liga 172
Lebeliūnas, Arvydas 35–41, 211
Leiris, Michel 60
Lenin, Vladimir Ilyich 13, 3–31, 42, 150, 212
Leningrad see St. Petersburg
Lermontov, Mikhail Yurevich 86
Liepāja Theatre 160, 188, 196, 212
The Lieutenant of Inishmore 131–132
Liniņš, Eduards 26
Līnis, Aivars 7
Lithuania 5–8, 11–12, 16–23, 25, 28, 30–92, 108, 123, 156, 184, 201, 204, 211
Lithuanian National Drama Theatre 6, 63, 211
Liūgą, Audronis 17, 22, 59–63, 65–66, 68, 70–71, 80, 132
A Long Christmas Dinner 43
Long Life 178, 181,184
The Lower Depths 182
Lūriņš, Valdis 158
Lūsēns, Jānis 164
Lutheranism (and Protestant) 7, 11, 25, 108, 119, 122–123, 156, 174, 196; see also Calvin

Index

Lydon, John (Johnny Rotten) 135–136
Lynch, David 198

Maculēvičs, Valentīns 158
Madagascar 90, 91, 107, 109
Madame Bovary 64
The Magic Christian 103
Magnier, Claude 48
Maironis 43
Mallarme, Stephane 60
Malmsten, Mait 143–145
Malthusian 149
Mamet, David 96
Manhood 60
Marazhanov, K.A. 157
Marcinkevičius, Justinas 31
Marcinkevičiūtė, Ramunė 81, 82, 211
Markevičiūtė, Elvyra 14, 44, 211
Marx (and Marxism) 20, 31, 68
The Masquerade 86–87, 90–91
Maugham, W(illiam) Somerset 201–203
McDonagh, Martin 131, 135, 205, 209
McGuinness, Frank 129, 152
Meeletu 96–101, 119, 121–122, 128
Mekas, Jonas 63
Melancholic Waltz 204
Merlin 47
The Metamorphosis 116, 118, 126–127
Meyerhold, Vsevolod 32, 49, 64, 120, 132, 139, 142, 157, 192
A Midsummer Night's Dream 82
Miller, Arthur 24
Miss Julie 184
Montalban, Ricardo 169
A Month in the Country 8
Moscow 25, 41–42, 63, 138–139, 142, 188–189
Mrożek, Sławomir 35, 107
Mykolaitis, Saulius 63

Nazis 1, 12, 20, 41, 94, 211
Nekrošius, Eimuntas 17, 21, 52, 60, 81, 120, 188, 197
Nemirovich-Danchenko, Vladimir 41, 64
The Netherlands 16, 184
New Drama Action 6–7. 52, 57, 60, 123
New Riga Theatre 157, 159, 172, 175–180, 182, 184–185, 192–193, 206
Nezlobin, K.N. 157
The Nice Feeling of Cleanness 211
Nietzsche, Friedrich Wilhelm 197, 199
Nietzsche: Basic Writings 199
Night of the Shooting Stars 36
Nomadism 2, 95, 124–125
Nora 184–187, 200
Nostalgia 36
Notos de Cochinas 148

Oedipus Rex 84–85
Ojasoo, Tiit 23, 28, 115, 131–132, 141–146, 196
Oleka-Žilinskas, Andrius 41
Onaitytė, Jūratė 44–45
One More Night and One More Morning 161, 169–172
Only Fakes Survive 135–136
The Open Circle 79–80
Orton, Joe 63, 104, 203
Orwell, George (Eric Arthur Blair) 127
Oskaras Koršunovas Theatre 63, 80
Ostrauskas, Kostas 43
Othello 87, 120

Paaver, Ene 7, 115–116, 121
Padegimas, Gytis 26, 32, 42–44, 63–64
Pampurs, Andejes 165
Paulus, Külli 23–24, 152, 212
Pedajas, Priit 115, 137–139, 141, 211
Pelevin, Viktor 117, 141, 148–149
Penelope and Dick 201–204
perestroika 11, 19, 35, 42, 153, 165
Pēteris Pētersons 172
Pētersons, Pēteris 26, 158, 174
Pillowman 135, 205, 209
Pinter, Harold 25, 42, 104
Pobedonoscevas, Leonardas 88–89
The Pocket Theatre 189
Pokštas, Kazy 91
Poland 6, 8, 30, 108, 156, 184
Poliščuka, Gaļina 28, 159, 161–164, 200
postmodernism 8, 76, 175, 197
Preminger, Otto 198–199
Priede, Gunārs 158, 193, 195
Priedīte, Anta 168–172
Proust, Marcel 19
Putņinš, Pauls 158, 211

Rabelais, Francois 50
Rähesoo, Jaak 6, 11, 12, 93–94, 139, 152, 156, 212
Raikh, Zinaida 192
Rainis, Janis 157, 162–163, 165
Rakvere Theatre 133, 212
Ramanauskas, Rokas 63
Rats 87
Raudsepp, Hugo 94
Ravenhill, Mark 59, 69–70, 80, 84
Reagan, Ronald Wilson 126
Red Desert 36
Reformation 23, 28, 124
Report 153
Returning to Father 152
Ribes, Jean Michelle 36
Riga (Latvia) 7, 16, 27, 156–210

Riga Russian Drama Theatre 157–158, 166, 193
Rijnieks, Juris 175
"The Rocking Horse Winner" 168
Roga, Indra 29,184–188, 200
Romeo and Juliet 84, 96, 142, 144–145, 167, 200
La Ronde 176–177
Rosencrantz and Guildenstern are Dead 152
Rozenberga, Elza (Aspazija) 157
Rubesa, Baņuta 176–177, 197, 206–209
Rubinovas, Stanislovas 48–51
Rudaitienė, Loreta 31–33
Rudzīte, Ilze 18
Rukov, Mogens 148
Rummo, Paul-Eerik 95
Russia (and Russian) 8, 16, 19, 25, 27–28, 30–31, 34, 68, 87, 93–94, 108, 114–115, 119–121, 124, 130, 138–140, 142, 154, 158, 174, 184, 188, 197, 212

Šabasevičinė, Daiva 69–71, 73
The Sad Ballad of Johnny Red and His Pretty Wife Cecilia 36
St. Petersburg (and Leningrad) 25, 41, 49, 66
Saja, Kazys 31–32
Sajūdis National Independence Movement 42, 211
Sakalauskas, Arūnas 82
Šaltenis, Saulius 31–32
Šapiro, Ādolfs 158, 166, 174, 188, 190–193
Saro, Anneli 24, 121–123, 126, 136–137, 211
Save Our Souls 154
Schilling, Arpad 59
Schnitzler, Arthur 176
Seneca (Lucius Annaeus) 206
Sepitko, Larisa 40
Sepp, Paul 115
The Sex Pistols 135–136
Shakespeare, William 20, 63, 82, 84, 120–122, 145, 147
Ship in the Swamp 113–114
Shopping and Fucking 59, 69, 73, 80, 82, 205
Simmul, Rain 98–99
Šimukauskas, Ramūnas 37, 40
Sinissaar, Triin 113–114
Skatuve *see* The Stage Theatre
Skendelienė, Rūta 22, 30, 66, 80, 211
Slovakia 8, 184
Smilģis, Eduards 8, 157, 174, 193, 212
Someone Who'll Watch Over Me 129, 152
Sometimes I Feel Life Is Over and There Is No Love 146, 196
Sorokin, Vladimir 178–179
Southern, Terry 103

Soviets (and Soviet Union) 2, 5, 6–7, 11–14, 16, 18–20, 22, 24–25, 27, 29–31, 41–44, 49, 63–65, 69–70, 72, 78, 81, 85–86, 94–95, 108, 115, 121–122, 126, 130, 136–138, 140, 142, 147, 152–154, 157–158, 160–161, 164–165, 173, 193, 200, 205–207, 209, 211
The Sphinx 161, 164–165, 168
Spielberg, Steven 41, 49
Sruoga, Balys 43
The Stage Theatre 188, 210
Stalin, Joseph Vissarionovich (and Stalinism) 41, 94, 114
Staniškytė, Jurgita 22, 28, 55, 60, 61, 66, 86
Stanislavsky, Constantin (and Stanislavskian) 8, 26, 28–29, 41, 64, 91, 120–121, 131–132, 138–140, 158–159, 174–177, 185
State Youth Theatre (Vilnius) 71–79
Storey, David 96
The Story of Kaspar Hauser 184
The Stranger (Blok) 49
Strindberg, (Johan) August 119
Stumbre, Lelde 158
Sundvor, Ingve 36
Sutkus, Antanas 41
Sweden 16, 54, 108, 113

Tailor Days in Silmachi 157, 161
Tallinn (Estonia) 6–7, 23–24, 114, 95–155, 160, 206
Tallinn City Theatre 23, 95–96, 98, 104, 113, 116–117, 126–129, 131–132, 141
Tammsaare, A. H. 94
Tarantino, Quentin 198–199
Tarkovsky, Andre 36, 40, 66
Tätte, Jaan 23, 29, 96–108, 122, 124–126, 128, 141, 212
The Taviani Brothers (Paolo and Vittorio) 36
Temple, Julien 135
Theatre Laboratory (Vilnius) 74
Theatre NO99 132, 146
Theatre TT 204, 210
Thirty Years War 23
thrashing house theatre *see* barn theatre
Three Sisters 189
Threepenny Opera 96
Tjarve, Baiba 16, 26–27
Tooming, Jaan 94–95, 138–140, 142
Toompere, Hendrik, Jr. 23, 28, 115, 141–142, 146–152
Top Girls 177
Torch, Chris 59
Touching the White Bear 205, 208
Tschapajev and Pustota 117, 126, 141

Tuminas, Rimas 21–22, 29, 60, 63, 81, 86–88, 90–92
Turgenev, Ivan Sergeyevich 8, 172
Turner, Scott 36
Türnpu, Anne 142
Twilight of the Idols 197

Ubu Roi 85
Unt, Mati 95

Vaičiūnas, Petras 43
Vaičkus, Juozas 41
Vaidila 30
Vaitkus, Jonas 21–22, 29, 42, 60, 63, 66–70, 72, 80–81, 87, 90, 92, 108, 119, 211
Vaivars, Regnārs 158, 161, 164, 174, 190, 200
Vakhtangov, Evgeny 32
Valmiera Drama Theatre 160, 175, 212
Vancevicius, Henrikas 41
van der Bosch, Jan-Willem 209
Varnas, Gintaras 28, 44–48, 87, 206
Vasinauskaitė, Rasa 83–84
Verdi, Giuseppe 121
Viesaitė, Irena 17
Viksna, Ingrida 206
Vilkarse, Ingrida 182
Vilnius (Lithuania) 6, 33, 35, 47, 51–92, 160, 206
Vilnius Little Theatre 63, 86–87

Vinterberg, Thomas 148
Von Krahl Theatre 23, 125, 127, 132–137, 141
Vrgoč, Dubravka 15, 212

Waiting for Godot 87
Warhol, Andy (Warholian) 201
Wasted Land 46–48, 88, 206
We Have to Wade Into the Sea 206
West Side Story 145
When Space Is Over-Crowded 153
Who's Afraid of Virginia Woolf 27
Wilder, Thorton 43
World War II 1, 11–12, 31, 43, 60, 95, 114, 158, 164, 206–207
Wysockij 85

Yeltsin, Boris Nikolayevich 31
Young Estonians 94

Zabriskie Point 36
Žalakevičius, Vytautas 40, 66
Zālīte, Māra 158, 164–165
Zappia, Larry 212
Zelionkaitė, Ieva 37, 39
Zeltiņa, Guna 27, 156, 158, 169, 181, 191
Zole, Ieva 159, 172–174, 180–182, 200, 209, 212
ZT Hollandia 59
Zukaitytė, Audra 80–81, 85

www.ingramcontent.com/pod-product-compliance
Lightning Source LLC
Chambersburg PA
CBHW032051300426
44116CB00007B/692